The Experience of God

*These volumes are dedicated to
the blessed memory of
Father Dumitru Staniloae
1903-1993
May his memory be eternal
Αιώνια η μνήμη αυτου
Veșnica pomenire*

The Experience of God

Orthodox Dogmatic Theology

Vol. 1: Revelation and Knowledge of the Triune God

Dumitru Staniloae

Translated and edited
by
Ioan Ionita
and
Robert Barringer

Foreword by
Metropolitan Kallistos Ware of Diokleia

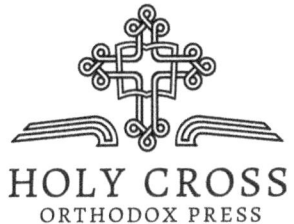

HOLY CROSS
ORTHODOX PRESS

Brookline, Massachusetts

Reprint 2022

© *Copyright 1994 by Holy Cross Orthodox Press*

Published by Holy Cross Orthodox Press
50 Goddard Avenue
Brookline, Massachusetts 02445

All rights reserved. No part of this publication may be reproduced, stored in a retrieval system, or transmitted in any form or by any means-electronic, mechanical, photocopy, recording, or any other without the prior written permission of the publisher. The only exception is brief quotations in printed reviews.

Library of Congress Cataloging-in-Publication Data
Staniloae, Dimitru.

[Teologia dogmatica ortodoxa. English]
The Experience of God/Dimitru Staniloae; foreword by Bishop Kallistos of Diokleia; translated and edited by loan Ionita and Robert Barringer.
P.cm.

Translation of: Teologia dogmatica ortodoxa.
Includes bibliographical references.
Contents: v. 1. Revelation and knowledge of the triune God. ISBN 0-917651-70-7 (pbk.)

Theology, Doctrinal. 2. Orthodox Eastern Church-Doctrines. I. Ionita, loan. II. Barringer, Robert. III. Title.
BX320.2.S7913 1989 230'. l 9---dc20
89-37264
CIP

Cover image by Ivanka Demchuk

Cover Design by Isaac Williams

ISBN 978-0917651700 (Paperback Edition)

ORTHODOX DOGMATIC THEOLOGY
by Dumitru Staniloae

Volume 1 Revelation and Knowledge of the Triune God
Volume 2 The World: Creation and Deification
Volume 3 The Person of Jesus Christ as God and Savior
Volume 4 The Church: Communion in the Holy Spirit
Volume 5 The Sanctifying Mysteries
Volume 6 The Fulfillment of Creation

CONTENTS

Foreword	ix
Chapter One: Natural Revelation	1
Chapter Two: Supernatural Revelation	15
Chapter Three: Scripture and Tradition	37
Chapter Four: The Church as the Instrument for Preserving Revelation	53
Chapter Five: Theology as Ecclesial Service	79
Chapter Six: Knowledge of God	95
Chapter Seven: The Being of God and His Uncreated Operations	125
Chapter Eight: The Super-Essential Attributes of God	141
Chapter Nine: The Spiritual Attributes of God	198
Chapter Ten: The Holy Trinity: Structure of Supreme Love	245

FOREWORD

True and living theology, according to Archpriest Staniloae, faces simultaneously in three directions: towards the past, the present and the future. It is at once apostolic, contemporary and prophetic. Its marks, he states, are "fidelity to the revelation of Christ given in holy Scripture and Tradition, . . . responsibility for the faithful who are contemporary with the theology as it is being done; openness to the eschatological future."

These are precisely the features that distinguish Fr. Dumitru's own master-work, his *Dogmatic Theology*, originally published in Romanian in 1978, and now translated into English. *The Experience of God*, as the English version is entitled, is in the first place firmly based upon apostolic tradition as interpreted by the Fathers. But it is at the same time an expression of what Fr. Georges Florovsky used to term "neopatristic synthesis." The patristic writers are treated by Fr. Dumitru always as contemporaries, as living witnesses whose testimony requires on our side a continual self-examination and rethinking, with present-day concerns in view. Faithful to the past, responsible to the present, *The Experience of God* is also a prophetic book, open to the future, creative, pointing towards paths as yet unexplored.

Dumitru Staniloae is widely regarded as the greatest Orthodox theologian alive today, and *The Experience of God* constitutes his crowning achievement, the fulfilment of his whole life's work. Its publication in translation by Holy Cross Orthodox Press is a notable event for English-speaking Orthodoxy throughout the world. This is a book, however, not only for the Orthodox themselves, and not only for non-Orthodox with a specialized interest in Eastern Christianity, but for anyone who is attracted by imaginative thinking on basic religious issues. It is particularly significant that this, the first major work of Orthodox dogmatic theology to appear in the English language, should have been written by a Romanian Orthodox. For Romania represents what Fr. Dumitru terms "oriental Latinity." As the only Orthodox Church that is Latin in its culture, it has always stood at the cross-roads: between East and West, between Orthodoxy and the Latin tradition, and also between Byzantium and the Slav world. Within Orthodoxy and within Christendom as a whole, the

Romanians see themselves as bridge-builders, whose special vocation it is to express balance, convergence and universality. And such indeed are the qualities evident in Fr. Dumitru's book. It is a bridge-building work, written by one who is profoundly Romanian in spirit, sensitive to the distinctive insights of Romanian poetry and folk-lore, yet who is also a "pan-Orthodox theologian," as Jürgen Moltmann has said,[1] and not only that, but in the best sense of the word an *ecumenical* theologian. Appropriately this English version is the fruit of inter-Christian co-operation, the work of a Romanian Orthodox in collaboration with a Canadian Roman Catholic.

* * *

Dumitru Staniloae was born on 16 November 1903 in the village of Vladeni in Transylvania, the westernmost province of modern Romania, bordering on Hungary. His roots are rural, and his early upbringing was in a relatively isolated agricultural community. He has never ceased to love the Romanian peasant culture that formed him in his childhood, and he has striven to incorporate its characteristic values into his religious thought. The sense of kinship with the earth, with the material environment of stream, hill and forest that he knew as a boy in the country, has continued to mark his theological vision. One of his central themes has always been the cosmic unity of all creation in Jesus Christ. The young Dumitru's parents, both devout Orthodox, exercised a lasting influence on his spiritual outlook. Something of the religious atmosphere in his home upbringing is conveyed by a story that he tells of how he came to read the Bible in its entirety when ten years old. "I found a Bible in the house of my grandfather who was a chanter in church. It was a Bible full of very striking pictures; these attracted me and I began to read. I read the text with close interest in order to understand the pictures. I read, sitting by the window, concentrated on my reading. ... Everyone, my mother, my father, all who came in, felt as if they were in church. No one spoke; they said: The child is reading the Holy Book. They all felt that here something holy was taking place."[2]

His mother encouraged him from his early years to think of becoming a priest. In due course he went to the seminary in Cernauti, where he studied for five years, from 1922 to 1927. Here he encountered the westernized style of "academic" theology, marked by

Scholasticism and by religious rationalism, which prevailed in the Romanian Orthodox Church at this period, and against which in later life he has strongly reacted. For his licenciate thesis at Cernauti he chose as topic "The Baptism of Children." From the start he was interested in the practical and pastoral implications of theology.

Newly graduated from the seminary, he spent a period abroad during 1928-29, studying in Greece at Athens, in Germany at Munich and Berlin, and in France at Paris, where he transcribed unpublished texts of St. Gregory Palamas from manuscripts in the Bibliothèque Nationale. He acquired a good knowledge of German, French, and also Greek, modern as well as patristic and Byzantine. In addition he learnt Russian, above all so as to read the works of Fr. Sergei Bulgakov. His doctoral dissertation, completed in 1928, was entitled *The Life and Work of Patriarch Dositheos of Jerusalem and his Relations with the Romanian Lands*. Once more the choice of subject was significant. Dositheos (1641-1707), himself a Greek, not only maintained close links with Russia but also devoted his energies to the establishment of printing presses in what is today Romania. The selection of Dositheos as his dissertation topic illustrates Fr. Dumitru's sense of the position of Romania as a meeting-place between the Greek and Slav worlds, and his awareness of its crucial role as a cultural centre during the *Turcocratia*, when it acted as guardian of the Byzantine heritage, as "Byzance après Byzance," to use the expression of the celebrated Romanian historian Nicolae Iorga.

In 1929 Dumitru Staniloae began his teaching career as a professor at the Theological Institute of Sibiu, and here he continued until after the Second World War, eventually becoming rector. In connection with his lectures at Sibiu, during 1930 he made a Romanian translation of the Greek *Dogmatics* by Christos Androutsos, originally published in 1907.[3] But the westernized, Scholastic approach of this manual, similar in its outlook to the theological training that he had received at Cernauti, satisfied him less and less as the years passed. When, nearly half a century later, he came to compose his own *Dogmatic Theology*, it was inspired by a very different spirit. While at Sibiu, in 1932, he was ordained priest. Although deeply interested in monastic spirituality, he is himself a member of the married clergy, the father of a family. Of his three children, two died young. The third, a daughter, well known as a writer and poet, is still alive and now resides in the West.

Fr. Dumitru's first major work, short but well-documented, *The Life and Teaching of St. Gregory Palamas*, was published in 1938. At this time Palamite theology was virtually unknown in the Orthodox world, while the learned studies devoted to it by the Roman Catholic scholar Martin Jugie had been written from a sharply hostile standpoint. In the revival of Palamism that has transformed Orthodoxy during the past fifty years, Fr. Dumitru may be seen as a decisive pioneer, along with Fr. (later Archbishop) Basil Krivocheine, whose own study, *The Ascetic and Theological Teaching of St. Gregory Palamas*, had appeared in Russian two years previously in 1936.[4] But whereas Fr. Basil relied exclusively on the limited range of Palamas' writings then available in printed form, Fr. Dumitru was able to draw also on unpublished works that he had consulted in manuscript at Paris. He has always remained a theologian in the Palamite tradition, ascribing — as readers of the present volume will discover — central significance to the distinction that Palamas made between the essence and the energies of God.

The second major work written by Fr. Dumitru during his Sibiu period, *Jesus Christ or the Restoration of Man*, appeared in 1943. Here his theme is Christ as the key to our human personhood. Only in the light of the incarnation, he maintains, can we discover our own authentic humanity. Christ is our ultimate meaning. Only through God incarnate can man become fully human. The famous statement of St. Athanasios needs to be extended: the Logos became man, not only so that man might become god, but so that man might become man.

A new era in Fr. Dumitru's life began after the Second Word War with his move from Sibiu to Bucharest, where he taught as professor in the Theological Institute from 1947 until his retirement in 1973. Shortly before his transfer to the Romanian capital, in 1946 he commenced the publication of what has been, along with his *Dogmatic Theology*, the main task of the second half of his life: the Romanian edition of the *Philokalia*. By 1948 this had reached the fourth volume, when publication had to be suspended due to Communist pressure on the Church. For a time Fr. Dumitru was obliged to limit himself mainly to articles in journals and to chapters in collective manuals of theology; a number of these contributions, however, are more than substantial, constituting original works in their own right.

In 1958, a time of persecution for Romanian Christians, Fr.

Dumitru suffered arrest and condemnation, spending the next five years in prison and concentration camp, and not returning to his post at the Bucharest Institute until 1964. "An experience like any other," he said later with a smile to Oliver Clément, "only somewhat difficult for my family." And he added that this was the only time in his life when he was able to practice and to "retain" in a semipermanent manner the invocation of the Name of Jesus.[5] "To carry one's cross" in this way, so he told Clément, "is the normal condition of the Christian, and so there is no need to talk about it."[6]

Another twelve years were to elapse after his return to the Bucharest Institute before the publication of the Romanian *Philokalia* could be resumed. Then, between 1976 and 1981, another six volumes were issued, making altogether a total of over 4,650 pages in ten volumes. Far more than simply a translation from the Greek, the Romanian edition by Fr. Dumitru includes theological introductions to each author and numerous footnotes to the text. The introductions and notes take full account of recent critical research, drawing on Western as well as Orthodox authorities.[7] As compared with the Greek *Philokalia* edited in the eighteenth century by St. Makarios of Corinth and St. Nikodemos of the Holy Mountain, the Romanian *Philokalia* assigns a larger place to St. Maximos the Confessor, whose writings occupy two entire volumes, three and four, and who has had on Fr. Dumitru's own theology an influence greater than that of any other patristic author.[8] The Romanian *Philokalia* also includes additional works by St. Symeon the New Theologian and St. Gregory Palamas, while volume eight ends with a survey of hesychasm in Romania, thus emphasizing the continuation of the Philokalic tradition into the post-Byzantine era.

The second outstanding production of Fr. Dumitru's "Bucharest period," his *Dogmatic Theology*, was published in three large volumes in 1978. This embodies the mature fruits of his theological reflection after more than half a century of teaching and writing. Versions in foreign languages have already begun to appear. The first volume of a German translation by Hermann Pitters, entitled *Orthodoxe Dogmatik*, was issued in 1985, while in the same year a French translation by Dan-Ilie (now Bishop Daniel) Ciobotea commenced publication in the series *Théophanie*, with the title *Le génie de l'Orthodoxie*.

If in this English translation Fr. Staniloae's original title *Dogmatic Theology* has not been retained, this is partly because of the negative associations of the word "dogmatic" in the mind of many Western readers. There is a danger that it might be taken to signify obligatory teaching, imposed from above by external authority. This, however, is not at all what the author means by dogmatic theology. He is never content in this work with a bald and exterior appeal to the Church's *magisterium*, but he seeks always to indicate the inner coherence of dogmatic truth and the significance of each dogma for the personal life of the Christian. It is the theologian's task to make manifest the link between dogma and personal spirituality, to show how every dogma responds to a deep need and longing in the human heart, and how it has practical consequences for society. Dogmas, he is convinced, do not enslave but liberate; theology is essentially freedom. Freedom, whether human or divine, is one of Fr. Dumitru's recurrent *leitmotifs*: God has made us partners and fellow-workers, who co-operate with him in full liberty; without freedom there can be no love and no interpersonal communion.

The title that has been chosen for the English edition, *The Experience of God*, highlights an aspect of theology that is all-important for Fr. Dumitru. "We need a concrete theology," he insists, "a theology of experience."[9] In his eyes theology, properly understood, is not an abstract system, not a philosophical theory, but the expression of personal experience, of a living encounter with the living God. It is not a "science" in the sense that physics and geology are scientific; for God is not an "object," to be dissected and analyzed with impersonal detachment. Theology, talking about God, presupposes a personal relationship. It presupposes faith and ascetic purification, the quest for continual prayer, the thirst for sanctity; the true theologians are the saints. It presupposes, furthermore, not only human effort but, much more fundamentally, divine grace and the illumination of the Holy Spirit; theology is a gift from God. The only genuine theology is that summed up by Evagrios of Pontos in a phrase which Fr. Dumitru likes to quote: "If you are a theologian, you will pray truly. And if you pray truly, you are a theologian."[10] Those, therefore, who expect a treatise on dogmatic theology to be a formal textbook, with precise definitions ranged in a strictly logical order, will be disconcerted and sometimes baffled by *The Experience of God*. But I trust that they will also be agreeably surprised.

The *Dogmatic Theology* was followed in 1981 by a study on *Orthodox Spirituality*. Despite his age, Fr. Dumitru continues up to the present to produce serious theological articles.[11] Unusually prolific as an author, he yet avoids superficiality. Metropolitan Antonie (Plamadeala) of Transylvania is right to speak of his "perfectionism": "He is a sort of 'perfectionist,' but not in that way of perfectionists who do not dare write anything, fearing that tomorrow will say it better. He writes all he thinks today, thinking that if he has new ideas tomorrow, these will complete and continue those of today."[12]

Through his lectures, articles and books, Fr. Dumitru Staniloae almost single-handed has transformed Romanian Orthodox theology, giving it a radically different orientation in the post-war period. Yet those who meet him for the first time would not easily guess how far-reaching his influence has been, for he is a humble man, gentle and unassuming. His learning and wide reading are never paraded in such a manner as to crush or intimidate. Attentive to others, warm and approachable, spontaneously he expresses a true Christian courtesy. When he speaks in *The Experience of God* about the humanity, tenderness and delicacy of the saints, unintentionally he has painted an icon also of himself. He has a face full of light, illumined by a smile as much in his eyes as on his lips. He moves swiftly from laughter to seriousness. He has the precious gift of conveying, simply through his presence, a sense of wholeness and peace. "He is a man who restores one's confidence in life," his friend Fr. Donald Allchin has justly remarked.[13] His life has been devoted to research, writing and teaching, and yet he has never been an "academic" in the narrow sense. He is not only a professor but a priest who loves the Liturgy, not only a scholar but a spiritual father. The link between theology and prayer, so often underlined in his works, is evident also in his own person. Theology is not merely what he studies but what he lives and is. He speaks with the wisdom of the heart.

* * *

The Experience of God appeared in the original Romanian edition in three volumes, but it is intended to publish the English translation in six volumes, subdividing each volume of the Romanian edition into two. This opening volume in the English translation covers three main topics: (1) Revelation, natural and supernatural; Scripture and tradition;the nature of theology. (2) The knowledge of God, both rational and apophatic; the distinction between God's essence or being and his energies or operations; the divine attributes. (3) The

Holy Trinity as an expression of mutual love.

The scope of the remaining five volumes will be: *Volume Two*: creation and deification. The meaning of creation *ex nihilo*; the creation of the angels, and the fall whereby some of them became demons; the creation and fall of humans; the origin and character of evil; our human solidarity with nature. *Volume Three*: the person of Jesus Christ. The presence and activity of the Logos in the work of creation and in the Old Testament; the incarnation, and the union between Christ's divine and human natures; his saving ministry in its three aspects: as teacher and prophet, as high priest and sacrifice, and as king. *Volume Four*: communion in the Holy Spirit. The Church as the mystical body of Christ in the Spirit; our salvation within the Church; divine grace and human freedom. *Volume Five*: the sanctifying mysteries or sacraments. *Volume Six*: eschatology or the fulfilment of creation. The second coming of Christ; the resurrection of the dead; the universal judgment; eternal life.

As Fr. Dumitru states in his preface, *The Experience of God* is a work of synthesis. It is such in the first place by virtue of the wide variety of sources which it brings together in unity. The author avoids overloading his text with footnotes, but sufficient references are given to indicate the richness of the material on which he draws. The book is founded, as we should expect, above all upon the Greek Fathers. The patristic era, in the Orthodox understanding — here Fr. Staniloae agrees with Fr. Florovsky — did not end in the fifth century with the Council of Chalcedon, or in the eighth with St. John of Damascus, or even in the fifteenth with the fall of the Byzantine Empire, but it has continued down to the present time. A contemporary Orthodox theologian is still basically "patristic" in his style of thinking, and it is therefore natural for him to quote side by side writers from the fourth, the fourteenth and the twentieth centuries. Two of the patristic writers particularly important for Fr. Dumitru's dogmatic synthesis have already been mentioned: St. Maximos the Confessor and St. Gregory Palamas. Other Fathers who are frequently cited include St. Gregory of Nazianzos, St. Gregory of Nyssa, St. Cyril of Alexandria and St. Dionysios the Areopagite. But the author's range of vision is not limited to the Greek East. He makes use also of Syriac writers, especially St. Isaak of Nineveh, known as "the Syrian." Latin Fathers are likewise mentioned, such as St. Ambrose, St. Augustine and St. Vincent of Lérins, as well as medieval Western theologians such as

Hugh of St. Victor.

The fact that Fr. Dumitru is patristic in spirit does not mean that he is enclosed in the past. On the contrary, he totally rejects a theology of mere repetition. He acknowledges that the Early Fathers are by no means exhaustive. In certain areas, he believes — most notably, in our understanding of the human person and of interpersonal relations — modern thought has given us new and vital insights not to be found in the writers of the ancient Church or of Byzantium. He sees tradition as open-ended and constantly creative, "not a sum of propositions learnt by heart, but a lived experience."[14] It is an unceasing invocation of the life-creating Spirit. Always the same, yet always new, tradition is not just a protective, conservative principle, but primarily a source of growth and regeneration. It signifies, not the passive and mechanical acceptance of what has been stated by others in the past, but an unremitting effort to relive this past inheritance in present-day conditions. Tradition is Scripture applied to human life, Scripture made contemporary. For Fr. Dumitru, tradition represents in this way the critical spirit of the Church. A "traditional" theologian, if he is genuinely such, is called to be bold and prophetic. He needs to ask not just "What did the Fathers say long ago?" but "What would they say if they were alive today?" Our aim as patristic theologians, rather than mere historians of doctrine, is not just archaeological exactness but "pneumatic anamnesis." We seek to present not just the letter of the Fathers but their vital spirit, their mind or *phronema*, what has been termed their "eternal youth."

From all this it follows that Fr. Dumitru, as a theologian loyal to the patristic tradition, is also "in communion with all generations," to use the phrase of Metropolitan Antonie.[15] Along with the Fathers, contemporary Orthodox authors make their appearance in *The Experience of God*. The major figures of the Russian diaspora are here: Lossky, Florovsky, Evdokimov, Schmemann, Meyendorff. From modern Greece Karmiris and Yannaras are cited, and Oliver Clément from the Orthodox writers of Western origin. Allusions to non-Orthodox are relatively infrequent, but the occasional references to Barth, Rahner, von Balthasar and Küng, among others, are sufficient to indicate Fr. Dumitru's familiarity with Roman Catholic and Protestant thinking.

One group of writings to which significantly Fr. Dumitru does not appeal are the so-called "Symbolic Books" of the Orthodox

Church, dating from the late sixteenth and the seventeenth century. In contrast they are regularly quoted in the standard Greek Dogmatics by Panagiotes Trembelas.[16] This omission on Fr. Dumitru's part is the more striking, in that his doctoral dissertation was devoted to Patriarch Dositheos of Jerusalem, himself the author of an *Orthodox Confession* that figures in the "Symbolic Books." If he refrains from citing Dositheos or Peter Moghila, the reason is undoubtedly his wish to escape from the Latinizing, Scholastic style of theology that they represent. Another source to which Fr. Dumitru makes little explicit reference is the Orthodox liturgical books. This is a more surprising omission, since the Church's worship is in fact of cardinal importance to him. Underlining as he does the integral connection between dogma and prayer, he certainly regards all dogmatic theology as liturgical and mystical.

There is also a second and more profound sense in which *The Experience of God* is a work of synthesis. Not only does the author draw together into unity a wide variety of sources, but he seeks also to indicate the coinherence and interpendence of all the dogmas. "Only connect . . .": in theology, as envisaged by Fr. Dumitru, everything connects with everything else; it all ties up. In consequence, even though the work has, as we have noted, a definite structure and a clearly articulated division of topics, yet the treatment is less consecutive, less organized in clear logical sequence, than the reader might anticipate. Discussing revelation in general, for instance, Fr. Dumitru speaks at once about the Trinity and the incarnation. There are many repetitions, but these are perhaps deliberate, not the result of inattention. The six volumes are systematic, in the sense that they present a coherent vision of the truth. But the system that the dogmas constitute, in Fr. Dumitru's words, "is not formed of abstract principles; it is the living unity of Christ."[17]

To convey this "living unity," Fr. Dumitru employs a style less academic, more personal and lyrical, than is customary in a work of dogmatic theology. In his use of words he is a true craftsman, a poet as well as theologian. As his disciple Fr. Ion Bria has remarked, he has "a total confidence in words, which he employs in their original, authentic sense," paying particular attention to their roots.[18] He has sought to restore value to the *Urwörte*, the primal words that are all too easily debased, such as love, joy, gift. His manner of writing, it has been said, is "paradoxically simple and complex,"[19] both lucid and demanding. For a full appreciation of the poetry, doubtless the reader needs to understand Romanian; but the translators deserve our gratitude for their skill in conveying both the simplicity and the complexity of Fr. Dumitru's writing.

* * *

What are the distinctive features that mark Fr. Dumitru's theology in general, and more particularly this first volume of *The Experience of God*? Four master-themes call for especial mention.

First and most fundamentally, his is a theology of *love and personal communion*. The only possible way to talk about God and humankind, he believes, is to use the language of love. As the God of love, our Christian God is involved and vulnerable, a God who suffers because of our inability to love; "there is a paradoxical union between the impassibility and the sufferings of God."[20] There is no true human person without communion in love: "The person without communion is not person." Communion is life; isolation signifies death. The gift of faith, the experience of the Spirit, and the understanding of the Bible are granted, not to individuals in separation, but to persons in relationship. "Faith, as a work of the Holy Spirit, comes to one person through another.... Scripture activates its own power in the communion between persons."

The "between" is all-important. One of Fr. Dumitru's favorite terms is "responsibility," used in its full and true sense of "response," "responsiveness": "this fire of responsibility, this fire that comes from the Holy Spirit," as he puts it.[21] Here, with his characteristic feeling for verbal roots, he draws attention to the literal sense of the Latin *cognosco* (*cum* + *gnosco*): I know only "with" (*cum*) others; all knowledge is interpersonal. Similarly in Romanian *cuvint*, meaning "word," is derived from the Latin *conventus*, a "coming together;"[22] there is no genuine word except in dialogue. "I do not know myself apart from a relationship with others," he writes; as he puts it elsewhere, "For myself, in so far as I am not loved, I am incomprehensible."[23] There are close parallels here with John Macmurray's *Persons in Relation*.[24] This insistence that the human person is primarily communion, meeting, repsonse, is perhaps the most significant affirmation in the whole of Fr. Dumitru's theology. Is not his message here of immediate relevance to our present age, which finds personal communication more and more problematic?

Secondly, and in direct connection with the first point, Fr. Dumitru's theology is strongly *Trinitarian*. For him the doctrine of the Trinity is not simply a piece of formal teaching accepted on authority, but something that makes a crucial difference to each one of us personally, affecting the way in which we regard our own selves and one another. The Holy Trinity is the plentitude of personhood in communion. The Trinitarian God of the Christian faith is to be understood above all in "social" terms, as *koinonia* or communion, as the supreme structure of interpersonal love. If God is love, then he cannot be merely one person loving himself alone, for self-love is not true love. As the God of love, he is shared, mutual love, a community of persons loving one another. This has immediate consequences for our understanding of the human person. Since humans are made in God's image, to be a person is to be an icon of the Trinitarian *koinonia*. If it is true that there is no real human person until there are at least two persons in communication with each other — if I need you in order to be myself — then the reason for this is precisely the dogma of the Trinity. What Fr. Dumitru terms the "divine intersubjectivity" of the Trinity constitutes the model and paradigm of all human relationships, and more specifically the model and paradigm of the Church. "The Trinity alone assures our existence as persons," writes Fr. Dumitru. ". . . Salvation and deification are nothing other than the extension to conscious creatures of the relations that obtain between the divine persons."

In the third place, Fr. Dumitru's theology is structured by the double truth of the *otherness yet nearness of God*. The Deity is totally transcendent and yet totally immanent, incomprehensible and yet the deep meaning of everything, infinitely beyond all participation and yet closer to us than our own heart. Fr. Dumitru's strong sense of divine transcendence and mystery makes him definitely an apophatic theologian. The greater our knowledge, he believes, the greater our sense of mystery; knowledge does no more than render the mystery immediate and inescapable. But at the same time he warns against a one-sided apophaticism. Human reason is a gift from God, to be used to the utmost. While stressing the antinomic and paradoxical character of Christian theology — "Paradox is to be found everywhere" — he does not advocate irrationalism. "Apophatic knowledge is not irrational but supra-rational, for the Son of God is the Logos and contains in himself the 'reasons' of all created things." The two ways, the apophatic or negative and the cataphatic or positive, are not alternatives but interdependent, and each presupposes the other. Apophatic theology is much more than a speculative technique, a philosophical method whereby we first make affirmations and then negate them. It is a way of ascent to personal union with God, leading not just to a theoretical awareness of God's transcendence, but to "a direct experience of his mystical presence." Apophaticism is to be interpreted in experiential terms; here, as so often, the experiential dimension is essential for Fr. Dumitru.

To express this saving dialectic of God's otherness yet nearness, Fr. Dumitru employs the Palamite distinction-in-unity between God's essence and his uncreated energies. The central place that he assigns to this distinction is a new and significant development, so far as works of modern Orthodox dogmatic theology are concerned. The Palamite teaching is ignored in the *Dogmatics* of Androutsos,[25] and allowed no more than a passing mention in that of Trembelas.[26] There is no reference to it in the main text of Fr. Michael Pomazansky's *Orthodox Dogmatic Theology*, although a few lines are devoted to St. Gregory Palamas in an appendix.[27] Fr. Dumitru's is thus the first dogmatics in which the distinction is seen as fundamental to the Orthodox understanding of God.[28]

Closely linked with Fr. Dumitru's teaching about the presence of God's uncreated energies throughout the universe, there is a fourth leading feature in his thought: his vision of *cosmic transfiguration*. More powerfully than any other Orthodox writer of our day, he presents a convincing theology of the world. One of the most impressive points in his world-view is the solidarity that he affirms between humans and the realm of nature. Once more his message is highly relevant for our present age, disillusioned as it is with scientific technology and seemingly helpless to check the growing pollution of the environment. Fr. Dumitru envisages the world in personalist terms, as a gift and a word from God, calling us to "interpersonal dialogue" with the "infinite creative subject." The world is a sacrament of God's presence, a means of communion with him, a theophany; all created things are God's "garments." With good reason *The Experience of God* has been termed "a confession of faith in an age of secularization."[29]

Fr. Dumitru takes as his basis here the cosmology of St. Maximos the Confessor, who discerns within each created thing a *logos* or inner principle implanted by the creator Logos. This indwelling *logos* makes each thing to be uniquely and distinctively that which it is, and at the same time draws that thing to union with God. Humanity, as high priest of the creation, has the vocation of rendering these *logoi* manifest, and so of offering the world back to God in thanksgiving. Matter is in this way to be seen not statically but dynamically, not as inert "stuff" but as living energy. Fr. Dumitru insists upon the holiness of matter, and is not afraid to speak of "mystical materialism." Matter is best defined as openness to the Spirit. It is the task of each human, as cosmic priest, to spiritualize the material creation without thereby dematerializing it. Creation is as yet unfinished; setting our imprint upon it through our creative imagination and our manual labor, we bring to fulfilment the potentialities hitherto unrealized within it. Fr. Dumitru puts forward here a strongly affirmative theology of work. Human labour, however fatiguing, is not just a burden or a reflection of our fallen condition, but should be viewed in positive terms as the expression of God's image marked upon us, a call to create after the likeness of the divine Creator, an opportunity for mutual love. The products of our handiwork and our intelligence are "like an echo of the great act of love by which God created the heavens and the earth."[30]

This belief in cosmic transfiguration makes Fr. Dumitru an "aesthetic" theologian, sensitive to beauty, who sets a high value on the gift of artistic imagination. In common with Feodor Dostoevsky, whose conviction it was that "beauty will save the world," Fr. Dumitru regards beauty as an objective principle in the creation, revealing to us the divine glory. Here again the contemporary relevance of his theology is apparent. One of the few ways — for many, indeed, the only way — in which women and men today are able to experience some sense of divine mystery is through a feeling for the beauty of the world.

Fr. Dumitru's "aesthetic" approach makes him also a theologian of joy. He sees joy as one of the specific characteristics of the Orthodox tradition: "Orthodoxy, through the joy of living in God, is doxological and not theoretical. It does not indulge in speculations about God, but it expresses the joy of living in God, and of participating in existence with the whole of creation."[31] More precisely, the joy which marks Orthodoxy is that of the resurrection: "The deepest foundation of the hope and joy which characterize Orthodoxy and which penetrate all its worship is the resurrection."[32] Our joy in the creation is not merely emotional or sentimental but firmly Christocentric, springing from our faith in God incarnate and risen from the dead. In his understanding of the incarnation, Fr. Dumitru sees it in cosmic terms, as not just a response to the fall but part of God's eternal purpose, an expression of the inner life of the Trinity, in this way upholding the standpoint represented in the East by St. Maximos and St. Isaak of Nineveh, and in the West by Duns Scotus.

Beauty and joy mean hope. Fr. Dumitru is definitely a theologian of universal hope. Indeed, he has sometimes been charged with an excessive ontological optimism, which in the opinion of his critics allows insufficiently for the brokenness of the world and the tragedy of sin. But in fact he has much to say about the fall, about death, repentance and suffering, and above all about the Cross. He does not neglect the need for ascetic renunciation, but at the same time he looks for a "new asceticism" that will be world-affirming, not disincarnate, as all too often Christian asceticism has tended to be in the past. Frequently he insists upon what he terms "the cross imprinted on the gift of the world," and he sees cross-bearing as a normal element in all Christian experience. He likes to quote St. Maximos: "All the realities which we perceive with the senses demand the cross. . . . All the realities which we understand with our mind have need of the tomb."[33] He also cites St. Cyril of Alexandria: "There can be no entry before the Father except in a state of sacrifice." "The cross is situated within each moment," he writes; "only through the cross can nearness be achieved." And again: "The Church rests upon crucified love."[34] If his ultimate vision is one of hope, then this is a cosmic optimism that he shares with such Greek Fathers as St. Gregory of Nyssa or St. Maximos the Confessor.

In his theology of the world Fr. Dumitru has given special attention to the meaning of time and space. He refuses to make a sharp dichotomy between time and eternity, between space and infinity, but sees them as interdependent. Time and space, while modalities of the created order, have their source in the uncreated life of God. He appeals here to St. Maximos: "The inner principles [*logoi*, 'reasons'] of time are in God." "The divine eternity," he writes, ". . . carries within itself the possibility of time, while time carries within itself the possibility of participating in eternity. . . . Eternity is as much in time as it is above time." In the divine plan, time is the means whereby God evokes and guarantees our human freedom. God's love always comes to us as an offer, and it is the dimension of time that enables us to respond to that offer in full freedom. Time is the interval between God's appeal and our answer: "For God, time means the duration of the expectant waiting between his knocking on the door and our act of opening it." We humans need this interval in order freely to love God and one another; time is given to us by God so that our love may ripen. The same is true of space: it affords us the possibility of "free movement ... the freedom to draw near or to move away." In a fallen world we experience time and space as distance and separation, as a prison, as fetters upon our liberty. But in their true nature, as created by God, they are the gateway to freedom, the safeguard of interpersonal communion in love.

* * *

Throughout *The Experience of God* there is a sense of balance and wholeness. It is a truly *catholic* work, total and all-embracing, expressing an Orthodoxy that is open and generous, not polemical and partisan. Fr. Dumitru believes in the "coincidence of opposites." Contrasting aspects of the truth are held together in harmony, as when the rational is accepted alongside the apophatic, or when time and eternity are understood as complementary. Faithful to the Trinitarian theology of the Cappadocians, he regards the Father alone as ultimate source of being within the Godhead; yet, while repudiating the *Filioque*, at the same time he finds a place for the Augustinian notion of the Spirit as the bond and communion between Father and Son.

Here is an Orthodox writer who faces the contemporary West, whether Christian or unbelieving, without aggressiveness and without fear. Even if his *critique* of Roman Catholic, Protestant or radical theology may at times appear sweeping and schematic, behind his strictures there is a positive intent. In the words of Fr. John Meyendorff, he "presents the truth of his convictions — uncompromisingly — as a liberating solution for all rather than as judgment upon others."[35] Oliver Clément sums him up: "A man who is not afraid."[36]

Fr. Dumitru Staniloae occupies, so it has been claimed, a position in present-day Orthodoxy comparable to that of Karl Barth in Protestantism or Karl Rahner in Catholicism. At a time when Orthodoxy is becoming firmly rooted in the West — ceasing to be a 'diaspora' and developing in many countries into a genuinely local Church — it is most important that basic Orthodox texts should be made available in the English language. Along with the translation into English of the Orthodox service books, and of such classic works as the *Evergetinos* and the *Philokalia*, the English publication of *The Experience of God* testifies to the "coming of age" of Orthodoxy in our Western world.

NOTES

1. Introduction to D. Staniloae, *Orthodoxe Dogmatik*, German translation by H. Pitters (Cologne/Gütersloh, 1985), p. 10.

2. M. A. Costa de Beauregard, *Dumitru Staniloae: Ose comprendre que Je t'aime* (Paris, 1983), p. 141.

3. Extensive quotations from Androutsos' book can be found in Frank Gavin, *Some Aspects of Contemporary Greek Orthodox Thought* (Milwaukee, 1923).

4. English translation in *The Eastern Churches Quarterly*, 3 (1938). Another pioneer work of earlier date is Gregorios Papamichael, Ὁ Ἅγιος Γρηγόριος ὁ Παλαμᾶς (St. Petersburg/Alexandria, 1911), a serious study which had, however, little impact on Orthodox theology at the time. It was of course Vladimir Lossky, in his *Essai sur la théologie mystique de l'Église d'Orient* (Paris, 1944; English translation, London, 1957), who first brought Palamism to the attention of a wider public, non-Orthodox as well as Orthodox.

5. Preface to D. Staniloae, *Prière de Jésus et expérience du Saint-Esprit* (Paris, 1981), p. 11.

6. Preface to D. Staniloae, *Le génie de l'Orthodoxie* (Paris, 1985), p. 12.

7. See 'Un moine de l'Eglise orthodoxe de Roumanie' (Fr. André Scrima), "L'avènement philocalique dans l'Orthodoxie roumaine," *Istina*, 5 (1958), 295-328, 443-74; Kallistos Ware, "Philocalie," *Dictionnaire de spiritualité*, 12 (1984), cols. 1346-47.

8. An edition of Maximos, *Mystagogia*, with a long introduction and copious notes by Fr. Staniloae, appeared in Greek as vol. 1 in the series Ἐπὶ τὰς Πηγάς ("To the Sources"), edited by Panagiotes Nellas (Athens, 1973). The first volume of a similar edition of Maximos, *Ambigua*, was published five years later (Ἐπὶ τὰς Πηγάς 4: Athens 1978).

9. Costa de Beauregard, *Dumitru Staniloae*, p. 156.

10. *On Prayer* 60 [61] (PG 79.1180B; *The Philokalia*, translated by G. E. H. Palmer, P. Sherrard and K. Ware, 1 [London/Boston, 1979], p. 62).

11. A valuable collection of his articles has been published in English by St. Vladimir's Seminary Press: D. Staniloae, *Theology and the Church*, translated by Robert Barringer (Crestwood, 1980). Further articles in English translation include: "Some characteristics of Orthodoxy," *Sobornost* (The Journal of the Fellowship of St. Alban and St. Sergius) 5:9 (1969) 627-29; "The Orthodox Conception of Tradition and the Development of Doctrine," ibid. 652-62; "The World as Gift and

Sacrament of God's Love," ibid. 662-73; "Orthodoxy, Life in the Resurrection," *Eastern Churches Review,* 2 (1969) 371-75; "The Cross on the Gift of the World," *Sobornost,* 6:2 (1971) 96-110; *The Victory of the Cross* (Fairacres Pamphlet 16: Oxford, no date [c. 1971]); "St. Callinicus of Cernica," in A. M. Allchin (ed.), *The Tradition of Life: Romanian Essays in Spirituality and Theology* (Studies Supplementary to Sobornost, no. 2: London, 1971), pp. 17-32; "The Foundation of Christian Responsibility in the World: The Dialogue of God and Man," ibid. pp. 53-73; "Unity and Diversity in Orthodox Tradition," *The Greek Orthodox Theological Review* 17:1 (1972), 19-36; "Jesus Christ, Incarnate Logos of God, Source of Freedom and Unity," *The Ecumenical Review* 26:4 (1974) 403-12; "The Role of the Holy Spirit in the Theology and Life of the Orthodox Church," *Diakonia* 9:4 (1974) 343-66; also (in a different translation) in *Sobornost* 7:1 (1975) 4-21; "The Cross in Orthodox Theology and Worship," *Sobornost* 7:4 (1977) 233-43; "Witness through 'Holiness' of Life," in Ion Bria (ed.), *Martyria/Mission: The Witness of the Orthodox Churches Today* (Geneva, 1980), pp. 45-51; *Prayer and Holiness: the Icon of Man Renewed in God* (Fairacres Publication 82: Oxford, 1982).

12. "Some lines on Fr. Staniloae's Theology," *The Altar: Almanach 1970* (The Romanian Orthodox Parish in London: London, 1970), p. 25. On Fr. Staniloae's theology, see also Ion Bria, "A Look at Contemporary Romanian Dogmatic Theology," *Sobornost* 6:5 (1972) 330-36; Isidor Todoran and others, "La théologie dogmatique actuelle. Ses problèmes et ses points de vue," in *De la théologie orthodoxe roumaine des origines à nos jours* (Editions de l'Institut Biblique et de Mission Orthodoxe: Bucharest, 1974), pp. 254-72; Dan-Ilie Ciobotea, "La théologie roumaine contemporaine," *Service orthodoxe de presse et d'information* (SOP) 27 (April, 1978), 9-11; I. Bria, "Hommage au Père Dumitru Staniloae à l'occasion de son soixante-quinzième anniversaire," *Contacts* 31 [105] (1979), 64-74; Istvan Juhasz, "Dumitru Staniloae's Ecumenical Studies as an Aspect of Orthodox-Protestant Dialogue," *Journal of Ecumenical Studies* 16:4 (1979) 747-64; I. Bria, "The Creative Vision of D. Staniloae. An introduction to his theological thought," *The Ecumenical Review* 33:1 (1981), 53-59; Daniel Neeser, "The World: Gift of God and Scene of Humanity's Response. Aspects of the Thought of Father Dumitru Staniloae," *The Ecumenical Review* 33:3 (1981), 272-82; D. -I. Ciobotea, "Une dogmatique pour l'homme d'aujourd'hui," *Irénikon* 54:4 (1981), 472-84; E. C. Miller, Jr, "Presentation of the Gifts: Orthodox Insights for Western Liturgical Renewal," *Worship* 60:1 (1986), 22-38.

13. Preface to Costa de Beauregard, *Dumitru Staniloae,* p. 10.

14. "The Orthodox Conception of Tradition and the Development of Doctrine," *Sobornost* 5:9 (1969), 653.

15. "Some lines on Fr. Staniloae's Theology," *The Altar* (1970), p. 26.

16. Δογματική τῆς Ὀρθοδόξου Καθολικῆς Ἐκκλησίας 1-3 (Athens, 1959-61); French translation by Pierre Dumont, *Dogmatique de l'Église orthodoxe catholique* 1-3 (Chevetogne, 1966-68).

17. Quotations from Fr. Staniloae, not otherwise identified, come from the first volume of *The Experience of God.*

18. D. Neeser, Introduction to D. Staniloae, *Dieu est amour* (Geneva, 1980), p. 18.

19. Metropolitan Antonie, "Some lines on Fr. Staniloae's Theology," *The Altar* (1970), p. 26.

20. Costa de Beauregard, *Dumitru Staniloae,* p. 52.

21. Ibid. p. 94.

22. Allchin, *The Tradition of Life,* p. 6.

23. Costa de Beauregard, *Dumitru Staniloae,* p. 24.

24. The Gifford Lectures for 1954 (London, 1961).
25. C. Androutsos, Δογματική τῆς Ὀρθοδόξου Ἀνατολικῆς Ἐκκλησίας (Athens, 1907), p. 45, makes a cursory reference to the divine energies, but without alluding to Palamas.
26. Δογματική 1, pp. 178-79 (printed in small type!); in the French translation, 1, pp. 213-14. Nothing is said about the essence-energies distinction in I. Karmiris, Σύνοψις τῆς δογματικῆς διδασκαλίας τῆς Ὀρθοδόξου Καθολικῆς Ἐκκλησίας (Athens, 1957); English translation by George Dimopoulos, *A Synopsis of the Dogmatic Teaching of the Orthodox Catholic Church* (Scranton, 1973).
27. M. Pomazansky, *Orthodox Dogmatic Theology: a concise exposition*, translated by Hieromonk Seraphim Rose of the St. Herman of Alaska Brotherhood (Platina, 1984), p. 394 (the Russian original was first published in 1963). The classic nineteenth-century Russian work of dogmatic theology by Metropolitan Makarii (Bulgakov) of Moscow mentions Palamas only in a footnote: see the French translation, *Theologie dogmatique orthodoxe* 1 (Paris, 1859), p. 179.
28. Fr. John Romanides, while professor at the University of Thessalonike during the 1970s, emphasized the distinction in his lectures on dogmatics, but unfortunately these have not been published in full.
29. Ciobotea, "Une dogmatique pour l'homme d'aujourd'hui," *Irénikon* 54:4 (1981) 473.
30. Neeser, "The World: Gift of God and Scene of Humanity's Response," *The Ecumenical Review* 33:3 (1981) 275.
31. "Some Characteristics of Orthodoxy," *Sobornost* 5:9 (1969) 628.
32. "Orthodoxy, Life in the Resurrection," *Eastern Churches Review* 2:4 (1969) 371.
33. *The Victory of the Cross*, p. 5.
34. Costa de Beauregard, *Dumitru Staniloae*, p. 93.
35. Foreword to Staniloae, *Theology and the Church*, p. 9.
36. Preface to Staniloae, *Le génie de l'Orthodoxie*, p. 13.

POSTSCRIPT

While this book was in the press, Archpriest Dumitru Staniloae died at Bucharest on 4 October 1993, in his ninetieth year. He thus had the joy to see, following the collapse of the Ceaucescu regime, the inauguration of a new era in the history of the Romanian Church and nation, full of dangers but also full of great hope. Although inevitably his energies had been diminished by his great age, he remained alert and active up to the end. Taking advantage of the new opportunities for apostolic work which existed from the end of 1990, he composed regular articles on pastoral and spiritual themes which appeared in the national press. The vast crowd present at his funeral — which was attended by the entire episcopate of the Romanian Orthodox Church — provided visible testimony to the profound respect and affection with which Fr. Dumitru was regarded. *Memory Eternal*!

Bishop Kallistos of Diokleia
Pembroke College, Oxford

Chapter One

Natural Revelation

The Orthodox Church makes no separation between natural and supernatural revelation. Natural revelation is known and understood fully in the light of supernatural revelation, or we might say that natural revelation is given and maintained by God continuously through his own divine act which is above nature. That is why Saint Maximos the Confessor does not posit an essential distinction between natural revelation and the supernatural or biblical one. According to him, this latter is only the embodying of the former in historical persons and actions.[1]

This affirmation of Maximos must probably be taken more in the sense that the two revelations are not divorced from one another. Supernatural revelation unfolds and brings forth its fruit within the framework of natural revelation, like a kind of casting of the work of God into bolder relief, a guiding of the physical and historical world toward that goal for which it was created in accordance with a plan laid down from all ages. Supernatural revelation merely restores direction to and provides a more determined support for that inner movement maintained within the world by God through natural revelation. At the beginning, moreover, in that state of the world which was fully normal, natural revelation was not separated from a revelation that was supernatural. Consequently, supernatural revelation places natural revelation itself in a clearer light.

It is possible, however, to speak both of a natural revelation and of a supernatural one, since, within the framework of natural revelation, the work of God is not emphasized in the same way nor is it as evident as it is in supernatural revelation.

Speaking more concretely and in accordance with our faith, the content of natural revelation is the cosmos and man who is endowed with reason, with conscience, and with freedom. But man is not only an object that can be known within this revelation; he is also one who is a subject of the knowledge of revelation. Both man and the cosmos are equally the product of a creative act of God which is above nature, and both are maintained in existence by God through an act of conservation which has, likewise, a supernatural character. To the acts of conserving and leading the world towards its own proper end, there corresponds within the cosmos and within man both a power and a tendency of self-conservation and of right development. From this point of view, man and the cosmos can themselves be taken as a kind of natural revelation.

But man and the cosmos constitute a natural revelation also from the point of view of knowledge. The cosmos is organized in a way that corresponds to our capacity for knowing. The cosmos — and human nature as intimately connected with the cosmos — are stamped with rationality, while man (God's creature) is further endowed with a reason capable of knowing consciously the rationality of the cosmos and of his own nature. Nevertheless, according to Christian doctrine, this rationality of the cosmos and this human reason of ours which enables us to know are, on the other hand, the product of the creative act of God. Thus, natural revelation is not something purely natural from this point of view either.

We consider that the rationality of the cosmos attests to the fact that the cosmos is the product of a rational being, since rationality, as an aspect of a reality which is destined to be known, has no explanation apart from a conscious Reason which knows it from the time it creates it or even before that time, and knows it continually so long as that same Reason preserves its being. On the other hand, the cosmos itself would be meaningless along with its rationality if there were no human reason that might come to know the cosmos because of its rational character. In our faith, the rationality of the cosmos has a meaning only if it is known in the thought of an intelligent creative being before its creation and in the whole time of its continuing in being, having been first brought into existence precisely that it might be known by a being for whom it was created, and that a dialogue between itself and this created rational being might thus be brought about through its mediation. This fact constitutes the content of natural revelation.

Christian supernatural revelation asserts the same thing when it teaches that, to God's original creative and conserving position vis-à-vis the world, there corresponds, on a lower plane which is by nature dependent, our own position as a being made in the image of God and able to know and to transform nature. In this position of man, it can be seen that the world must have its origin in a Being which intended through the creation of the world — and through its preservation continues to intend — that man should come to a knowledge of the world through itself and to a knowledge of that Being.

We appear as the only being which, while belonging to the visible world and stamped with rationality, is conscious both of the rationality it possesses and, simultaneously, of itself. As the only being in the world conscious of itself, we are, at the same time, the consciousness of the world; we are also that factor able to assert the rationality of the world, and to transform the world consciously to our own advantage, and able, through this very act, to transform ourselves consciously by our own act. We cannot be aware of ourselves without being conscious of the world and of the things in it. The better we know the world, or the more aware we are of it, the more conscious we are of ourselves. But the world, by contributing in this passive manner to our formation and to the deepening of our self-consciousness, does not itself become — through this contribution — conscious of itself. This means that we are not for the sake of the world, but the world is for us, although man does also need the world. The point of the world is to be found in man, not vice versa. Even the fact that we are aware that we need the world shows man's superior position vis-à-vis the world. For the world is not able to feel our need for it. The world, existing as an unconscious object, exists for man. It is subordinated to man, even though he did not create it.

The "reasons" or inner principles[2] of things reveal their light in human reason and through the conscious rational action of man. Likewise, our reason reveals its own power and depth even more richly by uncovering the reasons within created things. Yet, in this reciprocal influence, it is human reason and not the reasons within things which has the role of a subject working consciously. The reasons within things disclose themselves to human consciousness and must be assimilated by it and concentrated in it. They disclose themselves insofar as they have human reason as their virtual conscious center and by helping reason to become their own actual center. They are the potential rays of human reason on the way towards being revealed as its actual rays, and it is through these that human reason extends its vision farther and farther.

The fact that the world is understood within man and for man and through man shows that the world exists for man, not man for the world. But the fact that man himself, by explaining the world, understands himself for his own sake through the world demonstrates that man is in need of the world too. It is the world that has been created to be humanized, not man to be assimilated into the world or into nature. It is the whole world that has been created to become a Man writ large or at least to become the content of Man, a content which comprehends all things in each person; it was not man who was made to be part of nature, having no more meaning than any other part of nature, even to being swallowed up into nature. For if man were thus eventually to disappear into nature, the most important factor in reality would be lost, without nature gaining anything new, whereas, through the assimilation of the world into man, nature itself gains, for it is raised up to a plane which is entirely new, even though nature itself, properly speaking, does not disappear. Our disappearance into nature would represent no progress of any kind even for nature, whereas the continual and ultimately eternal humanization of nature does represent an eternal progress, quite apart from the fact that, through such a humanization, nothing, certainly not what is most valuable in reality, is lost. Our disappearance into nature would imply a static situation within a process that remains always essentially identical with itself and is, therefore, in its monotony, absurd.

Some of the Fathers of the Church have said that man is a microcosm, a world which sums up in itself the larger world. Saint Maximos the Confessor remarked that the more correct way would be to consider man as a macrocosm, because he is called to comprehend the whole world within himself as one capable of comprehending it without losing himself, for he is distinct from the world. Therefore, man effects a unity greater than the world exterior to himself, whereas, on the contrary, the world, as cosmos, as nature, cannot contain man fully within itself without losing him, that is, without losing in this way the most important part of reality, that part which, more than all others, gives reality its meaning.

The idea that man is called to become a world writ large has a more precise expression, however, in the term "macro-anthropos." The term conveys the fact that, in the strictest sense, the world is called to be humanized entirely, that is, to bear the entire stamp of the human, to become pan-human, making real through that stamp a need which is implicit in the world's own meaning: to become, in its entirety, a humanized cosmos, in a way that the human being is not called to become, nor can ever fully become, even at the farthest limit of his attachment to the world where he is completely identified with it, a "cosmicized" man. The destiny of the cosmos is found in man, not man's destiny in the cosmos. This is shown not only by the fact that the cosmos is the object of human consciousness and knowledge (not the reverse), but also by the fact that the entire cosmos serves human existence in a practical way.

The inferior chemical, mineral, and organic levels of existence, although they have a rationality, have no purpose within themselves. Their purpose consists in constituting the material condition of man's existence, and they have no consciousness of this goal of theirs. Within man, however, the order of certain conscious goals is disclosed. And it is only within the framework of these goals intended by man that the understanding of the goals of those levels inferior to him is also disclosed, for they have a place in reference to the purposes intended by him so that he can project, like a great arch over them all, an ultimate and supreme meaning to existence.

In contrast with the levels below him, man does not fulfil the goal of his own existence by serving another level above himself, for in the world no such level as this exists. Man follows his own goals. In this area, however, a great variety exists from man to man. Every man, depending on his own conscience and freedom, makes use of the different levels inferior to himself. And in order to make use of them, man organizes and transforms by his labor the data of the world, imprinting on them his own stamp. This adaptation of the world to man's needs — needs which are always growing and becoming more refined — demands, in the first place, that man have knowledge of the things of the world. But it likewise belongs to our nature — as the only being conscious of itself and of the world — to search for a meaning to our own existence and that of the world as well. And only the perspective of the eternity of our existence can give us this meaning. In our consciousness of self, there is implied, simultaneously with this search for the meaning of our existence, the will to continue in being forever so that we might deepen the infinite meaning of our own existence and that of the whole of reality.

According to this conception, we have been created for eternity inasmuch as we gasp, like suffocating beings, after eternity, after the absolute. We wish to love and to be loved more and more, striving after a love which is absolute and endless. But this we can only find in relation with a Person who is infinite and absolute, a conscious Person, if we may speak pleonastically. We strive to discover and achieve an ever greater beauty, to know an ever more profound reality, to progress within a continuous newness. In all these ways, we aim at the infinite because we are *person.* Yet all these aspects of an infinite reality we can only find in an infinite Person, or better, in a communion of Persons who are infinite in being, in love, in beauty. From an ever growing communion with this Personal reality,[3] newer and newer rays of reality, of beauty, and of innovation shine forth in us and — through us — upon all aspects of the world, while more and more dimensions and horizons of reality are being disclosed.

Communion with Personal reality or with the infinite Persons becomes for men the means of an infinite progress in love and knowledge and it is this which keeps continuously alive the interest of our own consciousness of self. Even though human self-consciousness might continue in endless self-replacing succession and transmit with this succession the meaning of existence as humanity comes to know it, if the meaning of his own existence for each member of this succession were not carried on into eternity in order to be eternally deepened, the meaning of our existence would appear to us as devoid of any real sense. In fact, subjects do not exist for the sake of some interrupted consciousness or even for the sake of an uninterrupted eternal consciousness; rather, consciousness exists for the sake of the subject and gives meaning to it. It is only through such a consciousness which is eternal and which becomes eternally more profound that we prove ourselves to be the purpose of all the inferior levels of existence, illuminating forever all the meanings and realities of the world and making them eternal. Only thus can it be seen that all things are for our sake and that we constitute for ourselves an eternal purpose, indeed the eternal purpose of all the things in the world.

Only thus is the purpose of all the inferior components of the world fulfilled in us. It is in the everlasting nature of our being that the meaning of all things — understood as the contents of a continuous enrichment and deepening of our eternal consciousness — is eternally being illuminated.

In fact, in everything we do we follow a purpose and for this purpose we make use of the things in the world. But we ourselves have need of a final eternal purpose, or better, we must ourselves be a final eternal purpose if we are to show ourselves as meaningful beings in everything we do. Through all the things we do, we manifest, directly or indirectly, an eternal purpose of this kind or we pursue the maintenance of our existence as an eternal purpose. Only in this do we find the meaning of our existence and of our deeds. We must, therefore, see the purpose of our existence projected beyond passing, earthly life, for if death were to bring a definitive end to our existence, we would no longer be a goal in our own right, but only a means within an unconscious process of nature. In that case, the entire meaning of our life and all the goals we pursue — and indeed all things whatsoever — would become meaningless.

According to our faith, however, the order of meanings cannot be left out of account. Meanings are real and man cannot live without them. He cannot endure to live without a consciousness of meanings and without pursuing them, for they culminate in a final meaning which man is convinced he will attain beyond death. If man were to dispute the reality of these meanings, his would be the unhappiest of existences. The animal has no knowledge of meanings, nor can it deny their reality. Through his consciousness, man is not content to lead an existence the meaning of which is to serve — without realizing it — a higher level of created reality, a level within which man would end his own existence. In a conscious fashion, man pursues his own meaning and, in the last analysis, he pursues an ultimate meaning which is the maintaining and perfecting of himself forever. He is a goal in himself for eternity. He is created for eternity and has in himself a kind of absolute character, that is, a permanent value which never ceases to grow richer. Man is open to meanings higher than the world, and through him, the world, too, is open to these meanings. Through understanding, through freedom, through action, and aspiration, man is open to an order superior to that of nature, although he makes use of nature in order to be able to achieve his own meaning as a being which is called to eternal perfection. Life on earth is only a preparation for that eternal order. Our being is an existence accommodated to that order and to the possibility of a continual spiritual perfection not subjected to nature and to repetition. That order is not produced by nature, for nature merely repeats itself, but rather it organizes the entire cosmos so as to render service to man as he works in view of his own purpose which transcends the earth.

We believe that, in the case of our being, the meanings of existence cannot reach their fulfillment within an immanent spiritual life, for the relative variety of this immanent life moves within a monotonous framework and ceases as a phenomenon of natural repetition with the death of the body. The meaning of existence can only reach its fulfillment within the ultimate and eternal life, of a life that is transcendent and free from all monotony of repetition and from all relativity. Only on that plane can our life develop to infinity within an endless newness which is, at the same time, a continuous fullness.

We aspire after an order beyond us but one which lies on a path similar to that of our own personal existence; we do not aspire to being swallowed up within some impersonal plan which lies, for a while, at our limited disposal but only so that afterwards we may disappear into it. Man strains towards an infinite personal reality higher than himself, a reality from which he can nourish himself infinitely, although, given his own limited possibilities, he cannot have it at his own disposal, nor, on the other hand, does he disappear into it himself afterwards.

The order of meanings is not the product of the human psyche nor does it end with the products of the psyche. For this order imposes itself on us without our willing it and, through the aspirations it instills within us, surpasses our own psychic possibilities. Man cannot live without it. But the order of meanings imposes itself as a personal horizon, infinite and superior to man, and it requires man's freedom if he is to have a share in that order. Even during man's earthly existence, the order of meanings does call upon him to participate in itself in freedom.

Saint Maximos the Confessor observed the fact that everything reaches its fulfillment in man while he realizes his own meaning in union with the Personal reality whose spiritual life is infinite.

The final meaning or goal after which man aspires must be understood in accordance with the freedom of human being and with its capacity for infinite development. If the rationality of the impersonal, lower order finds its fulfillment and sense in service of the being of man who transcends nature, man, in turn, as a conscious and free person, aspires to find the fulfillment of his own rationality and meaning not in some loss of his own being within an essence higher than any material and spiritual order, though still subject to monotony and immanent limitation, but in a communion with a transcendent and free person. For that being which is superior to man can likewise only be personal in character. And if the higher relationship between persons comes about in commuion, then our fully and eternally satisfying relationship must be communion with a being who is also personal in character and endowed with infinity and freedom. Only a being transcendent in this sense can be always new and life-giving in this communion with man. In the same way that man, as the highest being in the world, is a person and conscious of the meaning of the entire lower order, an order which he himself fulfills, so man must also find the fulfillment of his meaning, together with all the meanings of the levels lower than himself, in a person aware of this meaning and of all the meanings in the world inferior to him. Only a still greater person and, in the final analysis, only supreme Person can be conscious of the meaning of existence as a whole, as man is conscious of the meanings of the world inferior to himself. But the supreme Personal reality does not project this total meaning upon man, without man himself assimilating this meaning in a conscious way. The supreme Personal reality communicates it to man as to a person who assimilates it consciously and thus enriches his consciousness and his whole being, finding in this very act the fulfillment of his own meaning.

In this way, the supreme Personal reality fosters that character of our being according to which we are free and conscious persons.

Only a Person of a higher order can foster and satisfy the aspiration within our human nature towards the fulfillment of its own meaning, inasmuch as only such a Person can bring it about that our human nature is no longer an object swallowed up by a level which is said to be "superior" but which remains at bottom inferior because it is unconscious. If the levels inferior to man were personal, even he could not reduce them to the state of being objects. Neither could a person of an order higher than man reduce man to the condition of being an object by dissolving or swallowing him within himself.

Our being can find its fulfillment as person only in communion with a higher personal being. Such a being cannot, however, reveal its own greatness or bring our being to fulfillment either through a relationship with the various levels below the human reality or by reducing our being to the unconscious state proper to a passive object. This requires instead a relation in which man himself, in continuously new ways, freely and consciously assimilates the infinite spiritual richness of the supreme Personal reality.

This means that our personal reality remains free in relation to this higher being. Such a relationship is analogous to the relationship of one human person to another, a relationship in which the liberty of both is preserved. In this relationship, man exists for the sake of another person and is at the service of the other, although through this, he himself is enriched. Each man exists for the sake of others in a way that he does not exist for the sake of material things. However, he does not thereby fall to the level of becoming object, for in serving other persons, he commits himself freely and, through the effort of bringing joy to others, he himself grows in freedom and in the spiritual content of his being, to say nothing of that warmth of life that comes to him from the communion and love of those other persons. It is only with other persons that man can achieve the kind of communion in which neither he nor they descend to the status of being objects of exterior knowledge used always in an identical way. Instead, they grow as sources for an inexhaustible warmth of love and of thoughts that are ever new, brought forth and sustained by the reciprocal love of these persons, a love that remains always creative, always in search of new ways of manifesting itself.

But if through death human persons cease to exist, then not a single one among them will be able to communicate and to receive infinitely this warmth of love and thus grow infinitely, which is what, in fact, man desires. Human life ended definitively by death destroys any meaning and, therefore, any value of the rationality existing in the world and, indeed, of the world itself. The meanings pursued within the perspective of this earthly life are likewise stripped of all sense and value if any human life, in which everything seems to have found meaning, comes to a definitive end in death. For our cruellest grief is the lack of meaning, that is, the lack of an eternal meaning to our life and deeds. The necessity of this meaning is intimately connected to our being. The dogmas of faith respond to this necessity that our being have some sense. Thus they affirm the complete rationality of existence.

Only the eternity of a personal communion with a personal source of absolute life offers to all human persons the fulfillment of their meaning and affords them, at the same time, the possibility of an everlasting and perfect communion among themselves.

The rationality of the subject who — with a view to his own continued existence and proper development — makes use of the rationality of nature is infinitely superior to the rationality of the latter, inasmuch as nature develops rigidly in itself with no consciousness of its own purpose. According to our faith, the rationality existing in the universe needs to be completed by, and seeks an account of itself within, the rationality of a person. By itself, it does not exhaust all rationality. When the rationality of the world is seen in itself as the only one in existence, it has led many writers and thinkers to go so far as to think of the universe, which draws every person towards death, as one huge graveyard, a universe of the absurd, a place from which meaning is gone and where rationality is irrational. But the rationality of the universe cannot be irrational. It acquires its full meaning, however, only when it is considered to have its source in a rational person who makes it serve an eternal dialogue of love with other persons. Thus the rationality of the world, if it is to be fulfilled, implies the existence of a higher subject, following the analogy of the rational superiority of the human person. It thus implies the existence of a free subject who has created and imprinted on the world a rationality at the level of human understanding which makes possible a dialogue with man, a dialogue through which man may be led to an eternal and, in the highest sense, rational communion with the infinite creative subject. Everything which is an object of reason can only be the means for an interpersonal dialogue.

Hence, the world as object is only the means for a dialogue of loving thoughts and works between supreme rational Person and rational human persons themselves. The universe bears the mark given to it by its origin in rational creative Person and by its destiny to be the means for an interpersonal dialogue between that Personal reality and human persons so that these might remain for all eternity in the happiness of that same communion between them. The entire universe bears the stamp of a personal rationality intended for the eternal existence of human persons.

It is only through an eternal participation in the infinity of this supreme Personal reality that our being reckons it will see its own meaning fulfilled. This is how the Orthodox Christian doctrine of the deification of our being through participation in God or through grace is to be understood.

In other words, our being reckons that its own meaning and, simultaneously, the meaning of the whole of reality will be fulfilled only by virtue of the fact that between our persons and supreme or divine Person, there is no place for an intermediate existence: after God, man is also, in a way, immediate, able to participate immediately in everything God possesses as a degree of the supreme existence, all the while remaining man.

To reach this goal, or to fulfill this meaning towards which our being tends, we not only ascend to communion with supreme Person, but that Personal reality also descends to be with us. For love demands that each of those who love one another moves towards the other. Through all things, God gives himself to man, and man to God.

This is, in general, the content of the faith asserted by the meaning of existence, a faith which compels recognition on the basis of the evidence in nature. And far from hampering the development of creation, such faith assumes that this development is carried on infinitely and eternally, to the measure of man's own aspirations.

This faith expresses the incontestable fact that the world has been made for a purpose and, therefore, that it is the product of a creator who gives meaning and is guided by that creator towards the fulfillment of its purpose in himself. Moreover, with this goal in view, the creator himself leads our being towards the closest union with himself. These elements of faith are a kind of natural dogma and have their source in what is called natural revelation through which God makes himself known by the very fact that he created the world and man, and stamped on them certain meanings. These elements of faith constitute an acknowledgement of the fact that the world has its highest point in the human person who moves toward union with supreme Person as towards his final goal. These dogmas of natural faith affirm the maintenance of life on the superior level of meanings, just as they affirm the ascending dynamism of human persons as bearers of these same meanings towards that complete meaning which is eternity of existence in union with the supreme Personal reality.

Far from reducing existence to a closed horizon, they open for it the horizon of the infinite and look for ways of preserving existence from the narrow and monotonous horizon which ends in death.

Saint Maximos the Confessor describes the ascending dynamism of the world in these terms: "The final goal of the movement of the things that move is to reach the eternal and good existence, just as their beginning lies in the existence which is God. For he is both the giver of existence and the One who gives the gift of that good existence as its beginning and its goal."[4] The human being cannot rest until he achieves eternity of existence in the infinite and, thus, in the happiness of full existence. The blessed Augustine said: "*Inquietum est cor nostrum donec requiescat in te.*"[5]

But the meanings of existence, including its final sense, however evident they seem, do not compel the recognition of science in the way that natural phenomena do, for the latter occur in the same fashion repeatedly and can be subjected to experimentation. That is why the firm acceptance of these meanings has the character of faith. In other words, in their recognition, we see a paradoxical combination of their self-evidence and the necessity of accepting them by a deliberate act of will intended to preserve human existence on a level superior to that of a natural existence characterized by repetition ending in death. Thus, in the recognition of these meanings, the fact of freedom is also involved. The person of my neighbor discloses to me some of its meanings, but, on the other hand, their recognition depends on my freedom. And free acceptance of them presupposes faith.

This acceptance through faith belongs more properly to the domain of relations between the human person and divine Person and to the perfection of these relations in eternity, however self-evident the necessity of this relationship and of its perfection in eternity may appear to be as the meaning of existence.

This domain is a synthesis between self-evidence and faith because it is a domain of freedom and spirit. Thus, Saint Isaak the Syrian says: "For faith is more subtle than knowledge" or "faith is higher than knowledge."[6]

On the other hand, considering that faith is joined with the evidence of a higher domain, he also says: "Knowledge is perfected by faith and acquires the power to ascend on high, to perceive that which is higher than every perception, and to see the radiance [of him] that is incomprehensible to the intellect and to the knowlege of created things.... Faith, therefore, now shows us, as it were before our eyes, the reality of [that future] perfection. It is by our faith that we learn those things that cannot be comprehended, not by the investigation and power of knowledge."[7]

Nevertheless, both as content and as the power of acceptance, natural faith or faith based on natural revelation must be completed by the faith granted us through supernatural revelation.

NOTES

1. Cf. *The Ambigua*, PG 91.1128D-1133A, 1160B-D.
2. The Romanian phrase translated here as "the 'reasons' or inner principles of things" (*ratiunile lucrurilor*) corresponds to the Greek *logoi* and recurs throughout the work. These *logoi* are the objects of the first stage of contemplation (natural contemplation) and, as the intelligible structure of created things (cf. the Latin *ratio*), they are all contained within the Logos himself as the unitary and unifying cosmic principle; cf. *The Philokalia. The Complete Text,* trans. and ed. G. E. H. Palmer, P. Sherrard, K. Ware (London, 1979), p. 363. [Trans. note.]
3. The Romanian phrase translated here as "Personal reality" and in many other places through the text as "divine Personal reality" or "supreme Personal reality" or simply as "Person" without any article (*Persoana divina, suprema*) is characteristic of Father Staniloae's vocabulary for God. The plain English translation "a/the divine person" would, however, be a source of confusion in many of those same places, since it conveys to the English reader a unitarian concept of God which the author in no way intends and which his own Orthodox theology of the trinitarian life as communion of the three divine persons constantly belies. [Trans. note.]
4. *The Ambigua*, PG 91.1073C.
5. *Confessions* 1.1.1, PL 32.661: "Our heart is restless until it rests in you."
6. *Homily* 52; ET, Holy Transfiguration Monastery *The Ascetical Homilies of Saint Isaac the Syrian* (Boston, 1984), pp. 262 and 256.
7. *Homily* 52; ET p. 257.

Chapter Two

Supernatural Revelation

The Confirmation and Completion of Natural Faith

No matter how self-evident it appears, natural faith, which has its source in God's revelation through nature, is subject to doubt. This is true, first of all, because we are continuously tempted to take as the only existing reality that order of phenomena known through the senses and, through those instruments which prolong the senses, phenomena which offer bodily satisfactions connected with a transitory existence. It is true more completely, however, because the inevitable reality of death is opposed objectively to our thirsting after the fulfillment of the meaning of our existence in an eternal perfection. This doubt is nourished in turn by another fact, namely, that the order of meanings which shows man the prospect of perfection through communion with infinite Person does not seem to be confirmed within natural faith by the initiative of such a Personal reality.

Thus, the light of meanings or of the final eternal meaning of existence flickers in the dark. In this situation, supernatural revelation comes to our help. By it the infinite and eternal Personal reality, of his own initiative, enters into communication with man and also provides a foundation for our communion with our fellow men.

As, through supernatural revelation, we know the divine infinite Personal reality in his own clear initiative, we realize that there is a connection between the subjective, transient, and lesser temptations offered by nature and death as sorrowful objective reality. Further, we realize that these things represent not the natural state of existence, but a fallen state, for either death gives the impression that there is no other life beyond it, or, inversely, man weakens in himself the spirit called to eternal life by paying exclusive attention to passing pleasures of the flesh. These respective temptations represent a weakening in our lived pursuit of meanings and, therefore, a sin. Death is the result of this weakness or sin, however, for it is the ultimate collapse of reality into meaninglessness.

Hence, supernatural revelation strengthens the self-evidence of those points of natural faith in which the light of a higher and eternal meaning of existence is flickering. Supernatural revelation does strengthen natural faith because it completes it, both through the knowledge it brings to man that, because of sin and death, his nature now finds itself in an unnatural state, and also through the help it gives man to overcome this present unnatural state. Thus, supernatural revelation represents a bringing back of human nature to its own true state, while giving human nature, at the same time, power to reach the final goal towards which it naturally aspires. In this way, supernatural revelation confirms and restores natural faith or nature itself as natural revelation. Only through supernatural revelation do we fully know what nature, and the revelation it represents, are. Natural revelation appears to us in its full meaning only through supernatural revelation. Therefore, after the fall of the first man into sin, these two revelations must be seen as closely connected to one another. In fact, supernatural revelation reestablishes our nature and the nature of the world. It makes certain the self-evidence of natural faith regarding the goal of man and of the world, for, in his sinful state, man did not have complete certainty of these things nor was he able to make up his mind with ease.

If the first man's sin had not intervened, his nature, and with it the world itself, would have advanced naturally towards the goal of eternal perfection in God and been strengthened in communion with him even while on earth. But since this advancement was no longer possible either for him or for the world without supernatural revelation, the latter came to rescue our nature from the weakness in which it had fallen.

Due to supernatural revelation, both supreme Person — the final goal of the rational creature — and the way of advancing towards that supreme Personal reality are known by rational creatures clearly, just as they would have been known if the rational creature had held steadfast to natural revelation; for the light of supernatural revelation is cast now over the whole of nature. It is in this way that we must understand the affirmation of Saint Maximos the Confessor that natural revelation has the same value as supernatural revelation. But he specifies that it is for the saints that natural revelation has had the same value as supernatural revelation, that is, for those raised to a vision of God similar to that of supernatural revelation.[1] For the saints, the written law is nothing other than the law of nature seen in the personal types of those who have fulfilled it, while the law of nature is nothing other than the written law seen in its spiritual meanings beyond these types. Both are one when they are seen as leading towards the grace of the life to come.[2] Through Christ, his garments — the creatures — are themselves filled with his own light.[3]

From what has been said, however, it is at the same time clear that, consequent upon the weakness man contracted through sin, supernatural revelation is necessary if the content of natural revelation is to be fully developed.

In fact, supernatural revelation has accompanied natural revelation from the very beginning — first in the life of humanity, then, in a special way, in the life of the people of Israel. To Job and his interlocutors, God himself reveals his activity in nature (Job 38.41). David also says, through God's inspiration: "The heavens are telling the glory of God and the firmament proclaims his handiwork" (Ps 19.1). And the mother of one of the seven brothers in the Book of Maccabees tells him: "I beseech you, my child, to look at the heaven and the earth and see everything that is in them, and recognize that God made them out of things that did not exist. Thus also mankind comes into being" (2 Mac 7.28). She urges him to see from nature that man — God's creature — is created for God, because from nature itself it can be seen that God exists as Person above nature, and that man as a personal creature is created for eternal union with the supreme Personal reality and, by means of this, for union with his fellow men. To achieve this eternal union with supreme Person and with the persons of his fellows, man must also accept death from which he cannot escape, though he may be able to postpone it. Therefore, she continues: "Do not fear this butcher, but prove worthy of your brothers. Accept death so that by God's mercy I may get you back again with your brothers." But the certainty and clarity of this faith from nature is achieved by the young boy because of the fact that he knows the Law of Moses. For he answers: "I will not obey the king's command, but I obey the command of the law that was given to our fathers through Moses" (2 Mac 7.29-30).

Where supernatural revelation has no longer accompanied natural revelation and the latter has remained alone, serious obscurities of natural faith in God have occurred, giving rise to pagan religions with extremely unclear ideas about God. Most often these ideas confused God with nature, and made the continuation of the human person in eternity a matter of doubt.

This leads us to believe that it was only supernatural revelation, or the influence of it in certain cases, that has preserved natural faith from alteration. Under this influence, some endowed with a finer spiritual perception have grasped the truth about God found in natural revelation; indeed, they have even possessed a sensitivity for the voice of God speaking in their consciences and for his manifestation in nature. Elihu, Job's partner in discussion, says: "But it is the spirit in a man, the breath of the Almighty, that makes him understand" (Job 32.8). Some of the ancient Greek philosophers also arrived at the concept of the one God, but the god known by them did not so clearly have the personal features of the God known in the Old Testament, or known even from nature under the influence of supernatural revelation. This shows that, in principle, a more correct knowledge of God and of the meaning of our life through natural revelation taken by itself is not excluded; very rare, however, are those who grasp the content of its fundamental points and they never acquire full clarity or certainty regarding these points without some influence coming from supernatural revelation.

But the subjective attitude of those few, on account of their spiritual weakness, cannot do away with the objective revelation of God manifested in the self-evidence of the meaning of existence imprinted in their being. Therefore, in practice, many people live in a way that accords with this meaning, and when they do not, they feel guilty for not taking it into account. Saint Paul says this in the following words: "When Gentiles who do not have the law do by nature what the law requires, they are a law to themselves, even though they do not have the law. They show that what the law requires is written on their hearts, while their conscience also bears witness and their conflicting thoughts accuse or perhaps excuse them" (Rom 2.14-15).

God reveals himself objectively through conscience and nature. Subjectively, however, or on account of the sin within them that they have seconded with their own will, most people either resist the self-evidence of God and of that true meaning of their lives which is revealed to us naturally, or else they distort this evidence and refuse to make the contribution of their will necessary to accept it. In a general way, Saint Paul attests both these things: the fact of an objective natural revelation of God in human hearts and in nature, and the subjective refusal of many to accept the evidence of God revealed in this way. "For the wrath of God is revealed from heaven against all ungodliness and wickedness of men who by their wickedness suppress the truth. For what can be known about God is plain to them, because God has shown it to them. Ever since the creation of the world, his invisible nature, namely, his eternal power and deity, has been clearly perceived in the things that have been made. So they are without excuse" (Rom 1.18-20).

But the fact that those who were not under the influence of supernatural revelation could subjectively refuse faith based on natural revelation so easily meant also a weakening of objective self-evidence of God from natural revelation. This is due especially to death, which the weakness of man's spirit brought into the world. Hence it was necessary that God resort to supernatural revelation, not only as a kind of speaking in which his person might appear more clearly, but also as a series of supernatural acts through which he might, on the one hand, make evident his existence and his work and, on the other hand, make more sensitive the subjective perceptiveness of human beings so that they discern God as person and as the meaning of human life, and so facilitate man's decision to accept God through faith. Supernatural revelation has thus given clarity and certainty to natural faith, but it has also broadened knowledge of God and of the eternal meaning of our existence and that of the world. Moreover, through his supernatural acts, God has shown to the conscious creature the possibility of being raised up from the level of a nature fallen under the bondage of death, a slavery which was weakening man's faith that the eternal meaning of his own existence could be achieved. The supernatural acts of God's direct revelation provide conscious creatures with the hope of raising themselves above nature through God's grace and through freedom.

By means of the words of supernatural revelation, man has also learned what he can understand from natural revelation when this is enlightened by supernatural revelation. Through nature, the conscious creature sees the omnipotence of God, his goodness, his wisdom as creator and master of providence and, thus, himself learns to be good, to be intelligent, and to strive towards final union with God. Even death — and our inability to get used to death — teaches us not to be attached to this world, and shows that we are created for eternal existence. Many of the direct words of supernatural revelation teach us these same things. But man does not come to know the possibility of fulfilling his life's meaning except in the words and acts of supernatural revelation. Only these show him that he can escape the corruption of nature; they alone open for the man of faith both the perspective of avoiding dissolution within a nature subject to the corruption of all individual forms, and also the possibility of being saved. Only the dogmas of faith from supernatural revelation assure him the prospect of being free in the face of nature, even during his earthly life, together with complete freedom in an eternal existence.

From this it is clear that the acts of supernatural revelation do not suppress human nature as personal nature, but raise it from the state of weakness and of the corruption of its integrity in which it finds itself to that plane where it continues to all eternity in that perfection to which human nature aspires. Even the fact that these acts are accompanied by words which, at bottom, demand from man nothing more than a life oriented towards God and not totally submerged in the world — which is what natural revelation also demands — even this fact shows that the acts of supernatural revelation have no aim other than the raising of our nature from its fallen state and the fulfillment of our aspiration for perfection in eternity.

The words which have accompanied these acts have often done nothing more than require man to work during his earthly life in order to make himself fit for eternal life, the possibility of which was opened up and revealed by the acts of supernatural revelation. But this same demand is made by the natural law written in the conscience. Thus, when Saint Paul or Saint Maximos the Confessor speak of the equality of the natural law with the written law, they refer especially to the moral teaching of the Old Testament, not to the two modes in which God reveals himself, that is, through natural phenomena or through direct speech and supernatural acts.

In order to understand the fact that, on the one hand, supernatural revelation comes about through direct speech and through acts which transcend nature while, on the other, it does not contradict nature and natural faith but confirms and perfects them, we must first show what the two revelations have in common and what distinguishes supernatural revelation from nature and from the manifestation of God through nature.

The Convergence and Distinctiveness of the Two Revelations

The inseparability of the two kinds of revelation and their content which is, in part, common to both (indirectly provided by objective natural revelation and explicitly by supernatural revelation)[4] would not be comprehensible were we to hold, as Western theology has accustomed us to hold, that in natural revelation man is the only active agent.

This separation of God from nature, a nature through which God speaks and works, or rather through which he speaks by working and works by speaking, has easily led to various kinds of conceptions that have sought to explain the world exclusively on the basis of an immanent reality. But natural revelation is inseparable from supernatural revelation and the faithful feel themselves in immediate connection with God by means of the former as well. Yet this is true only if God manifests himself continuously in natural revelation by speaking and working continuously through all things, through all the combinations of things chosen by him, and through all the thoughts conveyed to him in these and, directly, in the human conscience, leading man in this way towards the fulfillment of the meaning of his existence in eternal union with himself.

In fact, God speaks and works continuously through created and directed realities, by creating circumstances that are always new, circumstances through which he calls each man to fulfill his duties towards God and his neighbors and through which he answers man's appeals at every moment. These realities and circumstances are so many thoughts of God made manifest, hence, so many words given concrete shape. But God speaks to our being especially through the thoughts he arouses in our conscience when we desire to do something or must do something or when, after we have done something wrong, he speaks to us through reprimands, difficulties, and illness. Through all things, it is God who is leading us, as in some ongoing dialogue, towards our perfection and opening up to us the perspective of total fulfillment for the meaning of our existence in communion with the infinite God.

The prophet David frequently affirms that God speaks through the greatness of nature, but he does not fail also to affirm that God speaks through the various troubles or joys which man experiences during his life. To illustrate the former, we have the words of Psalm 19:

"The heavens are telling the glory of God; and the firmament proclaims his handiwork. Day to day pours forth speech, and night to night declares knowledge. There is no speech nor are there words; their voice is not heard; yet their voice goes out through all the earth, and their words to the end of the world" (Ps 19.1-4). For the fact that God speaks through various troubles and through the help we receive, we have the following: "[The Lord] heard my cry. He drew me out of the desolate pit, out of the miry bog . . . " (Ps 40.2-3). Elihu first describes God speaking through various situations: "For God does speak, perhaps once, or even twice, though one perceives it not. In a dream, in a vision of the night, when deep sleep falls upon men, as they slumber in their beds, it is then he opens the ears of men and as a warning to them, terrifies them; by turning man from evil and keeping pride away from him, he withholds his soul from the pit and his life from passing to the grave. Or a man is chastened on his bed by pain and unceasing suffering within his frame, so that to his appetite food becomes repulsive, and his senses reject the choicest nourishment. His flesh is wasted so that it cannot be seen, and his bones, once invisible, appear; his soul draws near to the pit, his life to the place of the dead . . . He shall pray and God will favor him; he shall see God's face with rejoicing and thus he will get his pardon" (Job 33.14-22,26).

God's attitude towards us as persons is also shown sometimes in his refusal to answer. Perhaps it is God's refusal to answer those who do not call upon him with all their heart that explains how evidence of his presence and his activity in nature and in man's conscience can grow weak. Elihu continues: "Then they cry out, but he does not answer because of the pride of evil men. Surely God does not hear an empty cry, nor does the Almighty regard it" (Job 35.12-14).

Natural revelation goes on objectively at all times and in all places. It addresses itself to everyone; and those who recognize it in the light of supernatural revelation, and together with the teaching and the work of supernatural revelation, it helps in their progress towards eternal life.

Supernatural revelation specifies the goal of natural revelation as well as the ways of realizing it. In the light of supernatural revelation, Christians see how God is leading them to an ever greater communion with himself through things, through circumstances, through happenings both good and bad, through the voice of conscience, or through their own ideas as well. But Christians recognize that this communion is realized fully in Christ who has truly come down to us; they know that in Christ the sure foundation has been laid for complete union between God and the man who believes in him, the one in whom man's existence will be eternal. Thus, supernatural revelation makes specific the manner of this divine leading and helps our human reality, weakened as it is by sin and hindered by death, to advance effectively towards full and eternal union with God. Christians see how natural revelation is made specific and brought to completion through supernatural revelation which has its culmination in Christ. Both kinds of revelation lead toward God as the final and eternal goal.

By natural revelation, God leads the man who believes in him towards the goal of union with himself through indirect utterance and through things, making use of the various circumstances, problems, troubles, and pains that man faces and of the thoughts aroused in his conscience so that man can progress towards God through the way in which he faces up to all these things. In short, God makes use of what belongs to nature. By supernatural revelation, God causes his own words to appear directly in the conscience of the believer, or other words which manifest his own Person. In this, God does not work through nature but through a kind of utterance and action which makes more obvious the presence of his Person as he guides man towards union with that Personal reality as his final goal. Through this, God enters into direct and evident communion with the believer and this convinces him of God's existence and satisfies his thirst for communion with infinite Person, giving him proof at the same time that he is not left to the care of blind forces that will cause him to be lost, but is raised instead to a relationship with the supreme Personal reality who will lead him into an eternal existence in full communion with himself.

This more direct manifestation of God's Personal reality through his utterance and through the guidance of believers towards full union with himself is visible in the fact that God sends special and conscious instruments to whom he reveals himself in word so that they, in turn, may communicate to others God's thoughts and plans for them. In natural revelation, everyone has knowledge of God speaking through situations, circumstances, and personal events. But this communication with God is not sufficiently plain. Things themselves intervene too much between the human person and God, endangering communion between them.

In supernatural revelation, God makes himself known clearly as person, inasmuch as he calls and sends out a particular person to a particular human community. This person arrives with a responsibility awakened powerfully by God. On the one hand, God confirms the natural evidence that our being possesses about the future fulfillment of its meaning in union with God and, on the other hand, he shows man that this union will not come about nor is it being prepared in isolation, but rather in the solidarity of each man with his neighbor. Hence, this preparation does not come about only through situations interpreted by man in isolation, but through the mission of a person who draws the attention of all to the content of his mission. It is not isolated individuals whom God wishes to save through supernatural revelation, but the great multitudes of believers in a mutual and common responsibility towards himself, for all must help one another on the way of progress towards the goal of perfection and eternal life, and help strengthen their own communion based on communion with God. In fact, the communion among them is a constitutive part of their own perfection and of their progress towards that perfection.

In order to be seen more clearly as Person transcending nature and sovereign over it, capable of preserving our being from falling into slavery to nature, God makes himself known in supernatural revelation and through supernatural acts which cannot be treated as natural phenomena. These constitute another series of embodied words, a series above that embodied in the things and phenomena of nature. As such, these words do not occur continuously, for, in that case, they could seem to be the same as the natural phenomena which occur over and over again. These, however, are not only supernatural but also out of the ordinary. Generally speaking, along with the teachings accompanying them, they form a part of an ascending series in which God is manifested more and more clearly. For it is only by stages that God prepares our human nature enslaved to death by raising it spiritually to be able to pass over to the plane of communion with him — a plane not subject to death — and to understand this passing over.

In the Old Testament, at the beginning stages of the formation of the people of Israel, supernatural acts are concerned mostly with nature so that the community of the people of Israel may be strengthened by the knowledge that it is led by a God who transcends nature and so as to convince the community to attach itself closely to him. Once this faith has been unified and strengthened, God's activity upon souls to raise them to himself occurs during the time of the prophets through his words, although God does not by any means renounce his supernatural activity over nature. In the person of Jesus Christ, God's supernatural actions directed towards nature are concerned especially with human nature and correspond with the spiritual ascent of the latter. They make known the causal role the Spirit has within supernatural acts, as well as the highest spiritual level to which human nature is raised in Christ and the perspective Christ opens for all who unite themselves to him through faith.

The line of supernatural acts and the line of spirituality do not meet in Christ at the highest level, however, as if they constituted two parallel peaks. It is precisely the supreme spirituality of Christ which contains within itself the power to overcome the automatism of nature. The defeat of this automatism of repetition does not come about through an external victory over nature, as in mythology; it is the result of actualizing the higher power of the Spirit which overcomes nature without destroying it. Protestantism, for which spirituality is of lesser value, has no longer understood the supernatural acts in the life of Christ and has declared them mythological. This has led logically to the need to demythologize.

When explained through the climactic power of the Spirit, supernatural acts concerning the person of Christ, such as his supernatural birth and resurrection, do not nullify the nature he took from us with its own contribution; instead, they lead our human nature to the summit of its own realization, for our nature has the spirit as its highest component, and our spirit seeks, in a natural way, to expand its inherent potential in the divine Spirit. Christ's human nature thus remains within an eternal existence. Consequently, supernatural acts which touch his human nature, first and foremost among which is the resurrection, are to be understood rather as acts which restore the nature of man and that of the world in general. The incarnation of Christ represents, at one and the same time, both the descent of God to full communion with humanity and the highest ascent of the latter. God became man so that man might become God.

Christ has made himself the starting point for all who believe in him, as much through his transcending the laws of nature fallen into sin as through the fact that, in so doing, he leads towards its full realization that true human nature which, through the process of its spiritualization, was created to be in communion with God as an absolute Personal reality not subjected to the automatism of nature. Christ's words express his own condition as perfect man and are themselves intended to help us rise to a spiritual level similar to his own, one that corresponds to his risen state. For in Christ, there is made manifest the perfect relationship linking the highest spiritual level with that plane which transcends the laws of a nature tending towards death. The resurrection is the effect of that supremely spiritual level which, in Christ, humanity has attained through union with the deity.

God resorts to extraordinary supernatural acts especially at the beginning of new periods in the history of the plan of salvation. This was true during the time of the patriarchs, of Moses, of Joshua, of Elijah, and at all principal moments in the formation and protection of the people of Israel as bearer of the message of salvation. Nevertheless, the truly new and final period is inaugurated by the extraordinary supernatural acts of Jesus Christ. Through these acts, the people of God is formed in every part of the world and advances towards a state in which man can make his own everything that was given to human nature in Christ, and in which he can participate in God through direct and maximum communion with him.

If all the extraordinary supernatural acts of revelation are acts of great importance in the history of our salvation and guide us towards the final goal, then the supernatural acts achieved in Christ through the agency of our own human nature place that nature under the direct illumination of its final goal.

Clearly, the history of salvation does not consist of supernatural acts alone, because these do not occur continuously, just as God's supernatural revelation is not given continuously. These acts are found, however, within the order of an ascending spiritual progression and, in this sense, they have a history, which is the history of salvation. Between occurrences of these acts, the existence of the faithful is woven together from the words and supernatural acts of revelation. Thus, each stage of revelation carries within it a force which drives the spiritual life of our nature to a level where it is made capable of entering a new period, one inaugurated by a series of new and extraordinary supernatural acts and by the words of a higher knowledge and experience.

Supernatural acts worked upon particular created things or forces of nature, or the placing — in some extraordinary fashion — of certain created things and forces of nature at the service of those who believe, in order to guide them towards the fulfillment of their destiny, manifest more clearly not only the direct words of supernatural revelation, but also the words of God in nature. It can thus be seen that all of nature is called to become a more transparent milieu through which person is manifested, and to be brought under the power of the personal spirit.

In the periods between the occurrences of supernatural acts and their accompanying words, mankind lives not only from the light of supernatural acts and words of former times, but also from the natural revelation which occurs every day and has its own movement in history, enlightened by the former acts and words.

Thus, the whole history of salvation is guided, enlightened, and strengthened in good by divine revelation. But this does not mean that it consists only in the acts and words of that revelation; it is made up also of our responses to them. Our sensitivity to those acts and words and the power of our responses to them are frequently and to a great extent weakened and cut off by sin. But sin, too, in certain respects, is affected by the level of knowledge and spiritual subtlety mankind has reached through revelation. Sin can take on more sophisticated forms. Hence, revelation leads the world in a generally forward direction, both in the sense of good and of evil. In a certain manner, each of these serves the other.

The acts of supernatural revelation and the words explaining them have a prophetic character both because of the new periods they inaugurate as well as by reason of the perspectives they open towards the final goal. Prophecy is not only an external criterion which serves to prove some fact of supernatural revelation; it is also a part of its essence.

Revelation confirms and sustains our advance towards a final ascending goal and makes clear the loftiness of this goal. But even in its natural movement, creation is animated by a prophetic aspiration; that is, even natural revelation has a prophetic dynamism. But, given the sin which weighs down our human nature, we could make no progress towards the final goal — based as it is on natural revelation — in the absence of the illumination and help of supernatural revelation. Yet even supernatural revelation, in guiding creation towards its final goal, cannot dispense either with creation's own inherent aspiration or with the natural feeling that God urges and helps the world towards progress in continuously new circumstances.

Thus, God's acts and words in the two kinds of revelation form part of his plan to guide creation towards union with himself, that is, towards deification.

Christ represents the ultimate stage of supernatural revelation and the fulfillment of its plan. From him there radiates the power to fulfill this plan for the whole of creation and the entire universe. The period after Christ, therefore, is the ultimate stage in the history of salvation. History in its entirety is the interval during which progress towards the fulfillment of this plan occurs. The perfection of this fulfillment, however, takes place beyond history in the age to come. The moving force during this concluding period comes from Christ who attracts creation into the eschatological condition, that is, into the state of eternal perfection to which he led our human nature, namely, complete union with God.

Thus, Christ represents the climax of supernatural revelation and the full confirmation and clarification of the meaning of our existence through the fulfillment of this existence within himself, the one in whom our ultimate union with God, and thus our perfection also, is achieved. But simultaneously it can be seen that the absolute after which we aspire does not have an impersonal character, but is itself Person. Moreover, as we ourselves enter into ultimate communion with the Absolute as person, we also participate in the absolute. We are called to become an absolute by grace through our participation in the one who is personal Absolute by nature. The one who is personal Absolute by nature wishes to grant the human person a share in his absolute character, inasmuch as he himself becomes man. By the very fact of creation, the conscious person is already a virtual absolute through a certain participation. Hence, there can be no transcending of the person. Our person does not participate in the absolute by transcending its own nature as person, but by remaining man and by being confirmed in this quality. The incarnation of God as man leads our own absolute aspiration to its perfection through participation. That is why there can be no other essentially new acts of supernatural revelation beyond the incarnation and resurrection of the Son of God. The history of salvation now has as its purpose to provide believers with the opportunity of making themselves capable, with Christ or in Christ, of participating completely in the personal Absolute.

The Activity of the Word of God and of the Holy Spirit

Progress in the history of salvation, determined by revelation, is progress in knowing and fulfilling the meaning of our existence in God as direct and perfect communion with the Absolute as person, and in him, with all the persons of our fellow men. It is progress in knowing and fulfilling God's plan of salvation. In keeping with this, revelation is the work of the Son and Word of God after whose pattern man was created, inasmuch as the Son of God has his own origin in the Father and answers the Father's call. But revelation is also the work of the Holy Spirit as one who continuously makes us spiritual, strengthening us more and more in that loving freedom which is liberated from the automatism of nature. Progress in the believer's likeness to the Son and Word of God comes about by the fact that the Word himself draws closer and closer to us through the history of revelation. Then, as he takes our own image to himself in order to restore it, uniting it to himself as to the pattern, he lifts us up to our full realization by raising and exalting that humanity of ours which he assumed to be the basis of our own resurrection and ascension. This is at the same time a further step in our own becoming spiritual beings, for, if we are not spiritual in this sense, we will will not be able to be raised in glory or to ascend into heaven. This cooperation of the Word of God and of the Holy Spirit can be observed, first of all, in revelation down to the time of its conclusion in Christ, and after that in the Church, in Scripture, and in Tradition. The important role played by the Holy Spirit in the fulfillment of revelation, and in its efficacy afterwards, shows that the revelation of the Logos as the highest meaning of existence, and his incarnation in human nature, are one with this function of making human nature a spiritual reality brought about by the Holy Spirit, and that the two go forward together.

The Word of God, who prepares us to receive him through the revelation of the Old Testament, then becomes incarnate, rises from the dead, and attracts us also to resurrection and to eternal union with him; he reveals himself as the full meaning of our existence, who is himself filled with power to illuminate and attract. Our resurrection in Christ is, thus, the purpose of revelation and of the world. The Holy Spirit leads us to see the power of this meaning to our existence and gives us as well the capacity to make it our own and to be stamped by it. Saint Athanasios the Great said that the Word assumed a body in order that we might receive the Holy Spirit and that God became bearer of the body in order that man could become bearer of the Spirit.[5] Saint Symeon the New Theologian holds that the purpose of the entire work of our salvation through Christ is for us to receive the Holy Spirit, and Kabasilas, in turn, says: "What is the effect and result of the . . . acts of Christ? . . . it is nothing other than the coming of the Holy Spirit upon the Church."[6] The Savior himself said: "It is to your advantage that I go away. . . . And I will pray the Father, and he will give you another Counsellor to be with you forever" (Jn 16.7, 14.16).

The Word and the Holy Spirit are the two persons who together accomplish and jointly bring to fulfillment the whole of revelation and of its efficacy until the end of the world. To use the expression of Saint Irenaios, they are "the two hands of the Father," that is, the two active persons. Together they render the Father more and more transparent: "The brightness of the Trinity radiates outwards progressively."[7] Between the Word and the Holy Spirit exists a continuous reciprocity of revelation and both bring about a common revelation of the Father, and a common spiritualization of creation. The Word never lacks the Spirit who causes us to receive the Word; nor does the Spirit lack the Word with whom he unites us more and more. But each of the two has his own place in the act of revelation corresponding to his position in the internal life of the Holy Trinity. Hence, they are always together. Just as within the Holy Trinity, the Holy Spirit, by coming to rest upon the Son, or shining forth from him,[8] shows forth the Son to the Father, and the Son shows forth the Holy Spirit to the Father, because of the reciprocity existing between them,[9] in the same way within revelation and its subsequent effects, the Son sends the Holy Spirit forth into our innermost being, and the Spirit sends forth the Son or leads him before our spiritual vision, or even brings him directly within us. The blessed Augustine says: "Let us not think that the Son was sent in such a way by the Father that he was not also sent by the Holy Spirit."[10] And Saint Ambrose says: "Both Father and Spirit have sent the Son; in the same way, both Father and Son have sent the Spirit."[11] God draws near to us in his own condition and with the *élan* that characterizes it.

To this complementary work of revelation which is common to the

Son and the Holy Spirit there is a development. Paul Evdomikov sees this development as an alternation of the increasingly evident works of the Spirit and of the Word. In the Old Testament, the Holy Spirit prepared the coming of the Word in the flesh, and the Word, having once become incarnate, prepares the coming of the Spirit who will, until the end of the world, prepare for the second coming, in glory, of the incarnate Word, risen and exalted. "Through the mouth of the prophets the whole of the Old Testament is a preliminary Pentecost in view of the appearance of the Virgin and her Fiat."[12] Afterwards, "Pentecost appears as the ultimate purpose of the trinitarian economy of salvation. Following the Church Fathers, it could even be said that Christ is *the great Precursor of the Holy Spirit.*"[13] On the other hand, Evdokimov remarks that the Holy Spirit and the Word are always together, although in one period one of the two stands in the foreground, while at another period, it is the other of the two: "During *Christ's earthly mission,* men's relation to the Holy Spirit was brought about only through and in Christ. On the other hand, *after Pentecost* it is the relation to Christ which is brought about through and in the Holy Spirit. . . . The ascension does away with the historical visibility [of Christ]. . . . But, Pentecost restores to the world the interiorized presence of Christ and reveals him now not *before,* but *within* his disciples."[14]

In the Old Testament, God's word is still a word with limited spiritual effects and a word that has scarcely been revealed within the spiritual depths of man, because of the reduced level of his spiritual sensitivity. Thus, the power of God is manifested not only through the word itself, but also through accompanying acts exterior to the word, for these had a greater impression upon people at the lower spiritual level on which they found themselves. When Moses received on Sinai the Law — which might be called the concentrated word of God — the mountain "was wrapped in smoke, because the Lord descended upon it in fire; and the smoke rose from it as though from a furnace, and the whole mountain trembled violently" (Ex 19.18). This proved God's presence, on the one hand, to those who were waiting but, on the other hand, it placed a curtain between them and God. This very thing happened afterwards: "When Moses entered the tent, the pillar of cloud would descend and stand at the door of the tent, and the Lord would speak with Moses" (Ex 33.9).

Over the Word, or over Moses who represented him, there lay a veil until the incarnation of the Word as man. And the Spirit in the Old Testament did not shine forth in a visible way except on rare occasions. In the Old Testament, it was under the veil of the Law that the Word worked upon human subjects who were not sufficiently prepared in the realm of the spirit. Hence, in a parallel fashion, it was with acts of power that the Word impressed them. People were more impressed at that time by the radiance of the externals. Even the glory of God was shown to them in a more or less external manner. Saint Paul the Apostle says: "Since we have such a hope, we are very bold, not like Moses, who put a veil over his face so that the Israelites might not see the end of the fading [that is, exterior] splendor [by looking through the interior one]. But their minds were hardened; for to this day, when they read the old covenant, that same veil remains unlifted, because only through Christ is it taken away. Yes, to this day whenever Moses is read a veil lies over their minds; but when a man turns to the Lord the veil is removed" (2 Cor 3.12-16).

But in the case of persons from the Old Testament who had an increased sensitivity to the Spirit, the Spirit did also shine forth from the Word. In this way, the Holy Spirit not only prepared those in the Old Testament to receive the Word made flesh, but, through the Spirit, the Word himself was preparing his incarnation. After his ascension into heaven, moreover, it is still the Word who — through the Spirit who shines forth from him — prepares his own future coming in glory. "Just as the Word of God, before he came visibly and in the flesh, came spiritually to patriarchs and prophets, prefiguring the mysteries of his coming, so, likewise, after this appearance too, he comes not only to those who are children, feeding them spiritually and leading them to the age of their perfection in God, but also in those who are perfect, sketching in them secretly beforehand, as in an icon, the features of his future coming."[15]

In the Old Testament, insofar as men appear more capable of the Spirit because of their preparation through the Law, the work of the Spirit shines forth more intensely in them through the divine word. This is especially the case with the prophets. The Word himself who is communicated to them possesses more of the Spirit, that is, of an intrinsic spirituality. Men are, thus, prepared for the complete indwelling of the Spirit of the Son in human nature, simultaneously with the incarnation of the Son as man.

These events occur when men have been prepared to sense the

shining forth of the Spirit through human nature assumed by the Word, when this nature has itself been raised to such a capacity for the divine that, with all its own sensitivity, it can receive the Spirit and cause him to shine forth towards other men who have themselves become capable of perceiving the Spirit through what is human. The Holy Spirit has now made of human nature the center where he himself acts and from which he shines forth together with the Word of God. Now there comes to the forefront the Spirit's most proper role which is that of the sanctification and deification of human beings. Moreover, the human spirit is now revealed as possessing the greatest potential capacity to be conformed to the Holy Spirit.

The total return of the Holy Spirit to human nature takes place in Christ, for in him the divine hypostasis of the Word itself becomes the hypostasis of the human nature and reveals human nature to us as capable of union with God to the highest degree. From now on, the Holy Spirit has his center of irradiation in the Word made man, or in that Man who is also God. This constitutes the supreme spiritualization of the human being.

The complete result of the work of the Holy Spirit within the humanity of Christ remains, however, his resurrection. Thus, it is from Christ's risen state that the entire activity of the Spirit shines forth.

Before Christ's resurrection, the Holy Spirit shone forth from him in a more or less hidden fashion, rather in the way the illumination of the Spirit was included in the word of the Old Testament. But Christ himself felt the entire activity of the Spirit at work within him, since this was proper to their common nature, just as it was felt to a certain extent by the Apostles also and by all those who were closest to him. But for others, the Spirit remained hidden. Nevertheless, those who had eyes to see and ears to hear perceived the Spirit in Christ much more intensely than the people of Israel sensed him in Moses or in the prophets of the Old Testament.

From the time of the resurrection, however, the Spirit has suffused Christ's body completely, and from the time of Pentecost, those who believe in Christ are sensible of the full power of the Spirit shining forth from Christ. Yet they do not see his body because their own eyes are fleshly and they still see only what is shown to the flesh. Nevertheless, at their resurrection, when they too will have become entirely light, when their bodies will have been wholly suffused with the Spirit, they will discern the body of Christ wholly suffused by the spiritual, or, better, as the fully transparent organ of the Spirit. And this will come about through the spiritual sensitivity of their own bodies increased to the full so that they may respond to the presence of the things which are not seen.

This alternation is not a matter, therefore, of exchanging the direct presence of the Son and of the Holy Spirit for an indirect presence. It has to do, rather, with a progress in our own spiritualization, simultaneous with the progress of revelation itself. Revelation culminates in the descent of the Holy Spirit at Pentecost, for this descent is in function of Christ's resurrection and ascension in the body as its highest spiritualization. Through this begins the application to ourselves of the effect of revelation, that is, our being led by the Spirit of Christ — the Risen and Exalted One — towards resurrection and ascension in the body, not by the Spirit alone, therefore, but also by Christ himself.

In the resurrection of Christ, or in his body become transparent through and on behalf of the Spirit, there is revealed to us the purpose for which the world was created; and in our final resurrection, when our bodies too will be fully transparent through the Spirit in a perfect union with Christ, that same condition will be brought about for the whole of creation.

This demonstrates that revelation consists not so much in a disclosure of a sum of theoretical information about a God enclosed within his own transcendence, as it consists in God's act of descending to man and of raising man up to himself so that there might be achieved, in Christ, the deepest possible union and that this achievement might be the basis for extending between God and all the people who believe in him this same union. The various kinds of information given in revelation depict this act of God's descent and of the raising up of the man who believes. The words themselves merely explain this act of God and urge us at the same time to cooperate so that this union might also come about between each one of us and God. For the deepest union between God and the believer does not take place without the free cooperation of the latter.

Hence, revelation occurs through acts and words, through light and power; it is the act that enlightens and the light that transforms the one who believes. It reveals not only what God does for man, but also what man will become through God's action and through his own cooperation; it also reveals the meaning and the final purpose of human existence, or what might be called that final state for which we are destined and which itself constitutes our total fulfillment.

Revelation consists, therefore, not only in a sum of acts performed by God and in their interpretation through his words, but also in the anticipation and description of the final goal of creation, a goal which God has begun to bring about through the various acts he has performed. Revelation has a prophetic, eschatological character also. But in revelation God prophesies this final goal of creation not as through a science which objectively and passively sees beforehand the point creation will reach on its own, but by showing that — with its free cooperation — he himself will lead creation to that point through all the acts of power he performs. The acts of power and the words of God contained in revelation exert an effectiveness of their own until the time when their complete goal is fulfilled. That is to say, revelation remains active and contains in itself the description of that same effectiveness as it continues along. As he reveals himself in revelation as its active, saving factor, God also prophesies, at the same time, how he will lead creation to its final goal through his acts or, more precisely, through those dynamic states which he has brought into being in Christ as his own continuous acts. In revelation, God also presents himself as the prophet who is going to fulfill his prophecy.

Christ is the supreme prophet. In this sense, revelation remains active even though, on the other hand, its content has been closed, for in revelation the dynamic basis has been laid for all that will continue to be done and it has indicated all that was going to be done. God, who has been at work in the course of revelation, continues to work in the same way. The Son of God, who through his incarnation comes at the conclusion of revelation to the deepest intimacy with us and who through his resurrection becomes, as man, the means whereby the Holy Spirit can have the greatest possible effect upon us to lead us also to his own condition — this same Son of God remains within this intimacy and maximum effectiveness that transforms all created things. Through the incarnation and resurrection, and through the descent of the Holy Spirit, the Logos — as the meaning of all created things — has become their interior meaning and goal, a meaning and a goal that not only reveal what created things are going to be, but also lead them through the Spirit to what they ought to be, at the same time revealing in himself the fulfilled meaning of creation and of revelation.

In this sense, the revealed Christ remains and goes on working within creation, that is, he makes the entire revelation perpetually effective to lead believers towards union with himself and towards deification. He brings this about through a progressive spiritualization of the faithful in the Holy Spirit and to this end he makes use of three means which are concrete and unified: the Church, sacred Scripture, and holy Tradition.

NOTES

1. *The Ambigua*, PG 91.1149C-1152B, 1176B-C.
2. Ibid. PG 91.1152A-C.
3. Ibid. PG 91.1160C-D.
4. Ibid. PG 91.1152B-D.
5. Cf. *The Incarnation of the Word* 8, PG 26.996C.
6. *Commentary on the Divine Liturgy* 37, PG 150.452B; cf. Paul Evdokimov, *L'Esprit Saint dans la tradition orthodoxe* (Paris, 1967), p. 89.
7. Cf. Irenaios, *Against the Heresies* 5.1.3, ed. A. Rousseau, *SC* 153, pp. 26.83/28.85; Gregory of Nazianzos, *Oration* 31.26, PG 36.161D-164A.
8. Gregory of Cyprus [Patriarch of Constantinople 1283-1289], *Exposition of the True Faith against Bekkos*, PG 142.240C, 242B-C; *Apology*, PG 142.260B, 267A; *The Procession of the Holy Spirit*, PG 142.286A-B. Further discussion in D. Staniloae, *Theology and the Church* (Crestwood, NY., 1980), pp. 16-29.
9. Joseph Bryennios, *Twenty-Four Homilies on the Procession of the Holy Spirit*, (Buzau, 1832) [in Romanian]; cf. E. Boulgaris, Ἰωσὴφ μοναχοῦ τοῦ Βρυεννίου τὰ εὑρεθέντα (Leipzig, 1768), vol. 1, pp. 1-448 and the author's discussion of Bryennios' teaching on the relation of the Son and the Spirit in *Theology and the Church*, pp. 33-38.
10. *Against Maximinus* 2.20.4, PG 42.790.
11. *The Holy Spirit* 3.1.8, PL 16.811A.
12. Evdokimov, *L'Esprit Saint*, p. 87.
13. Ibid. p. 89.
14. Ibid. p. 90.
15. Maximos the Confessor, *Gnostic Chapters* 2.28, PG 90.1137B-C.

Chapter Three

Scripture and Tradition

Supernatural revelation came to its close in Christ. For in him, as in its first exemplar, the plan to save and to deify creation has reached its fulfillment. This plan cannot lead any higher. God draws no closer to man that he has in Christ. The union between God and man cannot advance any farther nor can we grow to any higher fulfillment than the one available to us in Christ.

But this does not mean that — by its very content — supernatural revelation can no longer be active. As God who came into the closest intimacy with us, as man raised to the supreme heights through union with God in a single person, as God's plan completed and given in him concrete expression to its uttermost fulfillment, Christ begins the work of extending to all of us that state which has been achieved in him.

His state has a dynamic character. As God, he wishes to achieve, in his humanity, intimacy with all men as partners equal to himself and to maintain the personal identity of each. In this way, he desires to raise each man to the level where his own humanity reaches its maximal realization. In other words, Christ wishes to extend God's plan already fulfilled in himself.

But Christ is above all. He is not a human person who stood in need of salvation and who, with this salvation in view, was united to God. He assumed human nature which was not hypostasized in itself but in his own hypostasis in order to make it the fundamental means through which he might extend to all men the deification to which his own human nature was raised. But precisely in this way, Christ can fulfill that work of saving and deifying all, as no other man could do it. He is not a human person united with the divine person; for any man could have been in that situation, inasmuch as he would not be the human center which is also God. In such a case, communion with Christ would not bring about that communion with God himself for which our being yearns. Christ is the divine person who — being man also — makes possible, through that communion accessible to us with himself as man, the communion of all with God himself, or with absolute Person. He is the center and foundation of that act whereby salvation and deification are extended to all who believe. In him, as in its foundation, the plan of salvation has been fulfilled.

The act of extending his plan is similarly carried out by Christ through the Holy Spirit; it was through the Holy Spirit that he communicated revelation and created and sustained the community of the people of Israel in its incomplete phase of existence. It is also through the Holy Spirit that the continuous efficacy of a revelation which has reached its conclusion is maintained through the creating and sustaining of the higher and universal community of the Church. The Church is the dialogue of God with the faithful through Christ in the Holy Spirit. This dialogue, conducted formerly by the Word from afar, becomes an intimate dialogue through the incarnation of the Son of God as man and begins to spread through the Church. The Church is, thus, that supernatural revelation concluded in Christ as it exercises its effect upon us in the course of time through the Holy Spirit. It is supernatural revelation — which has reached its fullness in Christ — in the act of spreading and bringing forth much fruit in those who believe. The Church is Christ united in the Holy Spirit with those who believe and over whom has been spread and through whom is spreading Christ's own act of drawing the faithful — by means of dialogue with them — into the process of growing into his likeness. Through the sensibility produced in them by the Holy Spirit within the Church, the faithful become aware of Christ's power by which the whole of revelation is fulfilled, and aware also of its action in themselves. But they do not discover a new revelation or some further revelation beyond the one fulfilled in Christ. Revelation continues to be active in the world through the Holy Spirit, in and through the Church, but it is not being continually completed by the addition of new parts. It is complete in Christ and from his power it is integrally at work in and through the Church on those conscious beings who believe and receive the faith. The light and power of revelation reached their zenith in that sun which is Christ.

The Church is Christ as fullness of revelation, having its continuous effectiveness from him. From him it continues to give light and warmth through the Holy Spirit to those who believe, and it does this not only until the end of time but to all eternity, in and through the Church on earth and in heaven, drawing light and warmth from Christ's Body as the form of their communion with him and among themselves. If revelation, which has become fully real in Christ, possesses in itself a prophetic dynamism, a kind of prophecy in motion, the action of revelation to the time of its final goal is entailed in that prophetic dynamism which finds expression in and through the Church.

Through the Holy Spirit, the Church has the mission, therefore, to put into effect not just any revelation at all but the revelation fulfilled in Christ, or, we might say, to make Christ effective as the embodiment of integral revelation and in the true prophetic tension implied in him. Hence, the Church has the mission to preserve, through the Holy Spirit, the revelation fulfilled in Christ who makes her capable of discerning the authenticity of revelation in its fullness and in the impulse that pushes it towards its true final goal. The Holy Spirit preserves the Church as witness to and as the competent means of making real the authentic revelation, and thus making human existence reach its fulfillment in Christ. Understood in such a way, this revelation is objectively unchanged in both Scripture and tradition. Therefore, the Church, through sacred Scripture and holy tradition, keeps revelation — in its true understanding — active. The action of the Church is nothing other than a putting of revelation, preserved in its integrity, into operation, and a preparation of the faithful to receive its work, or, better, the work of Christ who is expounded in sacred Scripture and communicated through holy tradition.

If Scripture and revelation become fully concrete in Christ, the Church cannot dispense with them by affirming that she has Christ himself. For they are the authentic expression of Christ, and the Church cannot remain with a Christ who has not been expressed. For a Christ who is not expressed cannot manifest his effectiveness. But because she has a Christ who is at work within her through the Holy Spirit, the Church alone is capable of understanding and interpreting Scripture authentically, that is, as something made up of stages, words, and acts which express the risen Christ and lead those who believe towards their fulfillment in the true Christ.

The Spirit of Christ makes us sensitive to Christ and unites us with him in the Church, because the fire of the Spirit which is spread from Christ cannot be separated from the common human sensitivity for Christ. He manifests himself as one who works through the fire of active faith. This fire is life within the continuous perfection of communion with Christ. Through the Spirit, the faithful are linked with Christ not in isolation, but together among themselves. Whoever attains to faith in Christ attains it through the faith or the sensitivity of someone else. The interpersonal sensitivity of faith in which the Holy Spirit is manifested links those who believe within the community of faith, that is, in the Church. The joyful sensitivity of communion with the absolute person of Christ spreads in the joy of communion and of works done in communion with others, and in the participation of others in the Personal reality of a God come down, in Christ, to the level of communion with human beings.

The Church is, therefore, more than just the only one who understands Scripture and tradition as the living and dynamic expression of the power of Christ — our final goal; she is also the only one who makes this power, or the warmth of this power, real through the sensitivity produced among all human beings by the Holy Spirit.

The Relation of Scripture to Church and Tradition

The living dialogue of the Church with Christ is conducted principally through Scripture and tradition. Sacred Scripture is one of the forms in which revelation keeps on being effective as God's continuous appeal. It is the written expression of the revelation fulfilled in Christ. It presents Christ in the form of his dynamic word and of the equally dynamic word of the holy Apostles concerning his saving works in their permanent effectiveness. But it also describes both the way God has prepared our salvation in Christ and the way Christ continues to be at work until the end of the world, extending his power so that we may grow in his likeness. Through the word of Scripture, Christ continues to speak to us also to provoke us to make a response in our deeds, and thus to be actively at work within us too. Through the word of Scripture, we sense that Christ continues to be at work in us through his Holy Spirit: "I am with you always, to the close of the age" (Mt 28.20). Sacred Scripture is the Son and Word of God who translated himself into words in his work of drawing close to men so that he might raise them up to himself, until the time of his incarnation, resurrection, and ascension as man. Through these words by which he is translated, Christ works upon us to bring us also to that state which he has reached. Scripture conveys what the Son of God in his condition as God and as perfect man continues to do with us and, therefore, Scripture interprets the work Christ is doing in the present. For Christ, who remains always alive and the same (Heb

13.8), interprets himself through the same words, but as the one who wants to make us also like himself.

Saint Maximos the Confessor, having mentioned these two expressions of Saint Paul speaking about us upon whom "the end of the ages has come" (1 Cor 10.11), and about the coming ages when God "might show the immeasurable riches of his grace in kindness toward us in Christ Jesus" (Eph 2.7), says: "Now that the ages arranged by decree beforehand to accomplish the work by which God was to become man have been brought to an end in us and God has truly achieved and fulfilled his perfect incarnation, we must henceforth wait for those other ages to come, which have been arranged to accomplish the work of man's mystical and ineffable deification."[1] But the riches that God will show us in the ages to come, the entirety of the goodness he has shown towards us in Christ, is described in Scripture. Sacred Scripture is, thus, not merely a book which helps us remember what God has done in preparing for the incarnation of his Son and in that incarnation itself; it is also a book that tells us what the incarnate Son of God is now doing and will continue to do until the end of the ages to bring us also to resurrection. For Scripture depicts not only God's coming down to us on earth even to the extent of his incarnation, but also the beginning of his raising us up to deification through the resurrection, and the beginning of the extension of this act of his spreading out within the early Church from the state of resurrection and providing the pattern for his action until the end of the world. For in Christ who is risen from the dead and seated at the right hand of the Father, God has shown us what he will give us also in the ages following the resurrection of his Son, a resurrection which is the foundation of our eternal life. For it is in Christ or with him that God has "raised us up . . . and made us sit with him in the heavenly places" (Eph 2.6). Sacred Scripture is, thus, a book which is always contemporary. "Heaven and earth will pass away, but my words will not pass away" (Mt 24.35; Mk 13.31; Lk 21.33).

Christ's words must be believed because they are God's words (Jn 3.34); so, too, must those of the Apostles about him, based as they are on his own words and deeds (Acts 4.29, 6.2, 7.8-14, 13.5,7,46, 16.32, 17.13). Hence, these words are fulfilled in those who obey them. For they are "spirit and life" (Jn 6.63); they are "the words of eternal life" (Jn 6.68). But they can be believed by, and bring eternal life to, those who hear them only if the Spirit is at work in them. "He who is of God hears the words of God; the reason why you do not hear is that you are not of God" (Jn 8.47). But the Spirit who produces faith in the one who hears them is the Spirit of Christ. Christ is our ultimate meaning; in him our ultimate meaning is fulfilled through the sensibility produced and maintained in us by the Holy Spirit. It is Christ himself, therefore, who is at work through the Holy Spirit in the one who hears his words and does not resist their content. Thus, Scripture is one of the forms through which the words of Christ are preserved, not only in the words spoken by him in the past, but also in the words which he is continually addressing to us.

Holy Scripture provides testimony to the work of the Spirit that was produced in those who listened to Christ's words or to the words the Apostles spoke about Christ after his ascension into heaven, based on his sayings and deeds. "But many of those who heard the word believed" (Acts 4.4). "While Peter was still saying this, the Holy Spirit fell on all who heard the word" (Acts 10.44).

Scripture does not tell us whether someone might have come to faith by simply reading the words of God contained in Scripture. This omission could be explained, of course, by the fact that no Scripture about Christ existed during the time from which the above testimony came. In general, however, the word of Scripture has power when it is communicated by one believer to another, whether by repeating it in the form it has in the Scripture, or by explaining it. For, in the faith which passes between them, the Holy Spirit is at work. Faith, as a work of the Holy Spirit, comes to one person through another, but only when this other communicates the word of Scripture assimilated and confessed with faith, or with the capacity of experiencing communion in the Spirit. Scripture elevates its own power in the communion between persons, in the transmission of its word with faith from one person to another down through the generations. From the very beginning, there must have existed persons who came to believe not by reading the Scripture, but through contact with a person who gave them faith in its content, and it was on this basis that they believed in the content, a content which was spoken first of all and afterwards set in writing. This person was Christ. Complete vision into the divine depths of Christ and the capacity to be sensible of them — these were the gifts of the Spirit of Christ who was at work in the communication of this vision and sensibility. Henceforth, the words of Christ or those about him, whether or not they were written in the Scripture, are the exterior means of expressing and transmitting the faith and of keeping it always fresh both within the framework of the Church and also spreading from the Church to those outside her, while it is the Holy Spirit who is concomitantly responsible for transmitting these words and keeping them ever fresh.

When we attribute this role to words, we understand more than just an exact reading or repeating of them; we have in mind, first of all, their content, which is a testimony about Christ. Yet even in this case, the continuous reading of Scripture by some person in the church community is implied, for this keeps the circulation of its undiminished and unaltered content alive and fresh within the church community. In this sense, Scripture guarantees the preservation of the living, unaltered faith in the Church, though, in its turn, Scripture is made fruitful by the Spirit of Christ, the Spirit of faith, and is preserved through that Spirit within the community of the Church ever since its foundation in accordance with the intense contact certain persons have with Christ.

Moreover, those who receive the faith from others, on the basis of the general content of Scripture communicated to them, penetrate more deeply into the richness of its spiritual meanings through subsequent frequent contact with Scripture. They are thus convinced more and more that its words can come only from God because they contain in themselves the infinite depths of the divine life. These spiritual meanings strengthen more and more the faith that was received through the other as a gift of the Spirit; they respond more and more to the thirst to know God and to the manner in which faith expects God to be. The condition created by the Spirit who brings forth faith in us is deepened by these meanings of the words of Scripture in such a way that no separation can be made between the work of the Spirit who comes to us through the other and the effect which the scriptural words have with respect to the content of the Scripture. In fact, the Spirit is transmitted to us from the other through the word of Scripture as it is believed by the other, and the enriching of my own faith through the reading of Scripture or through meditating on its content occurs in communion with others, that is, within the community of the Church. Apart from Scripture, faith would grow weak and in time its content would become impoverished and uncertain in the heart of the Church; but apart from the Church, the effects of Scripture would not have been made real, for Scripture would have been lacking that transmission of the Spirit which passes from those who believe to those who receive the faith.

Thus, the Spirit makes the words of Scripture real in the community of the Church. Even now Christ utters his words in the Holy Spirit, bringing more and more of their meanings to light in accordance with the level of the age and of the ecclesial community. As soon as we pass beyond the letter of Scripture and beyond reading it without spiritual understanding, it yields not only its own spiritual meanings but also the work of the Spirit of Christ achieved through these meanings in the one who is reading. We can even say that it yields Christ himself who discloses ever greater depths of his own spiritual richness. In this way the faithful comprehend more and more "what is the breadth and length and height and depth" and "the love of Christ which surpasses knowledge," that they may be "filled with all the fulness of God" (Eph 3.18-19). Saint Maximos the Confessor says: "Much [spiritual] knowledge is needed in order that, by removing carefully first the veils of the letters which cover the Word, we may be able with an unveiled mind to regard the pure Word himself, standing by himself and showing the Father in himself clearly, to the extent that human beings are capable of this vision."[2]

The words of Scripture are the inevitable occasion for us to enter through the work of the Spirit into relation with the authentic person of Christ who transcends them, but this certainty is effected not just by the reading of these words in their written form, but by grasping them in their content.

For this reason, the experience of the Apostles was the reverse: firstly, they knew the person and the deeds of Christ, some of which have been prophesied by him, and afterwards, "they believed the Scripture and the word which Jesus had spoken" (Jn 2.22). In this sense, faith in the person of Christ has been transmitted since the time of the Apostles through oral preaching and, subsequently, those who came to believe in him have confirmed and enriched their faith by reading the Scripture as well.

Nevertheless, as a means or an inevitable occasion through which faith in Christ is maintained and strengthened, and when it had taken shape, "all Scripture is inspired by God" (2 Tim 3.16).

Christ, who is at work in us through the Holy Spirit, communicating himself as the Scripture describes him, is also in the Church. The Church is the body of Christ in which he works throughout the course of time.

The Church is full of Christ as he goes about his saving work. But, if Christ is active in the Church, the Scripture that describes him, when it is actively at work, is also in the Church.

As a reality fulfilled in Christ, however, and manifesting the very same effectiveness through the Church down the course of the centuries, revelation signifies tradition. Hence, tradition is the Church herself as the very form of Christ's undiminished effectiveness through the Holy Spirit, or as the form of that revelation which is fulfilled in him over the centuries.

Therefore, "no prophecy of Scripture is a matter of one's own interpretation, because no prophecy ever came by the impulse of man, but men moved by the Holy Spirit spoke from God" (2 Pet 1.20-21). In the ocean of meanings which belong to the Spirit beyond the literal sense, no navigator can avoid going astray without the guidance of the same Spirit who hands down the understanding of them in the Church from generation to generation.

The Relation of Tradition to Church and Scripture

Tradition gives a permanent reality to the dialogue of the Church with Christ. The content of Scripture, received through the faith handed down from the Apostles in the community of the Church, is not a human product but something inspired by the Holy Spirit, and so it must be preserved on the one hand while, on the other hand, those unchanged meanings received from the Apostles must be deepened. Hence, Scripture requires a tradition which is unchanged from the Apostles. It represents another form of preserving and making use in its continuous effectiveness of that integral revelation fulfilled in Christ. Scripture has an intrinsic dynamism. Its content seeks to be made known, applied, and lived in an ever greater depth and intensity, for the very content of revelation — Christ, the incomprehensible one — seeks to be known and appropriated more and more deeply, and to be loved more and more intensely. Tradition keeps this dynamism of the Scripture contemporary without changing it, for tradition represents an application and a continuous deepening of the content of Scripture. At the same time as it preserves the authentic dynamism of Scripture, tradition, in its quality as true interpreter of Scripture, brings that dynamism to bear upon real life. This approach to Scripture and tradition is, in essence, the apostolic approach. For the understanding of his epistles, Saint Paul refers to his oral preaching which obviously remained in the community as tradition and through tradition (1 Cor 11.2, 15.3; 2 Thess 2.15, 3.6). This "apostolic teaching" or explanation of the faith must remain as a permanent model, as a rule not to be changed (Rom 6.17; Jude 3). From the beginning, the Church persevered in and was urged to persevere in "the apostolic teaching"; this reported the words and deeds of Christ, but it also constituted an explanation of them held in common and this, by its very nature, did not come about apart from the Spirit of Christ (Acts 2.42, 17.19; Rom 16.17; Acts 13.12; Tit 1.9; Heb 13.9; Rev 2.14). But, in its exposition, this teaching or explanation had a variety of forms (1 Cor 14.26; 1 Tim 4.2).

So the apostolic explanation, even though in essence it remains the same, has within it a dynamic principle. The essence is Christ as God-man, as humanity fulfilled in himself through resurrection and the culminating union with God. But the divine infinity which is communicated to humanity through Christ always requires explanation, because of the progress in the experience and in the understanding of it: "that you, being rooted and grounded in love, may have power to comprehend with all the saints what is the breadth and length and height and depth, and to know the love of Christ which surpasses knowledge, that you may be filled with all the fullness of God" (Eph 3.17-19). Tradition, which may also be described as the identity of the knowledge of Christ, consists in the continuous experiencing of his love, a love ever the same, yet always new, which surpasses all knowledge and limit. Nor can it be experienced except through a simultaneous experience of love among all the faithful (saints), which is to say, in the Church. Hence, it is made known through the Church. Through the Church, therefore, the true expression of this love in Holy Scripture is also made comprehensible (Eph 3.10). This is how we must understand the relation between the fact that revelation, which has reached its conclusion in Christ, is made a permanent reality, and the fact that it is continuously made new, a newness manifested through tradition, the basis of which was established by the Apostles. What, then, does tradition bring that is new, if it is not a continuation of revelation? "To understand, to use, that is, to integrate into our own destiny the elements of a revelation destined precisely to make present to us for all time the grace of which the Scripture spoke for the first time, and which already has a very long history. . . .

Through the revelation in Christ, something happened once and for all (Heb 7.27, 10.10). The Holy Spirit is at work. He is the One who, among other things, makes revelation contemporary. In a mysterious manner, revelation is, at the same time, closed and open; it comes to us through transmission."[3]

If Scripture had only a limited, literal, static meaning, it would have no need of tradition, of an explanation that would keep its original apostolic meanings unchanged. It would be absurd, moreover, to admit any application of Scripture to lived experience. If Scripture had no intention of making Christ pass into lives of human beings and to regulate their lives after the pattern of him, it would have no need of completion through tradition.

The apostolic explanation of the content of Scripture, the first and fully authentic explanation of it, coincides in its very nature with the application of the content of Scripture and the passing over of this content into the lives of human beings through the founding of the Church. This foundation was accompanied by concrete specifications for her modes of spiritual life and worship as well as for her hierarchical-sacramental structures based on the Lord's own indications, structures which correspond to the many appearances of the powers of Christ bestowed to meet the different needs of the faithful. In essence, the content of the apostolic tradition is nothing more than the content of Scripture applied to human life, or made to pass over into the reality of human life through the Church. Hence the Church preserves Scripture, applied through tradition as something which is always new and yet always the same. She preserves it through the hierarchical-sacramental structures specified by the Apostles as means whereby the content of revelation, or of Christ himself, passes over into the lives of men. She preserves it as something always new and always the same through the original tradition whereby the Apostles specified these structures, and whereby Christ truly communicates himself from one generation to the next, together with the inexhaustible richness of his bounties. The use of these structures of tradition means that through them, Christ, or the grace of Christ, is integrally received in the Church. This does not mean, however, that the integral Christ needs no further explanation or that further dimensions of his significance and other effects produced by him in the souls of men cannot be brought to light. Tradition, as an explanation of the same Christ, as explanation that is always growing in richness, can be separated neither from the reception of him as the unchanged content of tradition, nor from the outflow of this same grace of his, nor again from the reception of his identical person within the Church through the sacraments and the world that explains him.

Therefore, tradition has two meanings: a) the totality of the various ways by which Christ passes over into the reality of human lives under the form of the Church and all his works of sanctification and preaching; b) the transmission of these ways from generation to generation. Georges Florovsky says that the Apostles gave and, through their successors, the bishops, the Church received not a teaching only, by also the grace of the Holy Spirit. "Ultimately, 'tradition' is the continuity of the divine assistance, the abiding presence of the Holy Spirit."[4]

Tradition is the giving of permanent reality to the transmission of this same Christ who has been integrally revealed in the Church — that is to say, as incarnate, crucified, and risen. Thus, it is the permanent communication of the final dynamic condition to which God has come through revelation in drawing near to men. As such, it is the prolongation of the act of God in Christ which has been described in its essence in Scripture. Only through tradition does the content of Scripture become always vital, contemporary, effective, and dynamic in its entirety as the generations succeed one another throughout history. In this sense, tradition completes Scripture. Apart from tradition, the entire efficacy, or the continuous efficacy of Scripture or of revelation, is not made real. Without tradition, the whole content of Scripture can neither be penetrated nor lived out. All the canticles of the Church are steeped in scriptural texts, and all the liturgical and sacramental acts symbolize and make effectively real certain moments from Scripture, from the history of revelation. But by so doing, these liturgical hymns and actions also provide "a deep dogmatic and spiritual interpretation" to Scripture. Unless it is explained liturgically and applied in the liturgy and in the other sacraments, the Scripture becomes desiccated and disfigured.[5]

Apostolic tradition is a part of revelation, for the latter could not continue on if the manner in which the revealed Christ communicates himself to men were not itself made known.

Tradition has the role of putting and keeping the successive generations of Christians in contact with Christ because of the fact that tradition, by its very nature, is both the invocation of the Spirit of Christ (*epiklesis* in a broad sense) and the reception of the Holy

Spirit. The sacraments and other sacramental actions also come down to this, for, in them, through prayer, the graces and gifts of the Holy Spirit are asked for and received and these sanctify not only the soul but also the body of man and the nature that surrounds us. All the other sacred actions of the Church are to be found essentially within the framework of these two actions: the invocation and descent of the Holy Spirit. The moral and spiritual life, moreover, with all the abstinences, virtues, and the penitence that belong to it, as these are regulated by the canonical discipline of the Church, create the condition which renders believers fit to invoke the Spirit effectively and to have the sensible experience of receiving him. It is also the condition that makes the faithful who have received the Spirit capable of bearing fruit in a life that accords with the pattern of Christ's own life, and capable of advancing in their likeness to Christ towards the goal of full communion with him.

But the entire sanctifying work of the Church carried out through the invocation and reception of the Holy Spirit and through her own doxology, together with the entire moral and spiritual life of the faithful, are based on several things: on the saving works of Christ; on the power to which our humanity has attained in Christ; on the example of that help given by God in so many circumstances throughout the course of revelation; on the trust that the love of God in Christ for men will be made a permanent reality revealed in those many acts; finally, on the confidence that, in his risen state, Christ has remained close to us. The entire life of the faithful is an imitation of Christ made possible by his own power, a progress towards his holiness which comes about through their sanctification, and has in view their liberation from the automatism of nature and from the passionate attachment to the pleasures offered by nature — for it is this liberation which is the condition for true communion with the person of Christ whose love is infinite and with all human persons.

But this transmission of the integral Christ through tradition, the Christ who is presented essentially in Scripture, also provides the possibility of a continuous deepening and unfolding of the content of Scripture. This is a deepening and unfolding which remains within the framework of the tradition of the Church, of the fundamental unfolding of Scripture through the sacraments and through her liturgical and spiritual life, for it is a deepening in communion with the same Christ who is infinite in the spiritual riches that he communicates to us. This ecclesial tradition grows out of apostolic tradition and remains within its framework, as a tradition which is dynamic and identical at the same time, and as a tradition whose dynamism is nourished from the stable source of apostolic tradition, that is, from the integral Christ described and communicated through the apostolic tradition. It advances on a road whose landmarks are present in germ within apostolic tradition, as a summary of the essential ways of communicating the person of Christ and his saving work, who, by communicating himself to us, also opens our soul to him.

The development of tradition, says Vincent of Lérins, does not mean the changing of tradition, but an amplification within itself.[6] The continuous development of tradition is, on the one hand, what Scripture contains and, on the other hand, it is an illumination of the rich and unitary sense of revelation deposited in its essence within the Scripture. This development is found in brief in the Creeds, but it also takes place through the more extensive forms of the works of sanctification performed in the Church, and of the explanations of Scripture provided down through the history of the Church on the basis of the integral preaching of the Apostles, which has remained in the Church as apostolic tradition. Origen suggests that in the rule of faith there is to be found the hidden light of the dogmas, a light contained in the words of Scripture.[7] A contemporary Orthodox theologian says, "Tradition is a 'pneumatic' anamnesis which, beyond the often too human objectification of the texts, reveals the unity and meaning of the Scriptures and shows forth Christ who recapitulates and fulfills them."[8]

Inasmuch as it is in the general resurrection, in an eternal communion with the infinite person of Christ, and in our fulfillment in that person that revelation projects its final goal — a goal towards which we advance also through our own efforts in our continually improved human relations — and inasmuch as this goal is also disclosed in a concentrated way by Scripture, tradition makes explicit at every moment the road contained virtually in revelation as a road leading towards the goal of our perfection in Christ.

NOTES

1. *Questions to Thalassios* 22, PG 90.317D.
2. *Gnostic Chapters* 2.73, PG 90.1157C.
3. René Voeltzel in "Réligion pour le troisième millénaire. Lettre entrouverte à Jean Fourastié. Verses et controverses II. Actualité de la Révélation," *Réforme*, Nr. 1505, 19 January 1974, p. 12, observes: "One of the greatest mistakes committed by the churches is . . . to have declared arbitrarily the Revelation closed."
4. "The Ethos of the Orthodox Church," in *Orthodoxy. A Faith and Order Dialogue* (Geneva, 1960), p. 40.
5. A. Vedernikov, "Problema predaniya v pravoslavnom bogoslovii," [= The Problem of Tradition in Orthodox Theology] *Zhurnal Moskovskoi Patriarkhii* (1961) Nr. 9, 47-49 and Nr. 10, 68-71.
6. *Commonitory* 1.23, PL 50.667-668.
7. *First Principles* 4.1.7 and 4.2.2, eds. H. Crouzel/M. Simonetti, *SC* 268, pp. 286.196/288.200 and 300.47-56.
8. Olivier Clément, "Le renouveau de l'Église. Un point de vue orthodoxe," *Contacts* 16 (1964) Nr. 48, p. 266.

Chapter Four

The Church as the Instrument for Preserving Revelation

Tradition cannot exist without the Church. If tradition is in essence the invocation and descent of the Holy Spirit upon human beings, and the authentic and apostolic way of making the content of Scripture explicit on the basis of its sacramental and spiritual application in the lives of the faithful, then tradition cannot exist apart from the people who believe in revelation, that is, those who believe in Christ and his work within them through the Holy Spirit. But it is not in isolation that the faithful ask for Christ and receive him in the Holy Spirit. Nor is it in isolation from one another that they strive through their moral life to prepare themselves to ask for and receive the Holy Spirit and to be molded after the image of Christ. But all these things are performed and experienced by the faithful in community, that is, in the Church. This community had to have come into existence during the time of the Apostles or there would have been none to whom they might have communicated Christ in the Holy Spirit. Thus, if the preaching and the activity of the Apostles also belong to revelation, then revelation has continued to find its completion in the Church after the Church was founded. Hence, the Church is the subject of tradition, the subject which applies revelation in practice. The Church begins with tradition; tradition begins with the Church.

At the same time, however, the subject of tradition is also God. And insofar as her subject is God, the Church is a subject which bears tradition, or, rather, bears the work of the Spirit that is carried out and transmitted within her by means of and in the course of tradition. But the Church is also an active subject of tradition, inasmuch as, in the name of the faithful, she continuously requests and receives the activity of the Spirit through these same means and, moreover, prepares herself through them for this requesting and receiving of the Spirit, and makes efforts to model herself more and more after the pattern of Christ through the work of the Spirit.

Without the Church, as subject of tradition, tradition itself would not have begun to exist, and would have ceased to be practiced and transmitted; it would have ceased to exist. But, conversely, the Church would not have begun to exist and would not exist without tradition. As a continuous application of the content of Scripture, or more precisely, of revelation, tradition is an attribute of the Church. Tradition as content represents the way in which the fullness of Christ's revelation is maintained, or, rather, the way in which Christ is maintained as the fullness of revelation in its concreteness, while, as a form of transmission, tradition assures the continued existence of this content through faith. But both these sides of tradition are assured through the Church. In their rejection of the Church, Protestants have lost tradition both as transmission, that is, as a living succession of faith — for the faith of one person is born from the faith of another — and as plenitude of revelation, for Protestant Christians no longer receive the full understanding of Scripture which, through tradition, the Church has preserved in its integral application from the beginning. If tradition had not been put into practice with faith, moreover, the very content of Scripture would no longer be alive or effective or understood according to the Spirit. Scripture continues to be vital and effective through tradition, while tradition exists through the fact that it is put into practice by the Church. The Church is the milieu in which the content of Scripture or of revelation is imparted through tradition. Scripture or revelation need tradition as a means of activating their content, and they need the Church as the practicing subject of tradition and the milieu where the content of Scripture or of revelation is imparted. But the Church also needs Scripture in order to be quickened through it and grow in the knowledge and the experience of Christ, and to apply the Scripture more and more richly in her own life through tradition. Church, Scripture, and tradition are indissolubly united. Scripture is absorbed into the life of the Church through tradition. Scripture finds its end and takes on its form as concrete experience in the Church through tradition. But Scripture finds its end in the Church because, through the Holy Spirit, the Church possesses a continuing initiative through which she provides Scripture with its final end, and that is tradition. But the Church is also claimed by Scripture. The Holy Spirit is active in tradition because he is active in the Church where tradition is put into practice; and through his activity in the Church which puts tradition into practice, the Spirit also makes Scripture active by making

Scripture attract the Church. Church, tradition, and Scripture are woven into a whole, and the work of the Spirit is the soul of this integral unity. But within this unity, it is more to the Church that the Holy Spirit gives the initiative. She is moved by the Holy Spirit and her movement takes place in and through tradition, and is quickened through the link with Scripture.

The Church explains and applies Scripture in its authentic content through the apostolic tradition which she preserved, a tradition which has provided the true explanation and application of Scripture. This tradition has formed and maintains the Church, however, and the Church is obliged to preserve the content of Scripture in its authentic meaning, in that understanding transmitted to her by apostolic tradition from which she cannot turn aside.

Scripture exists and is applied through the Church. Apart from the Church, there would have been no Scripture. The canon of Scripture results from the Church, and is due to her witness. Scripture was written in the Church and it was the Church who gave witness to its apostolic authenticity. The Church has her direct origin in the work of the Apostles who were guided and animated by the Holy Spirit in making this initial application of revelation and of the apostolic tradition. The Church did not come into existence through the mediation of Scripture. Scripture arose within the bosom of the Church and for her benefit, as a way of fixing one part of the apostolic tradition or of revelation in written form in order to nourish the Church from and maintain her in Christ who is authentically transmitted through the tradition as a whole.

The apostolic tradition appears simultaneously with the Church, and the Church simultaneously with tradition, as the practical application of revelation. Hence, it is not possible to say which sustains the other, and any distinction between them can only be theoretical. Scripture, however, does not have its origin simultaneously with the Church, but arises afterwards and within the Church. The Church, from the beginning, provides guarantees about Scripture as an authentic part of tradition. As such, the Church defends Scripture, just as she defends tradition by providing guarantees for it. Yet, subsequently, the Church is nourished from Scripture just as she finds nourishment in the whole of her tradition.

The Church appears simultaneously with tradition because tradition is revelation incorporated into a community of believing people.

Revelation can only find incorporation concomitantly with the formation of a community of believers who will accept it and apply it in their life together. There exists no human community which accepts the application of revelation before it has begun to apply it as tradition. The authentic, fundamental, and normative form in which revelation is applied also belongs to revelation, a revelation which has been brought to its conclusion at the very point where its effectiveness begins. Hence, tradition cannot be changed or rejected, because to change or to reject it would be tantamount to mutilating revelation and its full and authentic application, and this, in turn, would mean a mutilation of the Church.

As revelation incorporated and lived out by a human community, the Church herself is a part of revelation, namely, the point where revelation has its final end and begins to bear fruit. In his resurrection and ascension as man, the Son of God had to reach the endpoint of his work of salvation and revelation so that he might send his Spirit through whom he imparts to men his own final state or revelation and might, thus, found the Church simultaneously with the descent of the Spirit into men. If the descent of Christ's Spirit — as manifestation of that effective power shining forth from the human as fully redeemed in Christ — is the ultimate act of revelation, or of the work of saving mankind in Christ, then the concrete appearance of the Church, as starting point for extending the effective power of the human fully redeemed in Christ, belongs also to the ultimate act in the disclosure of salvation in Christ. Revelation gives birth to the Church as the concrete and continuing means through which the humanity saved in Christ extends outwards in time and space. With this in view, the Church gives rise to the full organizing of her own essential structures, a work carried out and put into practice by tradition at its beginning, but described afterwards only in part within the Scripture of the New Testament. By preserving apostolic tradition in this way, the Church has thereby also preserved the integrity of revelation, even though, on the other hand, she is herself the work of revelation.

The Church is founded by Christ in whom the revelation of acts and words was concentrated and has its culminating point. But revelation continues to find its completion in the Church, in that part of it that has to do with the form in which revelation can crystallize as a union of believers with Christ, understood as the most fitting application of revelation, which is to say, in the form of the Church's essential structures organically linked with the content of revelation. Subsequently, the Church remains the milieu where revelation finds its application until the end of the world, and whence comes the gift of Christ's saving power through the Holy Spirit. The Church thus continues as milieu where some people seek for and receive Christ, grow in him, and conform themselves to him as model. In this sense, the descent of the Holy Spirit at the end of the fulfillment of the plan of salvation in Christ inaugurates and directs what is a new stage in the application of this plan, or of revelation itself, until the end of the world. This stage is that of revelation actively at work as tradition. The subject of this effective power of revelation is the Holy Spirit through the Church, or the Church through the Holy Spirit. Apart from the Holy Spirit, the Church would not have come into existence and would not continue on as a milieu where the effective power of revelation is prolonged. The Holy Spirit is the one who brought revelation to its conclusion — from the point of view of its content — and thus gives existence to the Church with her essential structures as the body of Christ, and it is also the Spirit who continues to sustain the effective power of revelation through the Church. Until the ascension of Christ, revelation in its fullness had its concrete embodiment in Christ. By bringing the Church into existence at Pentecost and in the period afterwards, the Holy Spirit makes Christ known to us in all that Christ contains on our behalf as well as in the work of extending the gifts of Christ within us. The act of bringing the Church into existence through the Holy Spirit and of specifying her structures through the Apostles is distinguished from revelation, for it represents the full goodness which God bears towards us now put at our disposal in Christ. This bringing into existence of the Church and the organization of her structures makes possible for us believers the transmission of the good things of Christ.

The Holy Spirit continues the revelation of Christ in this direction through the act of bringing the Church into existence and through the practical organization of her structures, that is, through the initial putting of them into practice. It is the same Spirit who afterwards maintains the Church as a permanent milieu for the effective power of revelation once this has been brought to a close in Christ, or rather perfected as both content and way of being put into practice. Thus, the Holy Spirit keeps the Church true to the revelation closed in Christ, and to Scripture and tradition which make Christ present and communicate him. And these three the Spirit maintains as parts and aspects of the same integral unity.

The Church moves inside revelation or inside Scripture and tradition; Scripture discloses its content inside the Church and inside tradition; tradition is alive within the Church. Revelation itself is effective within the Church and the Church is alive within revelation. But this interweaving depends on the activity of the same Holy Spirit of Christ. It was he who accompanied Christ in the course of revelation, that is, of his saving work, who led revelation to its end by bringing the Church into existence, and who was the inspiration behind having a part of revelation fixed in written form. It is this same Spirit who continues to bring about the union of Christ with those who believe and to cause them to grow in him, and who continues to maintain the Church as the body of Christ, to animate her in putting the unaltered content of revelation into practice as tradition, and to help her deepen the content of revelation and of Scripture through knowledge and experience.

The Church infallibly understands the meaning of revelation, because she herself is the work of revelation, of the Holy Spirit, and because she moves within revelation as one who is organically united with it. The Holy Spirit, who, together with Christ, is the author of revelation, the one who brought the Church into existence and the one who inspires Scriptures — this same Spirit is at work within the Church, helping her to understand and to appropriate, in an authentic and practical way, the content of revelation, that is, Christ in the fullness of his gifts. The Church understands the authentic meaning of the content of revelation because the Spirit sustains within her the evidence of the lived fullness of revelation made concrete in Christ. There can be no complete Church if this evidence of the theandric fullness of Christ is not found in her, nor can the evidence of this fullness be manifested or made active except in the Church. It is through the Holy Spirit, however, that this fullness is manifested and made active. That is why Saint Irenaios said: *"ubi enim ecclesia, ibi et Spiritus Dei,"* and again, *"ubi Spiritus Dei, illic Ecclesia et omnis gratia: Spiritus autem Veritas."*[1]

Saint Nikephoros the Confessor says:

The Church is clearly the house of God, as Saint Paul the Apostle considers in writing to Timothy, when he says that we should know "how one ought to behave in the household of God, which is the church of the living God" (1 Tim 3.15) . . . Thus, as the house is divine, it has been founded on the peaks of the high mountains (cf. Heb 12.18-20) that rise up into contemplation, peaks that tower over lower and earthly things, for these are the thoughts and reflections of the holy prophets and apostles, and they shine through brilliantly, and upon them, as upon the foundations of faith, the Church of God has been built and stands firm.[2]

The same saint declares that the very Apostles, finding themselves in the Church where the Holy Spirit was at work, were sent forth by Christ from within the Church, that is, by Christ working through the Holy Spirit in the Church. Starting from the text: "For out of Zion shall go forth the Law and the word of the Lord from Jerusalem" (Is 2.3), Nikephoros applies it to the Church as an image of the heavenly Jerusalem:

For out of this sensible Jerusalem, as one that is the image of the heavenly Jerusalem, the divine word has plainly come forth and encompasses all the ends of the earth. For here were wrought all the mysteries of our salvation . . . From here the holy apostles who would make disciples of all nations were also sent on their way in order to clear for the peoples that smooth, straight, and saving path.[3]

Dogmas as Doctrinal Expressions of Church

Christian dogmas are, according to their form, the points of the plan of our salvation and deification, points which are contained and made real in the supernatural divine revelation that culminated in Christ, and also are preserved, preached, applied, and explained or defined by the Church. As such, they represent truths of faith necessary for salvation. For Christianity, there exists a single all-comprehensive truth that saves us: Jesus Christ the God-Man. The all-comprehensive truth is, properly speaking, the Holy Trinity, the communion of the supreme persons, but the Holy Trinity brings about salvation through the Son of God, the divine hypostasis who unites in himself divinity and humanity, wishing to gather together all things in himself. It is in the divine Logos that all things have their origin and basis, their existence and meanings, and it is through his incarnation that he gathers all creatures to himself. The point of dogmas, therefore, is to make explicit Christ and his work of recapitulating all things in himself. Jesus himself said: "I am the truth" (Jn 14.6).

We have seen that even natural dogmas, as ultimate meanings of existence, have an intrinsic self-evidence, although they do need to be accepted by faith. To these ultimate meanings of existence — expressed in the dogmas — supernatural revelation gives precision and demonstrates concretely the possibility of their fulfillment; indeed, it shows that they have actually been fulfilled in Christ and that we make progress in appropriating them in our own lives by the help of God who has come down to us in Christ and in the Holy Spirit.

These more precise and more complete meanings, which have been fulfilled in Christ and are in the course of being fulfilled in us, have a self-evidence greater than that of natural dogmas. This is due to the experience of God lived out by the organs of supernatural revelation and by those to whom revelation is transmitted, just as it is also due to the supernatural acts which accompany this revelation.

But the fact that they are more evident does not make faith superfluous in the act of accepting them. Indeed, the more evident they are, the greater the faith with which they are awaited. Thus, there is a correspondence between the extent to which they are evident and the greatness of the faith with which they are received. Both the one and the other are effects of the work of the Holy Spirit.

In the case of natural dogmas, their quality of being evident, or their truth, depends on their meaning which imposes itself upon us naturally. In the case of supernatural dogmas, this self-evidence does not exist in function of their meaning, for this does not impose itself naturally, but depends on an act or a series of acts by which God reveals himself or makes himself evident. God reveals himself — or reveals these dogmas — through an initiative of his own perceived by the instruments of revelation. And it is this that makes them evident. Their meaning comes to be seen from the content revealed by this revelation. Revelation is fulfilled in such a way, however, that it makes itself evident as an act. If in natural revelation we have this order: meaning, hence, self-evidence, truth, or existence; in supernatural revelation we have the following order: the act of revelation (or existence, or self-evidence, or truth), hence, meaning.

In supernatural revelation, the personal saving reality of God asserts itself with a strongly accentuated pressure. The self-evidence, or the truth of what is being asserted, is proportional to the pressure exerted through revelation by the reality which lies behind it.

If, in the case of natural revelation, faith is produced, therefore, by the meaning of the self-evidence ascertained by man, then in supernatural revelation it is produced by the self-evidence or truth of the personal reality of God imposing itself on man without his effort. Thus supernatural revelation is the strongest motive for accepting the Christian dogmas.

The reality pressing upon us in supernatural revelation is the divine personal Logos. In the revelation of the Old Testament, this reality is not incarnate, whereas, in the revelation of the New Testament, the Logos is incarnate. In him are made known to us, as existing and working realities, all the truths of our salvation, and the meanings in all of them that must be fulfilled. In natural revelation, we reach the Logos through thought. But even upon this action of thought, pressure is exerted from the personal Logos, which takes the form of our own meaning.

Of course, the meaning that comes to light in supernatural dogmas is still more clear and more evident.

The meaning of the dogmas of supernatural revelation has a much greater clarity than that which attaches to natural dogmas, inasmuch as it makes God more easily seen as Person who has full meaning in himself and gives meaning to all things. But this is so because the instrument which receives the revelation, and whoever receives it in turn from him, comes into contact with the personal supreme existence, who is self-evident, and sees implied in this existence the assurance that the meaning of all things will be fulfilled, that eternal existence of theirs to which they all aspire.

But here, too, the truth of the reality which gives meaning to all things is only revealed to one who opens himself to it. The pressure it exerts, however strong, is not brought, in some physical way, upon the instrument of revelation, or upon anyone to whom this instrument communicates it. A person does not reveal himself or disclose himself, except to one who himself is open to the other. This is part of the very nature of revelation as a relation between persons. A person does not reveal himself to me if I do not open myself to him.

How much less, therefore, does a divine Person. But once the existence of a person has been revealed to me, he becomes for me — to the extent of this revelation — the meaning of my own existence and, to that extent, he shows himself as evident, true, and belonging to another level of existence, so that, in consequence, I can no longer find a meaning for my existence without him. I can live as the brutes, without meaning, but this existence is torment for me. The inferior levels of existence have a meaning because they exist for man. But if man wants to live for no one, he has no meaning to his existence. Hence, Saint Maximos the Confessor declares that each thing has a meaning, a rationality; only evil has no rationality because it exists for nothing in a positive way. Meaning is the foundation of existence. The truth and the self-evidence of existence is found in meaning. But the person has a meaning incomparably more important than those inherent in material things. The person gives meaning to things. According to Christian faith, that meaning which is absolutely necessary for all is to be found in the divine Personal reality who gives meaning to all. The existence of this Personal reality is not simply ontic, but ontological, and the supernatural revelation of this divine Person is necessary for us if we are to come to know him and our own meaning.

Self-evidence is entailed in the reality of supreme revealed Person, but the Personal reality does not impose himself without faith. For contact with supreme Person or with the supreme truth cannot take place without a free opening towards him. The self-evidence of supreme Person is a fact which is disclosed to free acceptance, to faith.

The person is a reality both near and far away; he opens his interior treasure and makes himself known, or does not open it and remains hidden. But he opens himself only to one who opens himself in turn to him. The truth of the Christian faith is the treasure of the supreme Personal reality, which he opens to the one who opens himself to him through faith. This opening up of self implies a free choice made on behalf of those things which I accept to take as true.

Faith is based on revelation, but revelation does not take place without faith. The two are complementary. Faith does not produce revelation; rather it grows up from a presentiment that supreme Person intends to reveal himself, and waits to be fully articulated in the moment when that Personal reality is revealed. There is something analogous here to the fact that it is not my faith that causes my fellow human being to reveal himself in those things which are intimate to him and quickening to me. Yet if there exists in me no kind of presentiment or expectation of his own capacity and disposition to reveal himself, a presentiment and expectation that become faith simultaneously with his revelation, then that revelation does not occur. Revelation and faith each calls forth the reality of the other even in their preliminary phases. Human nature has been made by God himself precisely so that it can receive his revelation through faith.

The primary foundation for the acceptance of dogmas is their communication through supernatural revelation wherein the divine Personal reality brings pressure upon human nature through its own initiative.

A second foundation is their preservation, preaching, application or fructification, explanation, and definition by the Church, that is, by the community of those who believe in Christ, a community that came into existence through the descent of the Holy Spirit and — on the basis of Christ's own commandment — through the Apostles, once supernatural revelation had come to its conclusion in him. The beginning of the existence of the Church was itself a fact of revelation that those who made the decision on that basis to become her first members had imposed on them with the same pressure as that belonging to a powerful spiritual initiative from on high. Revelation as word was communicated through the pressure exerted upon certain individual persons by an initiative from above. In the act of bringing the Church into existence, a similar pressure was also exerted upon a particular gathering of people. Something analogous occurred in those acts through which the people of Israel were welded together into the Church of the Old Testament, such as the exodus from Egypt, the crossing of the desert, and the occupation of Canaan.

But at Pentecost, the act of revelation does not weld a group together into a national religious community. Pentecost is more a matter of setting before the spiritual vision of an external heterogeneous gathering the entire significance of Christ as God incarnate, risen, and ascended to bring about the salvation of all through a common faith in himself, and of attracting them all to this common faith in him. In those acts of revelation through which the religious community of the people of Israel was created, the spiritual vision of this community was opened to recognize that it would be permanently led by God. At Pentecost, however, the universal Church came into existence through an act of revelation which, to the spiritual vision of those gathered together at that time, proposed the continuous saving presence of Christ in the midst of themselves and of those who would come after them so that all those who would adhere to her might be saved.

During the entire time of the Apostles, the Church was conscious of the unseen but effective presence of Christ in her midst, operating as a pressure equal with the pressure of revelation being exerted upon her as a community. The Church had this consciousness continuously, and she still has it even after that time, but the Church no longer experiences the pressure of revelation as a series of acts through which essential new contents are communicated to her. Rather, she experiences the pressure of revelation as a continuous act through which the same Christ is ceaselessly present in her midst with all his treasures of grace and truth. This consciousness is a sensitivity maintained in the Church by the Holy Spirit. The Holy Spirit gave concrete existence to the Church by placing the saving presence of Christ before the spiritual vision of those first people who believed and attached themselves to him. The Holy Spirit maintains the Church by keeping this same active presence of Christ continuously visible to the eyes of faith. The Church experiences the pressure from this active presence of Christ, just as the instruments of revelation and the people of Israel experienced the pressure of the acts of God's revelation. The difference lies in the fact that, through the former pressure, it is not something essentially new which is always being communicated to her, but instead the endless riches of one and the same Christ in whom the whole of revelation is concentrated and brought to an end.

The preservation, preaching, application or fructification, explanation, and definition of dogmas by the Church provide a further basis upon which they are accepted by her members and by those who open themselves with faith to their witness. For these acts of preserving, preaching, applying or making fruitful, explaining, and defining all constitute testimony to the experience of that same pressure exerted by the integral revelation concentrated in Christ, a pressure which those who became the first members of the Church at Pentecost experienced through the Holy Spirit. Revelation remains effective through the Church; the Church is the milieu where revelation goes on existing in its effective power. The Church keeps revelation vital; revelation keeps the Church vital. Thus, revelation receives an ecclesial dimension; its expressions or dogmas become the expressions or dogmas of the Church.

We have seen above that there is no salvation for the human person apart from communication with supreme Person. Apart from this communication, the power to strengthen oneself spiritually is nowhere to be found, nor the power to remain eternally as persons without being reduced to the level of nature, or virtually to that level.

The dogmas of the Christian faith specify, moreover, that the salvation of man is assured as an eternal, happy existence only if his relation with the supreme Personal reality is so close that the powers and attributes of God will be stamped indelibly upon him through what is called deification. For this deification makes man, together with God, a bearer of the divine attributes and powers that completely overcome that tendency which the human body has towards corruption.

Thus, the dogmas are necessary for salvation because they express Christ in his saving work. But Christ saves us only if we open ourselves to him, if we believe in him. Thus, the Christian dogmas express the powers of Christ in his saving action, provided only that we believe what they express.

In what has been said above, a number of things have been set in high relief: the character of God as Person revealing himself; the necessity of the human person to relate through faith to divine Person if the human person is to be saved; the possibility and the fact that this communication might be and has been achieved through the descent of the divine Personal reality to the human level in Christ.

It has also been shown that, for the Christian, dogma represents no constraint on the free spiritual development of the believing human being but, on the contrary, it is dogma that preserves the capacity for such development within human beings. Christian dogmas assure the freedom of the believer as person, and do not leave him subject to nature or dissolved within it. Rather, it is in freedom itself that Christian dogmas lay the foundation for the spiritual development of the believer, because dogmas are the expression of his communion with God as Person. Now interpersonal communion is the domain of freedom *par excellence,* although it is, at the same time, the domain of faith. That is why Saint Cyril of Alexandria says that those who become the sons of God are welcomed into the freedom of faith, which reigns in the court of God.[4]

We do not mean by this, however, that Christian dogmas do not themselves constitute a system, that is to say, a unified spiritual whole, comprised of various spiritual components, and differing from other systems inasmuch as it is permeated with its own meaning. To present the content of these components — that is, the dogmas — is the same thing as to present the system or spiritual organism which they comprise.

Their system, however, is not formed of abstract principles; it is the living unity of Christ, the person in whom there is united, and who himself unites, divinity and creation. Moreover, Christ — the theandric Person — is, as system, universally comprehensive in exactly the same manner as he remains open and dedicated to promoting freedom in those who wish to be saved through him.

Now, through freedom, the system is continually and actually open to what is new. It is open to those who want to know it in order to advance on the plane of that spiritual infinity which is to be found in eternal life; it is experienced from the very moment of entrance into that life, but it is lived in its entirety and in all its richness only through communion with God who is infinite Person. And it is lived in an experience and joy that are always new and inexhaustible, not a petrification, but a life transcending both petrification and motion in the sense we attach to them.[5] This opening towards eternal infinite life comes about through man's resurrection in Christ who is God who made himself man so that he might draw close to us and who, as man, rose again so that we might rise to an eternal communion with him as God, through the medium of his humanity which is common with our own. Saint Cyril of Alexandria says: "For Christ ... who rose again [as man] to an endless life, the common barrier of humanity has been transformed into incorruptibility."[6]

This is also the general idea that united all Christian dogmas within one system, that is, the promotion of an ever more intimate communion between ourselves and the personal God who became man for this purpose. Such perfect communion of all in Christ and, therefore, also among each other, is what is called the kingdom of Heaven or kingdom of God, that is to say, the perfected order of integral love. In other words, Christian dogmas express the plan of the deification of all created beings who have this as their desire, a plan fulfilled in its final perfected form in Christ. As it unfolds, moreover, this plan is nothing other than our own natural aspiration for union with God, given specific shape and actually accomplished.

Christian dogmas make up a unity which differs from any other unitary system, both because they hold out before the believer a perspective of infinite development, that is, true salvation, and because the power for this salvation and the perspective it holds out are actually given in Christ, the divine person, who is, at the same time, also the man existing in communion with the divine infinitude. In fact, in Christ, all that is expressed in Christian dogmas is integrally concentrated and realized: there is expressed that divine infinitude in which Christ's human nature participates and in which, through the medium of his common human nature, everyone has the possibility of sharing.

Christian dogmas are not a system of teachings, limited in its perspective and dependent on man for some equally limited realization; they are the interpretation of Christ's reality as this reality is being extended in the lives of human beings. Christian dogmas express, therefore, revelation in its greatest self-evidence, for, as perfect divine-human reality, Christ presses down upon us with his own love and power. Christ is, thus, the living dogma, universally comprehensive and at work to bring about the whole of salvation.

But through the reality of the person of Christ, come down to the plane accessible to human beings and bringing the pressure of his self-evidence to bear upon us, the Trinity itself exerts its influence or reveals itself completely. Through himself, Christ makes visible the Father and the Spirit and, together with them, achieves the task of raising humanity up to an eternal communion with the Holy Trinity, itself the structure of perfect communion.

At the same time, Christ is the perfect man through whom God is leading all human beings towards their recapitulation in himself, understood as a Church that is growing towards the kingdom of Heaven. Thus, Christian dogmas are many and yet one, because Christ is one, although in him are to be found all the conditions and all the means for our deification. The person of Christ as the incarnate Son of God, and thus his work too, proceeds outward from the Trinity in order to bring people back into communion with the Trinity. If this were not so, Christ would not be able to lead to eternal happiness, into an eternal communion with God and with one another, those who believe.

Outside Christianity, God is seen in two modes that do not assure an eternal communion of the human person with him. In the pagan religions, the persons of the gods are finally dissolved within an impersonal essence. This doctrine has received remarkable expression in the philosophy of Plotinos. In the end, this same fate awaits those who belong ultimately to the same essence, manifested, as it is, only temporarily in the form of persons. In Judaism and Islam, God as person is so enclosed in himself that for man no communication with him is possible, only obedience and a happiness God grants on the basis of this obedience. Between himself and creation a gulf remains. Lossky says that a single divine Person cannot communicate its nature.[7] But it could be said that the person thus loses the certitude of his existence, and is submerged in this nature which is one with that of the world. In fact, in the God of Judaism and Islam, only his power vis-à-vis the world is emphasized, and this would seem to imply that God does not have life in himself but only in function of the world. His life is the world. Hence, he does not have in himself a life he might give to the world, and, without the world, he has no purpose or possibility of existence.

For Christianity, God is a Trinity of persons who have all in common, that is, their entire being, yet are not confused with one another as persons. This implies a perfect love. For love seeks complete unity and reciprocal affirmation of the persons who love one another. Here the absolute is tri-personal, not something impersonal. But the person is assured through the perfect love between one person and the other who have their own basis in the common essence. A person in total solitude cannot be the absolute.

It is within this supreme unity and love which affirm the eternity of the divine persons that the foundation is laid whereby the interior love of the Trinity can be perceived in the work it directs *ad extra*. The creation wrought by the Trinity must also be touched by the effects of this unity in diversity. Moreover, human persons themselves have a common nature which comes into being through a multiplicity of persons.

The force of the perfect love entailed in the essential unity of the Trinity is manifested not only in the creation of a world which is one and diverse — and of a humanity with a common nature realized in a multiplicity of persons — it is also manifested in the will to achieve communion with this Trinity. In the plan of salvation, the Trinity reflects something of its own inner unity and love, yet without going so far in that direction as to unite creation or mankind to itself in essence — a union which would diminish the value of the persons of the Trinity and the love between them.

But precisely as human persons, united through a common finite nature, we can be tempted to accentuate a certain tendency we have to affirm ourselves beyond our own proper limits and, thus, to leave out of account both other human beings and God, from whom we have both our existence and the possibility of enriching our existence. Were we to succumb to this temptation, we would tear to pieces our common human nature. The common quality of this nature remains, nevertheless, the basis for its aspiration towards unity in love, however much the love between us has been weakened.[8] For this reason, God undertakes an action whereby he lays an immovable foundation for the communion between himself and us, uniting our nature with his nature within one of the divine persons.

The Son of God does not unite himself with a man. In that case, the man — in Christ — would be someone other than God, and this would leave human beings outside full communion with the divine person and, through him, with the other persons of the Trinity. The union of the two natures in him does not imply any confusion between the divine nature and human nature, nor does human nature unite itself with the divine nature borne by each divine person in his quality as bearer of the divine nature. In such a case, man would no longer be given the possibility of being, as man, in communion with God as son of God, through the fact that the Son of God became the Son of man. Each divine person would be at the same time also a human person.

This union between the two natures is characterized as the highest possible union on condition that the two are not blended, through the fact that they are united in a hypostasis. The hypostasis of Christ is the basis of this highest union between two different natures just as a common nature is the bridge that unites persons of the same nature.

Christ does not become a new species in this way, for he remains fully God and fully man, and, hence, the real mediator of our communion with God. Through his incarnation, he enters as man into perfect communion with God and, as God, into perfect communion with men. In communion with him, every man is in perfect communion with all the persons of the Trinity. In communion with him, every man, becoming the son of the Father through grace, enjoys the full love of the Father of Christ, while the Father can enjoy the perfect love of the man, Christ become his Son, a love in which the love of all who believe in him is united.

The knowledge of the Trinity of persons having a common nature and of the union of human nature with the divine nature in a divine person so far transcends our own possibility of thought that it can only be a revealed knowledge. And it is revealed as reality in Christ. Yet once revealed in the reality of Christ's person, that is, experienced in that person, the Trinity also reveals — as a real pressure upon us — its own quality as supreme meaning of our existence, as fulfillment of our yearning after ultimate meaning.

The basis of faith in the Trinity, however, is Christ, as a revelation of the Trinity made concrete and brought to its climax. Saint Cyril says: "That is why God says, 'Behold, I am laying for the foundations of Zion a chosen stone, a cornerstone, and precious' " (Is 28.16, LXX).

Only in the Trinity, which is a unity of distinct persons, is the character of being person fully assured. The person without communion is not person, while communion is conditioned by a common nature. We do not know what the divine nature is in itself, apart from the fact that it is all-perfect. But we do know that the divine nature is the basis of the all-perfect communion between the divine persons. No nature whatsoever of a spiritual character has subsistence apart from person; neither is the person fully person apart from nature, hence apart from the basis for communion. Properly speaking, the human person does not even exist except in the communion of nature with other persons.

The eternal communion after which we yearn has its origin and fulfillment in the one eternal co-essentiality of the divine persons of the Trinity. And if unity without confusion between the divine persons is assured by their sharing in a common nature, then certainly the communion between God and those who believe is assured by their participation, through grace, in the divine nature or in the energies irradiating from the common nature of the three divine persons, which is to say, from their loving community. But human nature, subsisting in a multiplicity of persons, must have some resemblance to the divine nature as this subsists in the three persons, if, in a divine person, it is to be able to be united with the divine nature. It is only because God himself is unity of persons who are not confused with one another, that he also wishes to attract rational created beings into communion with himself. It is only because a unity of nature exists respectively between the divine persons and between human persons that the divine persons and human persons can have a full unity without confusion of persons, and moreover, that a full union can be realized between the former and the latter.

The union of human nature with the divine nature in one hypostasis is the highest possible form of union between the two natures. In a certain way, we are all united through our nature in the hypostasis of the Word. To achieve this highest possible union God made his Son man so that just as he comes to rest, as God, in the loving bosom of the Father (Jn 1.18), so as Man, he, and together with him, all who are gathered in communion with him, can also rest in God. "Incarnation and trinity are thus inseparable, and against a certain Protestant criticism, against a liberalism which would oppose the Gospel and theology, we must stress the evangelical roots of the orthodox triadology. Can one indeed read the Gospel without asking the question: who is Jesus? And when we hear the confession of Peter: 'Thou art the Son of the living God' (Mt 16.16), when Saint John opens to us eternity with his Gospel, we understand that the only possible answer is the dogma of the Trinity, the Christ, only Son of the Father, God equal to the Father, identical divinity and different person."[10] That the incarnation is inseparable from the Trinity can be seen not only in the fact that in himself Christ makes visible the Father, but also in the fact that the Father reveals his own self in Christ, hovering above him and at times giving clear testimony about him as his Son (at the Epiphany, at the Transfiguration). Before the time of Christ the Father leads mankind towards Christ through the Spirit in a rather general way, but after the time of Christ, in a more evident way. Saint Cyril of Alexandria says: "Through knowledge and the gift of a divine vision, the Father leads those to whom he decides to give his divine grace towards the Son. When he receives them, the Son gives them life and to those whose own nature destined them to corruption he adds his own good grace, and pouring into them, as upon sparks of fire, the life-giving power of the Holy Spirit and transforming them utterly into immortality."[11] Or again: "For through both (the Father and the Son) is conveyed the understanding of the other; and with men the names wholly concur."[12]

The incarnation of the Word, as the manifestation of the love of the Holy Trinity for men, lays a foundation for our eternal communion with the Holy Trinity. But this eternal communion of ours with the Holy Trinity is reached through resurrection. In the resurrection of Christ the whole Trinity is active and reveals itself anew in a still more visible way, and thus remains disclosed forever with a view to full communion with us. According to Saint Cyril of Alexandria, the Trinity and the resurrection are the fundamental dogmas. Between Trinity and resurrection there is a link, for they are the alpha and the omega of our salvation, "because it was not this nature of the flesh that became the securer of life, but the deed was done through the work of the divine and ineffable nature, which has in itself the power to give life to all things naturally. Through the Son the Father has also acted upon that divine temple, not because the Word was unable to resurrect his own body, but because whatever the Father does, he does through the Son — for he is the power of the Father — and whatever the Son does most certainly comes from the Father. . . . Because, after the confession of the holy and consubstantial Trinity, the word of our hope and the power of blameless faith was turned to the mystery regarding the flesh, the blessed evangelist also places this return — and most helpfully — in his last chapters."[13]

The resurrection cannot be explained without the Holy Trinity. The entire economy of salvation undertaken by the Holy Trinity comes to its conclusion in the resurrection. On the other hand, it is through the resurrection that the eternal divine life common to the three persons is communicated, and thus those who believe are taken within the Trinitarian communion. It is hard to say whether we enter into eternal communion with the persons of the Holy Trinity and into communion among ourselves because we receive incorruptibility and immortality, that is, the divine life, or conversely, whether we receive this kind of life because we enter into communion with the persons of the Trinity.

The incorruptible divine life is communicated through the persons of the Holy Trinity and through the reception of believers into communion with them. The divine life has no actual subsistence apart from the Trinitarian persons. The communion between persons is not a non-substantial relationship, while the essence subsists only in the persons found in community. The paradoxical union between incarnation and Trinity which was pointed out by Lossky appears also in the case of resurrection and Trinity.

Living as they did in a period when the ideas of person and of interpersonal communion were still not very well developed, the Fathers, in their treatment of the resurrection, placed greater emphasis on the share that human nature had in the incorruptible divine life. The two aspects, nevertheless, form a single whole. Incorruptibility belongs to the perfection of communion, hence to the perfection of Trinitarian love.

Saint Cyril of Alexandria in his understanding of the resurrection seems to be emphasizing the incorruptible divine life communicated to human nature when he considers the resurrection as in fact a work of all three persons; he, nevertheless, also sees the human nature to which eternal life is communicated as subsisting in the person of the Word and then in human persons. In the understanding of the resurrection, Saint Cyril includes at bottom both the communication of the incorruptible divine life to humanity and the taking of the human nature personified in the Word into the communion of the Holy Trinity. The resurrection is a work common to the Holy Trinity because the eternal and incorruptible life is communicated to the human nature through communion, while this life is communicated by each divine person in union with the others. "For the fallen tent belongs to him who is from the seed of David, according to the flesh, that is, to Christ, and it was the first to be raised to incorruptibility by God the Father." [14]Saint Peter said the same thing: "God raised him up, having loosed the pangs of death, because it was not possible for him to be held by it" (Acts 2.24). The glory which Christ receives from the Father for the salvation of man is also received by the Father from man who is saved in Christ. For he has shown himself as Father of the one Son who raises man to such heights.[15]

If death is isolation, God, as incorruptible life, is perfect communion and He gives this life to those who believe in him, receiving them into this communion. The deeper the communion, the fuller the spiritual life. This life cannot be reduced to an empty communion, nor does communion consist in a relationship in which no life is communicated. These are two aspects of personal reality which are mysteriously and indissolubly linked.

In the communication of the divine life, therefore, Saint Cyril of Alexandria attributes a special role to the Holy Spirit. He communicates to human nature first of all the power to receive subsistence in the person of the Word by overcoming the laws of an endlessly repetitive nature. But this spiritual force exists only where there is full communion. The Holy Spirit then communicates to human nature the power to rise again by a new conquest of the laws of nature. The Spirit communicates this spiritual power because he is the Spirit of communion, and full communion exists moreover only where duality is overcome. If one person who does not communicate being loses the certitude of existence by being lost within nature, two persons likewise risk being submerged in monotony or in nature through an exclusive, closed, and selfish communion between themselves. Only the existence of three persons makes possible the maintenance of a continual freshness for each of the three persons as well as for any possible pairing of the persons. It is only in the existence of three persons that they do not become confused with one another nor are totally separated one from the other. Only a third person maintains the distinctive unity and breadth of love between two persons who can change as partners. And it is only in overcoming duality that life is truly rich and, in God, limitless. Christ receives the Spirit as man because, as man, he is received into the perfect communion of the Trinity, so that through him we too might be received into that same communion through grace.

Thus, the Holy Spirit fills Christ's humanity with divine life even after his birth. Saint Cyril of Alexandria says: "Because the Word of God was made man, he receives the Spirit from the Father as one of us, not receiving anything for himself personally, for he was the giver of the Spirit so that, having received the Spirit as man, he might preserve the Spirit on behalf of our nature, and that he who did not know sin might implant again in us that grace which had left us."[16]

Christ lives this full communion with the Father and the Spirit even in his body. Through this communion his body is filled with the incorruptible divine life and becomes a medium of his divine powers. "He fills his whole body with the life-creating work of his Spirit." His body becomes capable of being filled to such an extent with all his faultless sensibility for and through the Spirit, that his body itself is given the name of Spirit. "In fact, he calls his body here Spirit, but this does not change the fact that the body is body. By the very fact that it is united to the greatest extent with him and puts on his entire life-giving power, the body is also to be given the name of Spirit. . . . For through the Spirit his body too becomes life-creating because the Spirit transforms and transfigures the body in [the image of] his own powers."[17]

If this is true, the Spirit also has a role in the case of Christ's resurrection in the body.

Spirituality, communion, and power over repetitive nature work together. The body reaches the culmination of spirituality in resurrection. For it is in the body that the divine Spirit, who represents the fullness of the unconfused unity of the divine persons, has produced his full effect upon the humanity of Christ and raised it up to trinitarian participation, spirituality, and communion. He has done this not so that Christ's body only — having no hypostasis of its own — might participate in the communion of his divine hypostasis with the other persons of the Trinity, but also that, through it, Christ could realize perfect communion with us, by attracting us too into full communion with the persons of the Holy Trinity. To achieve this end, our own bodies must also increase in spirituality and, finally, appropriate that complete spirituality of resurrection in which the body of Christ is found. A body which lacks all spirituality is incapable of any communion. Moreover it hinders any effort towards communion that might still exist in the soul within it and thus is incapable of freeing itself even to a limited extent from the laws of nature which repeat themselves automatically.

On the other hand, Saint Cyril of Alexandria and all the Fathers also have knowledge of a resurrection that does not mean that the resurrected body is filled with a sensibility for God and for communion. Hence Saint Cyril does not present our resurrection as something produced in a particular way by the Holy Spirit, or at least he does not do this in all cases. In general he says that our resurrection is only a condition necessary for our body to become fully capable of receiving the indwelling of the Holy Spirit and, therefore, of receiving the sensibility for him. There exists, however, another state of resurrection to which the Spirit is not communicated, and this state does not give to resurrected bodies the capacity to receive the life-creating power of the Spirit. It is a resurrection that does not give life to the body through spirituality, but gives to the matter of the body the power of incorruptibility purely and simply. Once in Christ the matter organized into body has become incorruptible, the body is destined to become incorruptible in all human beings. "For to live again is something common to both saints and sinners . . . but to partake of the Holy Spirit is not at all something common to everyone, but is something additional and pertaining to superabundance of life and, as something beyond what is common to all, it will be given to those who have been justified through faith in Christ."[18]

This will be a resurrection to eternal solitude, not to communion;

a resurrection of a person whose nature has been reduced to a minimum, because it will not participate in the divine life or divine nature. If a negative state of existence could subsist in a hypostasis, as the holy Fathers say, it could have an eternal existence in that hypostasis too so that the respective hypostasis might suffer from this negative state in eternity. A hypostasis of this kind would stand at the margin of the plenary existence that subsists in the other hypostases. Its suffering is itself a certain participation in existence, and hence a participation in the others' resurrection to eternal life, thanks to Christ's resurrection. Without this exterior participation they would not suffer from the negative state of existence nor would they, in this fashion, pay homage to the fullness of existence in communion.

The Holy Trinity determined upon the incarnation, crucifixion, resurrection, and ascension as man of one of the persons of the Trinity so that this person might recapitulate all men in himself and thus bring all into eternal communion with God in Trinity. We have to do here with a circular movement that sets out from the Trinity towards men in order to lead them into the Trinity. It is a movement of the Trinity towards us which has as its goal the return into the Trinity itself in company with us. A divine person descends from the Holy Trinity in order to return to the Trinity — and to communion with the infinite Trinity — not only as divine person, but also as human person, having united to himself all of humanity that desires this.

Saint Cyril of Alexandria again: "The wise Paul, therefore, when he explains for us the unique, true, and most comprehensive purpose of the incarnation of the only begotten one, said that God the Father wished 'to unite all things' in Christ (Eph 1.10). And both the name and the fact of recapitulation indicate the bringing back to their original condition of things that had fallen away into diverse fates."[19]

It is not until this work of recapitulation that the operation of the Holy Spirit receives the principal role, although not in isolation from Christ and the Father. "For even though Christ had risen from the dead, the Spirit had not yet been given to humanity from the Father through him. For having ascended to God the Father, he sent us the Spirit. That is why he said, 'It is to your advantage that I go away, for if I do not go away, the Counselor will not come to you; but if I go, I will send him to you' "[20] (Jn 16.7).

Christ had to ascend in the body to the fullness of spirituality and communion with the Father so that, through his body which had come to the highest degree of spiritual irradiation, he might pour out the Spirit. On the other hand the ascension of believers to communion with God in Trinity occurs only when a divine person reflects in his activity both his communion with another divine person as well as the communion he shares with the other two persons together. Therefore, one person is always sent forth by the other two persons within their unity, a unity which knows no confusion.

The Spirit creates communion among us because in him there is the unconfused communion of the entire Trinity.

The Holy Spirit brings about the ascension of creation to the state of being Church. The Spirit always exists between God and the many people who believe. Through him revelation, or Christ, becomes effective in men, since through the Spirit God produces faith in these people. Through him revelation is unveiled in its entire clarity and effectiveness, and with a content that grows ever richer. Revelation reached its conclusion in Christ, but it is disclosed to all generations, and these cause it to bear fruit through the Spirit. It is through the Spirit that men are raised up to greater and greater participation in those infinite goods which are to be found in Christ, and which they receive through faith in him. And faith is never one man's faith only but the faith of many. Where one person is able to communicate faith and another to receive it, there the Holy Spirit is at work between the two of them and God. The Church comes into existence through the descent of the Holy Spirit for it is through him that faith is born. But faith is born in many and these are filled with the impulse of handing on the faith. That is why the Spirit descends in the form of many tongues of fire. The Church continues through him because it is through the Spirit that the faith is continuously passed on from one person to another, from one generation to another in words of fire.

The Church comes into being at Pentecost and it is then that the Spirit descends, who gives to the Apostles the fire of steadfast faith and the flame of preaching it fervently, just as he gives them an understanding of the whole treasury of the goods which are to be found in Christ. When those who knew Christ had to communicate the evangelical and saving message to every language and nation, he gave them the sign of tongues. As Saint Cyril of Alexandria says: "The Spirit apportioned the distribution of gifts in order that, just as this gross and earthly body is made up of particles, so too, Christ, that is, his body which is the Church, has its most perfect composition from the multitude of saints brought into spiritual unity."[21]

NOTES

1. *Against the Heresies* 3.24.1, eds. A. Rousseau/L. Doutreleau, *SC* 211, p. 474.27-29: "For where the Church is, there too is the Spirit of God, and where the Spirit of God is, there is the Church and all grace: and the Spirit is Truth."
2. *Defense of the Holy Icons* 41, PG 100.660B-C.
3. Ibid. 41, PG 100.661B-C.
4. *Commentary on the Gospel of John* 5 [Jn 8.35], PG 73.864B-D.
5. Maximos the Confessor, *The Ambigua*, PG 91.1220C-1221B.
6. *Commentary on the Gospel of John* 6 [Jn 10.10], PG 73.1033A.
7. Vladimir Lossky, *Orthodox Theology: An Introduction* (Crestwood, NY, 1978), pp. 27-32.
8. Maximos the Confessor, *Letter 2*, PG 91.396D: "and he [the devil], having thus split nature so far apart, divided it into many opinions and fantasies."
9. *Commentary on the Gospel of John* 4 [Jn 6.70], PG 73.629A citing Is 28.16 (LXX).
10. Lossky, *Orthodox Theology*, p. 36.
11. *Commentary on the Gospel of John* 4, [Jn 6.40], PG 73.545A.
12. Ibid. 5, [Jn 8.19], PG 73.792B.
13. Ibid. 12, [Jn 20.24-25], PG 74.724B-C.
14. Ibid. 4, [Jn 7.8], PG 73.644D.
15. Ibid. 9, [Jn 13.31-32], PG 74.153B-156A.
16. Ibid. 2, [Jn 1.32-33], PG 73.205D-208A.
17. Ibid. 4, [Jn 6.64], PG 73.604A-B,D.
18. Ibid. 6, [Jn 10.10], PG 73.1032C-D.
19. Ibid. 9, [Jn 14.20], PG 74.273B.
20. Ibid. 12, [Jn 20.16], PG 74.696C.
21. *Fragments on the Acts of the Apostles* 2.3, PG 74.757B.

Chapter Five

Theology as Ecclesial Service

As doctrinal expression of the plan of saving and deifying those who believe, a plan realized by Christ and the Holy Spirit through the Church, or as doctrinal expression of the "treasures of wisdom" and of divine life put at our disposal in Christ so that we might appropriate them gradually during our life on earth and fully in the life to come, the dogmas need to have their infinite content continually disclosed. This task is accomplished by the Church through *theology*.

The results of this theological explanation which enter into permanent use by the Church become the teaching of the Church and this is identical with ecclesiastical tradition in the broad sense and contains within itself an enriched understanding of holy Scripture and apostolic tradition that is placed in the service of the Church's work of preaching, sanctification, and pastoral care.

The faithful cannot remain at the level of merely repeating dogmas in their schematic formulae. On the contrary they seek entry into the infinite depths of meaning of the dogmas and are helped by an explanation which is based on both holy Scripture and holy Tradition. In this sense theology is a necessity imposed by the Church's need to explain to the faithful the various points of Christian belief.

This need for theological explanation of the dogmas as definite points of the faith arises in the first instance from the fact that dogmas are concise formulae comprising both the infinite God's relation to the finite creature on the latter's endless path towards the infinite, and God's uninterrupted action on behalf of the salvation or deification of the creature. Dogmas as such, therefore, although in form they are defined, have a content that is infinite. This content seeks to be continously and ever more adequately disclosed, despite the fact that it can never be brought totally to light. In his action of making us perfect and receiving as response our own activity towards perfection, God also takes into account the new circumstances in which we live as he orients himself towards us, and this unending action of his, therefore, is itself always understood by us in a new light.

The defined character of dogmatic formulae does not contradict their infinite content, but secures it. In face of that which does not exist, the very fact that something does exist gives that something definition. Only nothingness does not define itself in any way. The physicist Bernard Philberth rightly observes: "The ultimate boundary that grounds the existence of that which is, however, is that boundary which faces on *nothingness*. That which is is distinction from *nothingness*, it is alteration over against nothingness. Nothingness itself has no boundary, no distinction, no alteration; otherwise it would not *be* nothingness. In nothingness boundary, distinction and alteration are also equally void."[1]

The dogma of the union of the divine nature with the human nature in a single person — without any alteration or confusion of either of the two natures — places a precise and rigorous boundary between itself and any other affirmation (and hence definition), and simultaneously unites two great mysteries, namely the fundamental mysteries of existence. Precisely through the dogmatic definition of this union, both divine infinitude and human participation in this infinitude are affirmed and preserved. To renounce this dogmatic definition would be equivalent to admitting the suppression either of the divine infinitude and absoluteness, or of a human participation in that infinitude in which the human would not be swallowed up by the divine.

For it should be mentioned that this dogma affirms the evident fact that through participation in the infinite divine existence, man is assured as an existence in his own right, not only over against *nothingness*, but also before God. The Christian dogma of the union of the divine and human natures in the person of God the Word does not presuppose man's disappearance within the infinity of God. It makes clear our preservation as human beings even at the level of this supreme union between the divine and the human. Indeed it goes even farther and assures the human element its maximum development. The mystery of communion between persons is marked by this very paradox: the union and the preservation of persons through it. Love between persons brings about the highest possible degree of union between them, but at the same time it produces the joy which the one has in the other as well as the distinction between them. God as person remains always a "Thou," distinct from the man united with him. In the communion of persons each one remains at the same time a boundary for the other; each has the other in himself, but as a distinct person. In their interiority to one another there is otherness. According to Christian faith man remains defined as man even within the highest degree of union with God and even as he participates in God's infinity. To express the matter more exactly, in union with God the believer is strengthened to the greatest possible extent precisely in his own character as a creature distinct from God. The different structures are strictly maintained, despite the fact that they become interior to one another or, to put it another way, they are maintained by the very fact that they are reciprocally interior to each other. This fact is also proper to the world in the unity and variety of its component parts, or in its eternal and perfect relationship to God. The most profound meaning of God's transcendence is to be found here. If no transcendent absolute reality existed, but the absolute were instead immanent and impersonal, then all things would be transformed into all things, for in such an absolute, as in the ground of their same essence, all things are indistinctively one.

Dogmas are definitions or strict "delimitations" (horoi). Yet, dogmas delimit God's infinity over against what is finite and they delimit man's infinite capacity for advancement, that is to say, the infinity of God and finite man's capacity for the infinite, a capacity which exists in solidarity with the infinity of God and draws endlessly closer to it.

To renounce the delimitation of either of these realities or to renounce their common delimitation — for neither the one nor the other lacks the principle of movement — would transform the fathomless depths of their combined existence into a meaningless slough where anything was possible, but nothing was truly new and profound. Dogmas are rather general formulae; they do not enter into details, yet this is precisely how they assure the breadth of the infinite content they contain. Their general character does not mean, however, that all precision is lacking. The fundamental structures of salvation are well specified within their general contours.

The paradoxical character of the dogmatic formulae has already been mentioned. God is one in essence and threefold in persons. He is unchangeable but alive, active and new in his providential action of saving the world. Christ is God and man; man remains a created being, and yet is deified. The paradox is to be found everywhere, but it belongs particularly to the person in general because person is not subject to a law that makes everything uniform and because person can embrace all. The person is a unity but one of endless richness; person remains the same and yet is endlessly different and new in its manifestations and states. Relations between persons show this same paradoxical character even more strongly. Man is autonomous and yet he cannot live or realize his own being except in communion with others. Any forced reduction of one of the aspects of human existence to another produces suffering within that aspect because such reduction is contrary to its existence. Even in relations with the world, the person shows this inner paradoxical character: person embraces the world in all its variety and brings it into a unity, yet person itself remains distinct and one, and preserves the world in its variety. How much more inevitable this paradox becomes in the domain of the infinite God's relations with the limited and created world: the one God, who has life in a manner beyond all understanding, exists within an interpersonal love.

The dogmatic formulae are paradoxical because they comprise essentially contradictory aspects of a living and inexhaustibly rich reality. In themselves, therefore, dogmas express all: the infinite and the finite united — without loss of their own being in all their dimensions.

Theology has an object of unending reflection in the all-comprehensive and infinite content of the dogmatic formulae, for these delimit and strictly secure this infinite reality in the unconfused richness of its own dimensions of inexhaustible depth and complexity.

But theology, in its turn, has to remain within the framework of the general and yet precise formulae of the dogmas precisely so as to maintain them as objects of unending reflection and deepening. The divine nature and the human nature — especially as these have been united in a climactic but unconfused manner in the divine person of Christ — comprise and offer to reflexion an infinite content. We can never exhaust the explanation of the divine and human natures in their richness of life and, simultaneously, in their unalterable character, just as there can be no end to depicting the depth and complexity of their union in one person, who is himself an inexhaustible mystery, always new and yet unchangeable.

Every theology which — within the framework of the precise formulae of the dogmas — makes explicit their infinite content is a broadened expression of those dogmas. There has often been talk of a distinction between dogmas and *theologoumena*. In this view dogmas would be the formulae established by the church while *theologoumena* would refer to various theological explanations which have not yet received an official ecclesiastical formulation, but which arise from the dogmas. This implies, however, alongside the distinction between dogmas and *theologoumena* a further distinction between those explanations which are taken as *theologoumena* and other kinds of explanations, these latter depending organically on the dogmas. In such a case, however, why would the *theologoumena* not also depend organically on the dogmas if they arose from them?

In fact, all the explanations of dogmas, so long as they remain within the framework of the dogmatic formulae, depend organically on the dogmas. Moreover, if they do not remain within the framework of those formulae, they cannot be considered as *theologoumena* either, nor can they hope to be invested with the character of dogmatic formulae at some undetermined point in the future. They are explanations which the Church does not make her own in the explanation of her dogmas and so in time they become obsolete.

However, although any true theology constructed within the framework of the Church makes the content of her dogmas more explicit, the Church does not invest any and every such explanation with the authority of her teaching. Alternatively, these explanations have authority by the very fact that they are implied in dogmas which have been formulated. The Church unceasingly multiplies her dogmatic explanations, but she concentrates — in a strictly dogmatic formula — the deeper explicitation of an older formula only when this deep explicitation is confronted by non-organic interpretations of the older formulae or when these kinds of interpretations are beginning to produce confusion and schisms within the Church.

When theological explanations are organic explicitations of the dogmas and are useful for renewing ecclesial life — and as such enter into the general and permanent preaching of the Church — they are included in the teaching of the Church understood in a broad sense. In the case of the Fathers of the Church, that is what happened with almost the whole of their theology. A basic identity exists on the one hand between dogmas and the teaching of the Church, while, on the other hand, they are formally distinct. Church teaching, as the content of the dogmas made explicit, depends on the dogmas. Nevertheless, until the teaching has been officially defined by the ecumenical synods and appropriated by the consensus of local synods, it remains as ecclesiastical teaching in this broad sense.

Teaching has the authority of Church tradition if it has entered into the general use of the Church, but it does not have the authority possessed by dogmatic definitions and by those elements of the faith upon which local synods have expressed their voice officially in consensus. That is to say, such teaching has ecclesiastical authority in its general content, but it does not have the authority of certain dogmatic formulae.

In this way the Church causes her teaching to grow, while at the same time preserving the fundamental terms of her unvarying doctrine. She causes her teaching to grow through theology because she brings these terms to light for each generation of believers in a way that corresponds to its understanding as this is determined by the level of spiritual development in which the faithful find themselves.

Theology is reflection upon the content of faith inherited from that witness and initial living out of revelation which we possess in the Scripture and in apostolic tradition. Its purpose is to make that content effective as a factor of salvation for every generation of believers. Theology, in this sense, is something that has been done by all the members of the Church at all times. It is something that the Apostles also did, for they were not merely receivers and transmitters of revelation; they lived it and — as it passed through their own experience — expounded it according to the way of understanding of the people of their time. Theology is something that was done by the Fathers and is still done by every priest as he interprets the revelation so that it can be lived out by his people.

Not all theology, however, becomes Church teaching, but only that which the Church takes to herself by unanimous consensus in time and space. And the Church takes to herself only those teachings which time shows have been organically assimilated to the previous way Christians have lived out that content contained in Christ, only those teachings which time shows have translated into the lives of the faithful the same experience of that same revelation concentrated in Christ. Even in theology as it is done by theologians, many things remain unassimilated into the teaching of the Church, and prove themselves in this way to have no permanence.

A distinction exists, therefore, between ecclesiastical teaching with its obligatory and permanent character and theology which may contain explanations linked to a certain period of history and current within the Church only for a particular time. This is not the theology that is done by the Church in her character as a single body, but a theology done by particular members of the Church — hierarchs, priests, lay people — in a way which is somehow individual to themselves. Church teaching, on the contrary, is made up of those elements that the Church, as the one body of Christ, retains from the theological thinking of individuals as something of permanent value even though these elements may have been provoked by the needs of different historical periods. This is what proves itself a theology of the Church precisely in her quality of being one body.

And so it is in the Church that theology is done and from it the Church maintains as permanent teaching those things which authentically develop and make explicit the plan of man's deification. Theology is done in the Church through the personal thinking of her members, and her teaching is constituted from what remains over permanently from their thinking when this latter has become a common possession and has proven itself as theology of the Church understood as the one body. Theology and Church teaching do not fall, however, under the competence of two distinct and partial sectors of the Church, as they do in Catholicism. There, theology is done by theologians who are specialists, while Church teaching is fixed by the magisterium of the Church or the hierarchical body and, in the last analysis, by the Pope. The latter claims that he exclusively has a "charism" which the Church as a whole does not have, and on the basis of this charism, he alone without the Church establishes ecclesiastical teaching. In Orthodoxy, the Church cannot err by virtue of the fact that she is guided by the Holy Spirit and also because of her quality as body of Christ in its entirety, which preserves "the deposit" inherited through experience and represented in synods of bishops. Through the Holy Spirit, the Spirit of communion, the Church in her entirety makes real a symphonic interconditioning of personal thoughts. All the members of the Church are part of this body and all do theology to a greater or lesser extent. From their reciprocal conditioning within the Church results the infallible teaching of the Church which is verified as such, however, only after the passage of sufficient time.

True theology, as the expression of theologians, is also guided, on the one hand, by responsibility for the salvation of the faithful, a reponsibility the Church leaders also have (and particularly with respect to the faithful who live during the period when that particular theology is being done); on the other hand, theology as the work of theologians is guided by the faith and spiritual experience of the Church. "Arbitrary option" (*hairesis* — heresy) can be characteristic at certain periods even of some members of the hierarchy. But the Church in her totality as body of Christ is the one who does not err and who receives what is not erroneous, that is, what does not jeopardize the salvation of her faithful, whether this emanates from theologians, from hierarchs, or from the laity.

The progress of theology is made possible by the divine infinity in human form which has been placed at man's disposal, but it is made necessary by the need to render this infinite reality accessible to the faithful in every age whose level of understanding and spiritual life has been built up by the spiritual efforts of previous generations. These faithful belong to the Church and their salvation is achieved within their solidarity in the Church. Theologians must integrate their own service with this work of saving the faithful of the Church in every age. Hence personal theological reflection must be animated not by the desire for originality at any price, but by the need to explain what constitutes a common inheritance and ministers to the salvation of the Church's faithful in that age. It must remain intimately bound to the Church's life of prayer and service so that it may deepen and renew that service. Where this is not the case, service in the Church can become a matter of form only, and theology something cold and individualistic.

The results of personal theological reflection will be integrated that much more surely within the teaching of the Church to the extent that this reflection is fed by a teaching inherited from the whole of the past and is nourished by being conducted in prayer, in worship, in the authentic spirituality of the Church, and in the Church's living dialogue with Christ — and to the extent that personal theological reflection harmonizes itself with this living dialogue, for it too is a dialogue with Christ and renews and enriches the dialogue of the Church. That is why it has been said, "If you are a theologian, you will pray truly. And if you pray truly, you are a theologian."[2] "First is prayer, then the word" [of theologizing], according to Saint John Chrysostom. "So said the Apostles too: 'But we will devote ourselves to prayer and to the ministry of the word' " (Acts 6.4).[3] Yet prayer is more fervent when it is made in common. And in common prayer community of thought also comes about. St. John Chrysostom also says: "It is possible to pray at home too, but it is impossible for you to pray there as you do in church. . . . You will not be heard when you call upon the Master by yourself as you are heard when you pray with your brothers. For here there is something more: there is unity in thought and in words; there is the bond of love and the prayer of the priests."[4]

The theologian must take part in this prayer and in the life of the Church, for theology wishes to know God from the experience of his saving activity among men. But the theologian will never know this if he does not enter into a personal relationship of love with God and with the faithful through prayer. Hence one who prays together with the other members of the Church is that much more a theologian. For in their common love for God, the saving and perfecting work of his love reveals itself all the more. In the prayers of the Church and in her worship there breathes her single spirit, and her eschatological horizon — her goal of perfection in Christ — is transparent. A theology which feeds on the prayer and spiritual life of the Church is a theology which expresses and deepens the Church's thinking, her spiritual life, and her work of sanctification and serving.

More than this, the theologian must aspire to live in a still fuller way the spirituality that is so characteristic of the Orthodox Church. All the Fathers of the Church have affirmed that no one can approach God with understanding unless he is purified from passions. St. Gregory of Nazianzos says: "Do you wish ever to become a theologian and someone worthy of God? Keep the commandments, proceed by way of the precepts, gain purity through purification. First cleanse yourself; then draw near to the pure one."[5] That is why the Cappadocian Fathers speak about the "mystery of theology." Saint Gregory of Nyssa says: "The knowledge of God (*theologia*) is a mountain steep indeed and difficult to climb — the majority of people scarcely reach its base."[6]

The Greek theologian Karmiris remarks in connection with these patristic expressions: "It is clear from them that only the faithful, devout, and purified theologian can approach to some extent the one who is absolutely pure, to draw near to God and to speak about him." On the other hand the breath of the Holy Spirit is necessary for true theologizing. "Without the breath and collaboration of the Holy Spirit there can be no authentic Orthodox theology. That is why contemporary Orthodox theologians also must become, through faith and the sanctity of their lives, worthy vessels of the Holy Spirit [true pneumatophors — 'full of the Spirit,' Acts 6.3] who will enlighten and guide them to theological contemplation and to climb the 'heights of theology . . . in the power of the Spirit' and who will grant to everyone in a totally unique and personal way 'according to the measure of Christ's gift' his illuminating grace.''[7]

Theological process is also explained by the spiritual progress of mankind through the course of time and by those new problems mankind faces in function of which this progress comes about. In summary, the real progress of theology and its consequent justification as a living theology — for without this kind of progress theology does not seem to be justified, and constitutes an inadequate repetition of the old formulae — are linked to three conditions: fidelity to the revelation of Christ given in holy Scripture and tradition and lived uninterruptedly in the life of the Church; responsibility for the faithful who are contemporary with the theology as it is being done; openness to the eschatological future, that is, the obligation to guide the faithful towards their true perfection in that future. If one or the other of these conditions is not fulfilled, theology arises which is inadequate and to a great extent useless, at times even damaging to the Church and to the faithful.

An inadequate theology is one that consists in a literal repetition of the words and formulae of the past. A damaging theology is one that remains fixed in the formulae of a past system and confuses these with revelation itself. Catholic theology did this for centuries in its repetition of the scholastic formulae, and sometimes even Orthodox theologians have done this, comfortably repeating the by-now opaque formulae of certain nineteenth-century manuals influenced by scholasticism, and making them into infallible criteria of judgement for Orthodoxy. This was a theology that hindered any spiritual revival and any spiritual progress, a theology devoid of all dynamic meaning and reflecting a static and exterior order which it continued to think of as perfect. Furthermore, it implied a lack of responsibility shown towards the faithful of its own time, and consequently also towards theology's duty to work for religious renewal in its own time. This, in turn, implies also a lack of responsibility shown for the richness of revelation expressed in holy scripture and in apostolic and patristic tradition.

Such a theology was guilty of a threefold infidelity: infidelity to the unlimited character of revelation, to its own contemporaries, and to the future.

In its different periods theology is inevitably linked to a certain extent with the concepts that belong to those periods. Hence, to stick to concepts which, with the passing of the period from which they were taken, have lost their validity and to insist on maintaining them permanently as a basis for theology — these are attitudes which make the formulations of such a theology into objects that are lifeless and foreign to the life of the Church and of the faithful in succeeding periods. This applies particularly to the point mentioned above, namely, that not everything from theology is assimilated within definitive Church teaching. The Church assimilates into her teaching only what has in fact its own relevance for every period. That is why it is a good thing when, from the thought of each age, theology retains what is permanently valuable.

Even more damaging, however, is theology which entirely abandons the revelation in Christ which has been preserved in holy scripture and in the tradition of the Church in order to adapt itself to what it thinks representative exclusively of the spirit of the age. The Protestant Bultmannian theology which declared that all the essential events from the beginning of Christianity are myths was of this kind, as were the similar views of the Anglican Bishop J. A. T. Robinson, and the theory of a Christianity without God put forward by the "God is dead" theological movement in America.

Christianity cannot be of use to any age, nor consequently to the present age either, if it does not bring to it what it alone can bring: the link with the infinite source of power, that is, with God become man. Only in this way can Christianity contribute to progress by means of an unending process of spiritualization. We, the theologians of today, can and must reveal, even more than was done in the past, what the principal acts of divine revelation culminating in Christ — the incarnation of the Son of God, his sacrifice on the cross, his resurrection and ascension as man — what these contribute as a vision of Christian humanism and what consequences flow from them for the service of progress and of the process of spiritualization in general. This is the positive meaning of theology's openness to the world, while remaining faithful to itself: that it give full attention to the *saeculum*, in the sense of recognizing the world's stability and value, and of helping the world, as it should, towards a genuine development of what constitutes true Christian humanity. The dogmas of incarnation, resurrection, and deification contribute greatly to this progress of what is authentically human.

Contrary to Docetism (the theory of an only apparent humanity of Christ), the hypostatic union of the two natures in Christ serves only to strengthen — for all eternity — what is relative, hence, what is created, through what is absolute.

To the same extent that a theology fixed in the formulae of the past is damaging, so a theology which clings exclusively to the present is inadequate.

Yet just as damaging and productive of just as much disorder is a theology which pays attention to nothing but the future, and is dominated by an exclusively eschatological spirit that neglects the reality of the present life and the help which must be given it. Protestant theology often manifests this character when, through an exclusive preoccupation with eschatological hope, it depreciates the present, man's obligation to grow spiritually in time, and his call to discharge the duties he has towards his contemporaries. The intense expectation of the life which will come after the end of the world receives almost all the emphasis, particularly in some newer Protestant denominations.

A Christian theology that is complete and open to genuine progress must certainly also be animated by hope and by the perspective of the eschatological future, yet this hope and this perspective are sustained by the actual experience in the present time of continuous progress in spiritualization and in improving the relationship of love among men. Theology advances toward this future through the spiritual progress it makes in the present time, fed from the source established fundamentally by the revelation which culminates in Christ and which was achieved two thousand years ago, as the biblical documents of that revelation and the witness of the Christian centuries down to our own time assure us.

Through its very fidelity to the deeds and words of Christ as these are known from apostolic preaching, theology can still advance in understanding without going beyond the content of revelation.[8]

Like the Church too, theology must be apostolic, contemporary with every age, and prophetic and eschatological. But as it progresses, theology must not break with the Church, but rather advance together with the Church which is being led forward towards the kingdom of heaven. Theology must be apostolic because it has to be an unceasing testimony about Christ, the complete revelation, just as the preaching of the apostles was a testimony about Christ as the definitive revelation. At the same time theology must be eschatological for in Christ and in the apostolic preaching the eschatological element is also included. But theology is not to be prophetic in the sense that it predicts some future stage higher than that represented by the revelation in Christ. It can be prophetic only in the sense that it outlines future steps in the discovery of those treasures which are hidden in Christ. Theology can be prophetic in its explanation of the risen Christ as one who represents our state in the life to come, but it does not promise a future stage that goes beyond Christ. This character of theology can be termed prophetic/eschatological rather than simply prophetic because it prophesies nothing other than a future given in Christ, a future in which we too will be participants in the life to come.

A Christian theology which meets all the conditions mentioned above promotes progress and thus facilitates the effectiveness of revelation in uninterrupted continuity. In this sense, it is a theology of faith, of love, and of hope. Through faith it manifests certainty in the real revelation of God in Christ; through hope it gives believers a perspective that opens out into complete assimilation of the good things of Christ who has been revealed; through love it helps them even now to be united with Christ and with one another. Through faith theology is faithful to the revelation achieved in the past; through hope it is open to a future of full participation in the good things of Christ and guides the advancement towards him, while through love it sustains the present participation in these good things through a communion with Christ and our neighbors that increases continuously. Because of these three factors, theology is traditional and at the same time both contemporary and prophetic/eschatological. It is faithful to the past, but not enclosed in the past; it is faithful to the contemporary world but its vision goes beyond the present situation of mankind today. Theology must be anchored in the fixed foundation laid down by Christ, but at the same time it makes the good things of Christ accessible to the people of today and prepares them to participate in them fully in the age to come. Theology thus constitutes a ferment for progress in every age.

Progress in the understanding of dogmas is possible, on the other hand, because their content is infinite and hence apophatic (ineffable), that is, it can never be comprehended in notions or words that might exhaust it. Apophaticism of the Eastern tradition "teaches us to see above all a negative meaning in the dogmas of the Church: it forbids us to follow natural ways of thought and to form concepts which would usurp the place of spiritual realities. For Christianity is not a philosophical school for speculating about abstract concepts, but is essentially a communion with the living God."[9]

Progress takes the form of an emphasis placed more strongly now on one aspect of the inexhaustible richness of dogmas and now on another, according to the preoccupations and the spiritual development of the faithful at a particular time. But the aspect that receives this greater emphasis opens up an increased understanding of the whole content of the dogmas and gives promise of future advancement in understanding it. "The history of theological thought is composed of different periods or doctrinal cycles in which one aspect of the Christian tradition takes precedence over others, in which all doctrinal themes are treated to a certain extent as a function of the one question which has become central in the dogmatic consciousness."[10]

Through the theology which is done within her, the Church advances under the light of "the Sun of righteousness" which is continually growing and filling her with an ever greater light. The continuous journey under this same sun, that nevertheless goes on increasing in brilliance, is the tradition of the Church, while the authentic light of the sun — which accumulates as a dowry and as a permanent good interpreted by theological insight — becomes the teaching of the Church. This light from which theology grows and which in turn theology makes grow by interpreting it in the ever more brilliant light of revelation, enriches the tradition of the Church and — imprinted on the being of the faithful as a force of transformation — makes them into more and more spiritual beings. Such a process of spiritualization is the gradual appearance, through the very being of the faithful, of the presence of Christ. This being is changed into an ascending meaning or refined continuously as understanding, as sensibility, decency and love in relationships, as penetration into the complexity and profundity of the divine and human realities united together.

Theology grows under the sun of revelation, which, having once appeared in the person of Jesus Christ, shines forth always in the

Church and in her members with that light which is called tradition; moreover, the interpretation of tradition, undertaken by theology and assimilated by the Church, is the teaching of the Church. Theology follows the trajectory of this sun and its growth as communion in the reality of the Church, increasing the very consciousness of the Church and expressing the fresh nuances in which — at every step and without any essential change — the growth of this sun can be seen. Theology opens up, therefore, the prospect of the full manifestation of Christ at the end of time.

Theology promotes progress as it helps the spiritual progress of Christian people towards an eschatological communion which is universal and perfect. Theology is a part of the movement of the human spirit towards full union with God and — through its task of explaining this movement — has a particularly effective role within it.

Saint Maximos the Confessor defended this movement of the human spirit against Origenism which held that motion itself was produced by the fall of spirits from primordial unity.[11] If it is through the spiritual experience of the Church that this movement finds its practical realization in the most enduring way, then theology — which particularly has the task of explaining this movement and hence of helping it forward — is called to help in a general way the entire movement of creation towards God. It succeeds in doing this by opening up the vision of God today, and a more complete vision tomorrow, as it takes power from God who, through creation, gave this impulse to man and who, through the incarnation, crucifixion, and resurrection of his Son, gave it also to the Church and to theology. Theology will be effective if it stands always before God and helps the faithful to do the same in their every act: to see God through the formulae of the past, to express him through the explanations of the present, to hope and to call for the advancement towards full union with him in the life to come.

NOTES

1. Bernhard Philberth, *Der Dreieine*. Anfang und Sein. Die Struktur der Schöpfung (Stein am Rhein 1980), p. 103. God is distinct from *nothingness*, and in a way that is incomparably greater and more definitive than is any other existence, because he is not threatened in his existence by *nothingness*. But, through God, man too is called to be distinct, totally and definitively, from *nothingness*. God and man are the two fundamental realities definefd in dogmas. Because the latter is linked to the former, he constitutes together with God one dogma. God and man are defined as fundamental dogmas because they are the fundamental existences, at once manifest and yet not understood. They are manifest because without them nothing has meaning; and they are full of mystery because they are of an inexhaustible content. In the existence of God, which is radically distinct from *nothingness*, there is given the infinity of his existence. But in his relationship with us there enters the possibility of giving definition to his activity. In God's radical boundary over against *nothingness* lies the infinity of his existence and the impossibility of ever understanding it fully, while in the fact that we too receive a real and definitive boundary facing *nothingness*, we too, in a form which is properly human, participate in an existence which is infinite in development and inexhaustible in ˙nowledge.
2. Evagrios of Pontos, *Prayer* 60, PG 79.1180B; ET Palmer/Sherrard/ Vare, *The Philokalia*, vol. 1, p. 62.
3. *The Incomprehensible Nature of God* 3.6, PG 48.725; ET Paul W. Harkins, *St. John Chrysostom. On the Incomprehensible Nature of God, FC* 72, Washington 1984, p. 111 [= 3.35].
4. *The Incomprehensible Nature of God* 3.6, PG 48.725; ET Harkins [=3.34], pp. 110-111.
5. *Oration* 20.12, PG 35.1080B.
6. *The Life of Moses*, PG 44.373D-376A; ET A. J. Malherbe/E. Ferguson, *Gregory of Nyssa. The Life of Moses* (NY, 1978), p. 93 [=158].
7. "Advice to Theologians," Ὀρθόδοξος Τύπος (Athens), 1 February 1974, a lecture delivered at the Theological Faculty in Thessalonike, 14 November 1973.
8. The theologian T. M. Parker says: "Even the profoundest theologian has never fully plumbed its depths [revelation] and all of us spend our lives growing slowly into what can at best be only very incomplete knowledge of the faith. We accept it [the word of God] as a whole, because it is the word of God, who cannot deceive or be deceived. . . . But however great our education or our natural genius, we remain . . . incapable of taking the full riches of the faith into our small minds. . . ." ("The Creeds IV," in *Report of the Sixth Anglo-Catholic Congress. Subject: The Church. London: July 1948* (Westminster,1948), p.74.
9. Vladimir Lossky, *The Mystical Theology of the Eastern Church* (London, 1957), p. 42.
10. Vladimir Lossky, *The Vision of God* (Leighton Buzzard/Clayton WN, 1963), p. 124.
11. The theme of motion recurs throughout *The Ambigua* (PG 1032A-1417C); cf. P. Sherwood, *The Earlier Ambigua of Saint Maximus the Confessor and His Refutation of Origenism* (Rome, 1955), pp. 72-109.

Chapter Six

Knowledge of God

Rational and Apophatic Knowledge of God

According to patristic tradition, there is a rational or cataphatic knowledge of God, and an apophatic or ineffable knowledge. The latter is superior to the former because it completes it. God is not known in his essence, however, through either of these. We know God through cataphatic knowledge only as creating and sustaining cause of the world, while through apophatic knowledge we gain a kind of direct experience of his mystical presence which surpasses the simple knowledge of him as cause who is invested with certain attributes similar to those of the world. This latter knowledge is termed apophatic because the mystical presence of God experienced through it transcends the possibility of being defined in words. This knowledge is more adequate to God than is cataphatic knowledge.

Rational knowledge, however, cannot simply be renounced. Even though what it says about God may not be entirely adequate, it says nothing which is opposed to God. It is just that what it does say must be deepened through apophatic knowledge. Moreover, even apophatic knowledge, when it seeks to give any account of itself at all, must resort to the terms of the knowledge of the intellect, though it does fill these terms continuously with a deeper meaning than the mind's notions can provide.

Apophatic knowledge is able to accomplish this since for it the attributes of God are not merely objects of thought, but are to a certain extent experienced directly. For instance, in apophatic knowledge the infinity or omnipotence or love of God is not just an intellectual notion, but a matter of direct experience. In the act of knowing apophatically the human subject experiences in a real way a kind of submersion into the infinity, the omnipotence, or the love of God. Through apophatic knowledge the human subject not only knows that God is infinite, omnipotent, or loving, but also experiences this. Yet within this experience, the infinity of God actually appears so overwhelmingly that man realizes that this infinity is wholly other than the one he can conceive in his mind, that it is ineffable. It is also true that in the course of rational knowledge man realizes that God's infinity is greater and other than what he is able to comprise within an intellectual concept of it. Hence he corrects this knowledge by a negation of it. But this negation is equally intellectual as an expression. Man knows that the infinity of God is other than the infinity he conceives with his mind, but the subsequent negation always refers to what has been affirmed. This is the *via negativa* of Western theology. In Eastern patristic tradition, however, apophatic theology is a direct experience. It is true that it too must resort to this negative intellectual theology in expressing itself, but in itself it differs from the other.[1]

In our opinion these two kinds of knowledge are neither contradictory nor mutually exclusive, rather they complete each other. Strictly speaking, apophatic knowledge is completed by rational knowledge of two kinds, that which proceeds by way of affirmation and that which proceeds by way of negation. It transfers both these ways of rational knowledge to a plane more in keeping with its own nature, but, when it needs to express itself — in however unsatisfactory a way — apophatic knowledge in its turn has recourse to the terms of rational knowledge in both of its aspects (affirmation and negation). One who has a rational knowledge in both of its aspects (affirmation and negation). One who has a rational knowledge of God often completes this with apophatic knowledge, while the one whose apophatic experience is more pronounced will have recourse to the terms of rational knowledge when giving expression to this experience. Thus when the Eastern Fathers speak of God, they pass frequently from one mode to the other.

Like the rational knowledge of affirmation, apophatic knowledge too comes about from regarding the world, even while it goes beyond this regard. Sometimes it has no need of any actual vision of the world in order to arise, even though apophatic knowledge does presume knowledge of the world and the enrichment of the soul that comes about through it. The mystical presence of God is able to emerge in the experience of apophatic knowledge at whatever moment it arises, whether this is through the world or directly. Affirmative rational knowledge is, however, always connected with the world. The world remains always a term that is kept in the thought of one who knows God by way of deduction, as cause of the world and invested with attributes similar to those of the world. The fact that in apophatic knowledge the soul is absorbed in discerning God's presence caused the Eastern Fathers to speak on occasion of a "forgetting" of the world during this act. This does not mean, however, a factual withdrawal from the world. Even while remaining in the world a man can contemplate God as the one who is totally other than the world, whether this becomes apparent to him through the world itself or apart from it.

What further distinguishes the apophatic, direct, and mystical knowledge of God from rational, deductive knowledge is that, in the former, the human subject experiences the presence of God as person in a more pressing way. Nevertheless, the understanding of God as person is not excluded in affirmative, rational knowledge either, although the mystery of God as person is not revealed as clearly, profoundly, and pressingly. Yet it must be kept in mind that, in both these kinds of knowledge, supernatural revelation mediates to us, as a certain fact, the knowledge of God as person. Even apophatic knowledge, when it lacks supernatural revelation, can experience the ineffable presence of God in the way of an impersonal depth. We must not, therefore, distinguish apophatic knowledge from affirmative, rational knowledge only on this basis that the former would be a revealed supernatural knowledge while the latter would constitute a purely natural knowledge. Both are grounded in supernatural revelation when it is a matter of knowing God as person.

Rational knowledge, however, does not make use of the entire content of supernatual revelation. In this sense it resembles the knowledge of God in Judaism and Islam, since these too have part of the supernatural revelation at their base, but not all of it. By the fact that this is a poorer knowedge of God and as such, does not need the entire supernatural revelation, it sometimes happens that this same knowledge can also be seen in some people who have not shared in any part of supernatural revelation.

Finally, the third thing which must be mentioned with regard to the relation between these two kinds of knowledge of God is that, to the extent that man progresses in the spiritual life, the intellectual knowledge about God — as creator of the world and source of its rovidential care — which comes to man from the world, is imbued with the direct and richer contemplation of him, that is, with apophatic knowledge.

This is a further reason why the Fathers often alternate their discussion of the affirmative rational knowledge of God with talk about apophatic knowledge. Or, perhaps, inasmuch as in their case affirmative rational knowledge was overwhelmed by apophatic knowledge, they speak more about the latter, although they do show that the former is not excluded.

In his discussion of the affirmative rational knowledge of God that comes from the things of the world, Saint Gregory of Nazianzos says: "Now our very eyes and the law of nature teach us that God exists and that he is the efficient and maintaining cause of all things: our eyes, because they fall on visible objects, and see them in beautiful stability and progress, immovably moving and revolving, if I may so say; natural law, because through these visible things and their order it reasons back to their author. For how could this universe have come into being or been put together unless God had called it into existence, and held it together? For everyone who sees a beautifully made lute, and considers the skill with which it has been fitted together and arranged, or who hears its melody, would think of none but the lutemaker, or the luteplayer, and would recur to him in mind, though he might not know him by sight. And thus to us also is manifested that which made and moves and preserves all created things, even though he be not comprehended by the mind. And very wanting in sense is he who will not willingly go thus far in following natural proofs. . . ."[2]

Saint Gregory the Theologian rightly remarks that the rationality of the world is inexplicable in the absence of a person who conceived it as rational and that, inasmuch as, in such a case, this rationality would not be following any purpose, it would at bottom be meaningless and lack true rationality. It would be an absurd rationality. At the same time, Saint Gregory finds that God has not made a world petrified within a static rationality or an endlessly circular movement. Rather this is a world through which God produces a canticle that advances in its melodical themes. That is to say, God continues to speak to us through the world, and to lead us towards a goal. He is not only the creator of this vast lute but also the one who plays on it a canticle of vast proportions and complexity.

But for Saint Gregory this intellectual knowledge of God which has been rationally deduced from the world is still insufficient. Such knowledge needs completion through a higher knowledge which is an acknowledgement of the very mystery of God, an apophatic knowledge, a superior way of grasping his infinite richness — one which, precisely because of its infinity, cannot be understood or expressed. Speaking as if in the name of Moses who, in his ascent of Mount Sinai, became the image of all who raise themselves above a knowledge of God derived from the creatures to the knowledge of his limitless and mystical presence, Saint Gregory talks of this apophatic knowledge too, but he alternates his description with a description of cataphatic or affirmative, rational knowledge. He says: "I was running to lay hold on God, and thus I went up into the Mount, and drew aside the curtain of the cloud, and entered away from matter and material things, and as far as I could I withdrew within myself. And then when I looked up, I scarce saw the back parts of God; although I was sheltered by the rock, the Word that was made flesh for us. And when I looked a little closer, I saw, not the first and unmingled nature, known to itself — to the Trinity, I mean; not that which abides within the first veil, and is hidden by the cherubim; but only that nature which at last even reaches to us. And that is, as far as I can learn, the majesty, or, as holy David calls it, the glory which is manifested among the creatures, which it has produced and governs [Ps 8.2]. For these are the back parts of God, which he leaves behind him, as tokens of himself, like the shadows and reflection of the sun in the water, which show the sun to our weak eyes, because we cannot look at the sun himself, for by his unmixed light he is too strong for our power of perception."[3]

As we can see, to rise above the things of the world does not mean that these disappear; it means, through them, to rise beyond them. And since they remain, the apophatic knowledge of God does not exclude affirmative rational knowledge. But, as Saint Gregory can go from the one to the other, the latter knowledge is imbued with the former. In apophatic knowledge the world remains, but it has become transparent of God. This knowledge is apophatic because the God who now is perceived cannot be defined; he is experienced as a reality which transcends all possibility of definition. Yet, even this is a knowledge of the God who descended to us, not a knowledge of his own being in itself. Such knowledge is combined with the affirmative rational kind of knowledge to so great an extent that it is hard to say when Saint Gregory is speaking of the one or of the other.

How impossible it is to enclose the radiance of God's mystical presence — together with certain characteristics attributed to God — within the notions of the human mind has been shown by Saint Gregory of Nazianzos in another description of Moses' experience on Mount Sinai. Here, again, it is hard to distinguish between the two kinds of knowledge: "God always was, and always is, and always will be. Or rather, God always Is. For Was and Will be are fragments of our time, and of changeable nature, but He is Eternal Being. And this is the Name that He gives to Himself when giving the Oracle to Moses in the Mount. For in Himself He sums up and contains all Being, having neither beginning in the past nor end in the future; like some great Sea of Being, limitless and unbounded, transcending all conception of time and nature, only adumbrated by the mind, and very dimly and scantly ... not by His Essentials, but by His Environment; one image being got from one source and another from another, and combined into some sort of presentation of the truth, which escapes us before we have caught it, and takes to flight before we have conceived it, blazing forth upon our Master-part, even when that is cleansed, as the lightning flash which will not stay its course."[4]

The presence of God as person — a presence that presses upon us and from which shines forth his infinity — is not the conclusion of a rational judgment, as in the case of knowledge that is intellectual, cataphatic, or negative; rather it is perceived by one in a state of revived spiritual sensibility and this cannot come about so long as man is dominated by bodily pleasures or passions of any kind. It demands that man rise above the passions and be purified from them. After lengthy purification, the fineness of this kind of spiritual sensibility, which is capable of perceiving the mystical reality of God, itself becomes an enduring thing. An entire gradation exists both with respect to purification and with respect to the depth and duration of the apophatic perception of God. This does not exclude, however, the knowledge of God as creator and source of providence but is combined together with it. Apophatic knowledge is not irrational but supranatural, for the Son of God is the Logos and contains in himself the "reasons" of all created things. But it is supra-rational in the same way that the person — as one who is the subject of reason and of a life which has its own meaning forever — is supra-rational.

Saint Gregory of Nazianzos says, still speaking in the name of Moses: "Now when I go up eagerly into the Mount — or, to use a truer expression, when I both eagerly long, and at the same time am afraid (the one through my hope and the other through my weakness), to enter within the cloud, and hold converse with God, for so God commands — if any be an Aaron, let him go up with me, and let him stand near, being ready, if it must be so, to remain outside the cloud. But if any be a Nadab or an Abihu, or of the Order of the Elders, let him go up indeed, but let him stand afar off, according to the value of his purification. But if any be of the multitude, who are unworthy of this height of contemplation, if he be altogether impure, let him not approach at all, for it would be dangerous to him; but if he be at least temporarily purified, let him remain below and listen to the voice alone, and the trumpet, the bare words of piety . . ."[5]

That cleansing from the passions and the acute sense of one's own sinfulness and insufficiency are necessary conditions for this knowledge shows that it is not a negative, intellectual knowledge as has been understood in the West, that is, the simple negation of certain rational affirmations about God. It has to do with a knowledge that comes through experience. In fact, the Eastern Fathers prefer the term "union" to "knowledge" when dealing with this approach to God. In the experience of this apophatic knowledge God *is* perceived on the one hand, but, on the other, that which is perceived gives one to understand that there is something here beyond all perception. Both perceptions are expressed through the terms of affirmative and negative theology.

Saint Gregory continues: "It seems to me that, through what is perceived, he attracts me to him (for the one who is totally unperceived gives no hope and no help); and through what is unperceived, he stirs up my admiration; and being admired, he is longed for again; and being longed for, he cleanses us; and cleansing us, he gives us divine image; and so becoming, he speaks with us like with his household; the word even dare say something bolder: God unites himself with gods and is known by them, namely as much as he knows those who know him. Therefore God is infinite and difficult to be contemplated. And only this is perceived of him: infinity."[6]

The Fathers insist on stressing that even this experienced infinity is not the being of God, for it could be identified with the essence of the universe or of the human spirit, or seen as being in a continuity of nature with these, as in the thought of Plotinos. But God is neither the essence of the world nor of the human spirit; he transcends these because he is uncreated while they are created. His transcendence is assured by his character as person, capable of surpassing an infinity which is not itself person.

Only transcendent Person assures an infinity, the essence of which is not continuous with the essence of the world or of the human spirit; rather, it exists within a continuity made possible by grace and through a human participation that depends on the benevolence of divine Person and the effort of our own nature. In this case, for our nature to participate in infinity implies the joy of communion, without being annihilated as person, in the prospect of such communion becoming an eternal reality. If this were not so, infinity would only secure personal reality in a momentary way. That is why St. Maximos the Confessor says: "... the works of God which began to exist in time are all those that exist through participation.... Moreover, the things of God which did not begin to exist in time are those which are participated in, a participation through grace, by those things that share. Such, for example, are goodness — and all that is contained in the *logos* of goodness — and, in short, all life, immortality, simplicity, permanence, infinity and all things that are conceived as existing in their essence around God."[7] We know these works through a conscious participation in them — although the things themselves do not depend on our being — but do not know the very being of God; rather we realize that we are in communion with his divine Personal reality.

Neoplatonism held divinity to be identical with these things and hence confused divinity with the essence of the world or of the human spirit, reckoning that the human spirit, once raised up from its preoccupation with the multiplicity of things, would actually identify itself with divinity as a unity and a simplicity that were devoid of all determination and, hence, apophatic. Neoplatonism held, therefore, that divinity is known in its essence. This was the basis for the Eunomians' claim to have exact knowledge of the being of God. This implied, however, a denial of the transcendental and personal character of God. If God is transcendent, he is personal. Christian apophatic knowledge implies that God came down to meet man's capacity to grasp him as much as it also implies God's transcendence. God comes down through his energies while his personal character assures his transcendence. His person transcends even his infinity.[8]

In this sense God is not identical with any of those things we name as his qualities; he is identical neither with infinity, eternity, or simplicity, but transcends all of these. They are neither the essence of God nor the persons in whom his being subsists integrally, but they are "around God's being." Thus the idea that in our knowing God's infinity we do not know God fully, Saint Gregory the Theologian bases on the fact that the being of God cannot be identified with simplicity, just as ours is not identical with composition. If this were true, the distinction between the divinity and ourselves would be one of mode only, not of essence.

As God is person, between him and us a relationship of love is established that maintains both God and ourselves as persons. We do not experience this love as an infinity that is always self-identical, but as an infinity that has a perspective of continuous newness, as an ocean of richness always new where we will advance continuously. Our knowledge of God makes us seek to know him even more; and our love for him stimulates us to an even greater love. Because God is person, knowledge of him through experience is related to the extent of our purification from the passionate and blind attachment to finite things. But this is precisely what makes us see that, beyond that ever new richness which we perceive, its source exists and this source does not enter within the range of our experience.

We can say that there are two kinds of apophaticism: the apophaticism of what is experienced but cannot be defined; and the apophaticism of that which cannot even be experienced. These two are simultaneous. What is experienced has an intelligible character also, inasmuch as it is expressed in intellectual terms — though these are both affirmative and negative. Yet, this intelligibility is always inadequate. The being which remains beyond experience, which yet we sense to be the source of everything we experience, subsists in person. Subsisting as person, being is a living source of energies or of acts which are communicated to us. Hence, the apophatic has, as its ultimate basis, person; and thus even this apophaticism does not mean that God is wholly enclosed within himself.

Saint Gregory of Nyssa speaks in a similar fashion about the two types of knowledge of God, sometimes distinguishing them and at other times combining them. But he says more about apophatic knowledge, for in his view, cataphatic (affirmative rational) knowledge is included within apophatic knowledge. The first chapters of *The Great Catechetical Oration* are dedicated to the rational knowledge of God. But even while speaking of cataphatic knowledge, Saint Gregory says that God reveals himself in it too as a mystery that cannot be defined — which makes it equivalent to the beginning of apophatic knowledge and to the desire for a more profound experience of the latter. "And so, one who severely studies the depths of the mystery, receives secretly in his spirit, indeed, a moderate amount of apprehension of the doctrine of God's nature, yet he is unable to explain clearly in words the ineffable depth of this mystery."[9]

But Saint Gregory of Nyssa, persisting in the description of apophatic knowledge, does not see it as forever separated from the contemplation of created things. On the other hand, he too requires, as a condition for this knowledge, the purification of the soul from passions so that whoever wishes to contemplate might remain no longer enclosed exclusively within the visible horizon of material things.

Saint Gregory also makes use of Moses' ascent of the mountain as an image of the ascent of the soul towards intimacy with God: "When he who has been purified and is sharp of hearing in his heart hears this sound (I am speaking of the knowledge of the divine power which comes from the contemplation of reality), he is led by it to the place where his intelligence lets him slip in where God is. This is called *darkness* by the Scripture, which signifies, as I said, the unknown and unseen."[10] "Wherefore John the sublime, who penetrated into the luminous darkness, says, *No one has ever seen God* (Jn 1.18), thus asserting that knowledge of the divine essence is unattainable not only by men but also by every intelligent creature."[11]

But Saint Gregory of Nyssa gives us a deeper reason why there must first be a passage through the knowledge of created things before that darkness is reached and incomprehensibility of God is confronted. In that darkness Moses saw the tabernacle not made with hands, and this is "Christ who is the power and the wisdom of God" (1 Cor 1.24) who "encompasses everything in himself." "For the power which encompasses the universe, in which *lives the fulness of divinity* (Col 2.9), the common protector of all, who encompasses everything within himself, is rightly called 'tabernacle.'"[12] But it is through the contemplation of all things that we grow towards being capable of contemplating everything in him who encompasses all things in a simple and concentrated way. The sound of the trumpet that Moses hears from above — before he enters into the darkness where God is and where he sees the heavenly tabernacle, that is the power of God who encompasses all things. This Saint Gregory interprets as the manifestation of God's glory in creatures. Without seeing this, no one can rise to the experience of God's incomprehensible presence. "When he who has been purified and is sharp of hearing in his heart hears this sound (I am speaking of the knowledge of the divine power which comes from the contemplation of reality), he is led by it to the place where his intelligence lets him slip in where God is. This is called *darkness* by the Scripture (Ex 20.21), which signifies, as I said, the unknown and unseen. When he arrives there, he sees that tabernacle not made with hands. . . ."[13]

It should be observed that, following the Scripture, Saint Gregory of Nyssa holds that Moses reached the vision of the heavenly tabernacle after he had entered into the darkness of the consciousness of God's incomprehensibility. This leads us to understand that once Moses reached the experience of the incomprehensible mystery of God, he sees it either through or apart from created things, or else he passes from the one to the other, on an always higher plane. The things themselves become more and more transparent for the glory of God who reveals himself through them — for between the "reasons" of things and God there is no contradiction. "Then as he rises higher in his ascent he hears the sounds of the trumpets. Thereupon, he slips into the inner sanctuary of divine knowledge. And he does not remain there, but he passes on to the tabernacle not made with hands (Heb 9.11). For truly this is the limit that someone reaches who is elevated through such ascents."[14]

The knowledge of God always preserves its paradoxical character: to the extent that one ascends in the knowledge of God, he ascends at the same time in the understanding of the mystery of God as that which is not to be understood. "This is the true knowledge of what is sought; this is the seeing that consists in not seeing, because that which is sought transcends all knowledge, being separated on all sides by incomprehensibility as by a kind of darkness."[15] "When, therefore, Moses grew in knowledge, he declared that he had seen God in the darkness, that is, that he had then come to know that what is divine is beyond all knowledge and comprehension. . . . The divine word at the beginning forbids that the Divine be likened to any of the things known by men (Ex 20.2), since every concept which comes from some comprehensible image by an approximate understanding and by guessing at the divine nature constitutes an idol of God and does not proclaim God."[16]

This transparency keeps the ascent to the knowledge of God permanently open. Every understanding that touches upon God must have a certain fragility and transparence; it cannot be something fixed once and for all, but must itself urge us to call this understanding into question and stimulate us to seek one further along in the same direction. If such an understanding does remain fixed in our mind, we place limits on God corresponding to the boundaries of this particular understanding. We may even forget God entirely and find that our whole attention is concentrated on this particular understanding or upon the words which express God. In such a case our "understanding" becomes an "idol," a false god. The understanding or the word we use must always make God transparent, as one who is not contained within it, as one who transcends all understanding and reveals himself now under one aspect of his infinite richness and now under another.

Dionysios the Areopagite says: "That is why so many continue to be unbelieving in the presence of the explanations of the divine mysteries, for we contemplate them solely by way of the perceptible symbols attached to them. What is necessary is to uncover them, to see them in their naked purity. By contemplating them in this manner we can revere that 'source of life' flowing into itself. We see it remaining within itself, a unique and simple power, source of its own movement and activity, which is never failing and which is the knowledge of all knowledge by virtue of its own perpetual self-contemplation."[17] In fact it is through words and meanings that we must always pass beyond words and meanings. Only thus do we perceive the presence of God which is full of mysteries. If we hold too much to words and meanings — and this occurs when we stay always with the same words and the same meanings — then they come between us and God and we rest in them, treating these things as if they themselves were God.

On the one hand we do have need of words and meanings because they are borrowed from God's creatures and it is in them that his powers are manifested and through them that he came down to our level; on the other hand, however, we must go beyond them so that we can ascend above God's creatures and his works and find ourselves before God himself as their source. Even the works of God, experienced as powers that made and guide created things, are themselves superior to these created things and hence also to words borrowed from them.

On the one hand, we must ascend to the ever more sublime meanings of things and of the words which express these things — even the words from holy Scripture. On the other hand, we must rise beyond these to the experience of the mystery of God and of his operations. All created things and the words borrowed from these are symbols in comparison with God's operations and his Personal reality as their source.[18] But within these symbols there are numerous levels of meanings, levels that are superimposed on one another and — until we reach them — quite unsuspected by us. We must always be ascending to further meanings of these symbols and to further levels and, ultimately, we must rise above all their meanings. The more we use words of greater subtlety and the more we ascend to their more sublime meanings the greater is our understanding of God as the one who transcends all things and as the one who — as single source of their reasons — is full of all their potential depth and complexity. It is precisely for this reason that he calls upon us to leave all symbols behind, to abandon the words and their meanings. Even when the words refer to the operations of God's economy, we must still ascend in our understanding of their meanings and pass on continuously to others which are more adequate and then leave these behind as well; for even these operations themselves are boundless: "His judgments are inscrutable," says Saint John Chrysostom, "his ways are unsearchable, his peace surpasses all understanding, his gift is indescribable, what God has prepared for those who love him has not entered into the heart of man, his greatness has no bound, his understanding is infinite. Are all these incomprehensible while only God himself can be comprehended? . . . The heretic answers that Paul is not talking about God's essence but about his governance of the universe. Very good, then. If he is talking about the governance of the universe, our victory is all the more complete. For if his governance of the universe is incomprehensible, then all the more so is God himself beyond our powers of comprehension."[19]

God is the source of power and light who draws us always higher up into knowledge and perfection of life. He is not a ceiling that puts an end to our ascent. He is the Supreme One, but his is a supremacy which is endless and inexhaustible in the attraction he exercises over us and the gifts he pours out upon us. In fact, none of this is possible unless God is person and our relationship with him is a relationship of love. An impersonal nature is in many respects finite. Otherwise it would not be subject to a law. The love of the human being, moreover, develops through virtue and this development implies freedom. Hence progress in the union with God has more than just the character of a theoretical knowledge. The understanding is nourished by the free effort of virtue (and vice-versa), while, in relationship with God, man receives the power he needs for this. We see here again that apophatic knowledge is not achieved by closing the spirit off from the reality of the world and from the persons of our fellow men. It is in relation with them that we grow in virtue.

This is the teaching of both Saint Gregory of Nyssa and Saint

John Chrysostom. The first says: "Similarly, the soul moves in the opposite direction. Once it is released from its earthly attachment, it becomes light and swift for its movement upward, soaring from below up to the heights. If nothing comes from above to hinder its upward thrust (for the nature of the Good attracts to itself those who look to it), the soul rises ever higher and will always make its flight yet higher — by its desire of the heavenly things *straining ahead for what is still to come* (Phil 3.14), as the Apostle says. Made to desire and not to abandon the transcendent height by the things already attained, it makes its way upward without ceasing, ever through its prior accomplishments renewing its intensity for the flight. Activity directed toward virtue causes its capacity to grow through exertion; this kind of activity alone does not slacken its intensity by the effort, but increases it."[20]

Only through an effort of purification does the subtlety of the spirit increase and it is only this subtlety that can renounce any understanding about God that has already been achieved, or the slothful tendency to remain fixed in it, or the further tendency to make it into an idol and thus immobilize the spirit with the worship of its limited reality. The soul is borne upwards by a continual thirst and "it prays God to show himself to it." Things already attained are always symbols or images of the archetype and it is towards increased knowledge of the archetype that that soul strives unceasingly. Now the archetype is God as supreme Personal reality. The basic symbols are the things of the world and these are always being penetrated by light from more sublime meanings.

Saint Gregory of Nyssa describes this ascent in part as follows: "Such an experience seems to me to belong to the soul which loves what is beautiful. Hope always draws the soul from the beauty which is seen to what is beyond, always kindles the desire for the hidden through what is constantly perceived. Therefore, the ardent lover of beauty, although receiving what is always visible as an image of what he desires, yet longs to be filled with the very stamp of the archetype. And the bold request which goes up the mountains of desire asks this: to enjoy the Beauty not in mirrors and reflections, but face to face."[21]

God cannot be captured in notions because he is life or, more precisely, the source of life. Moreover, no person can be defined either, because each person is alive and, to a certain extent, a source of life. How much less, then, the supreme Personal reality. Anyone who thinks that he knows God, which is to say that he limits God by his own notions, is — from the Christian point of view — spiritually dead. That is how Saint Gregory of Nyssa interprets the words in Exodus 33.20, "For man shall not see me and live." "Scripture does not indicate that this causes the death of those who look, for how would the face of life ever be the cause of death to those who approach it? On the contrary, the Divine is by its nature life-giving. Yet the characteristic of the divine nature is to transcend all characteristics. Therefore, he who thinks God is something to be known does not have life, because he has turned form true Being to what he considers by sense perception to have being. True Being is true life. This Being is inaccessible to knowledge. If then the life-giving nature transcends knowledge, that which is perceived certainly is not life. . . . He learns from what was said that the Divine is by its very nature infinite, enclosed by no boundary. If the Divine is perceived as though bounded by something, one must by all means consider along with that boundary what is beyond it."[22] "Therefore, no consideration will be given to anything enclosing infinite nature. It is not in the nature of what is unenclosed to be grasped. . . . This truly is the vision of God: never to be satisfied in the desire to see him."[23]

Dionysios the Areopagite is considered to have laid more emphasis on apophatic knowledge than any other Church Father. Yet if we read his writings attentively, we see that he everywhere combines apophatic knowledge with cataphatic. This follows from the fact that he too speaks of a spiritual progress in one who knows God. In knowledge that can be given expression, therefore, he does not merely see a sum of intellectual affirmations, partly positive and partly negative — as scholastic theology practiced these two modes of knowing — but rather, and above all, knowledge from experience that has recourse to terms of affirmation and negation only in expressing itself, inasmuch as the consciousness of God's mystery is simultaneously implied in the things which are known about God. It is only by their belief that Dionysios separates knowledge which can be expressed from apophatic knowledge that Catholic theologians have been able to reproach the Eastern tradition with appropriating only the apophatic theology of Dionysios, and that precisely as a negative intellectual theology.[24]

In his work *The Divine Names*, Dionysios the Areopagite lays particular emphasis on the terms of affirmation in rational knowledge. But even here Dionysios does not separate off affirmations from negations, for these affirmative terms too are either based on an apophatic experience which simultaneously gives evidence of the mystery of God or else are linked with the experience of his mystery, since, on the one hand, all the powers that created and sustain the various aspects of the world come from God and, on the other hand, God is a unity higher than these. "Hence, with regard to the supra-essential being of God — transcendent Goodness transcendently there — no lover of the truth which is above all truth will seek to praise it as word or power or mind or life or being. No. It is at a total remove from every condition, movement, life, imagination, conjecture, name, discourse, thought, conception, being, rest, dwelling, unity, limit, infinity, the totality of existence. And yet, since it is the underpinning of goodness, and, by merely being there, is the cause of everything, to praise this divinely beneficent Providence, you must turn to all of creation."[25]

Nor are the attributes of God known only from rational deduction but from his operations reflected in the world through the world's participation in them. Their light is projected into the world and, in a way, experienced. This does not conflict with the consideration that God is the cause of the world. This latter consideration is the reason why even Dionysios the Areopagite does not completely separate rational knowledge from apophatic knowledge — a separation not made by the other Fathers either — but alternates in speaking about them both, even describing the experience of these operations in the terms of an intellectual theology of affirmation. Speaking of the beauty of God, Dionysios says: "But the 'beautiful' which is beyond individual being is called 'beauty' because of that beauty bestowed by it on all things, each in accordance with what it is. It is given this name because it is the cause of the harmony and splendor in everthing, because like a light it flashes onto everything the beauty-causing impartations of its own well-spring ray."[26]

Dionysios always speaks of a certain participation in God. But, in what is communicated to us from God, we experience the fact of not participating in him or, rather, the fact that, in his essence, God remains for us as one in whom we cannot participate. Yet through what he does communicate to us, God attracts us higher and higher into the mystery of the knowledge of his existence: "Many Scripture writers will tell you that the divinity is not only invisible and incomprehensible, but also 'unsearchable and inscrutable,' since there is not a trace for anyone who would reach through into the hidden depths of this infinity. And yet, on the other hand, the Good is not absolutely incommunicable to everything. By itself it generously reveals a firm, transcendent beam, granting enlightenments proportionate to each being, and thereby draws sacred minds upwards to its permitted contemplation, to participation and to the state of becoming like it."[27]

Thus in union with that light which is beyond nature, purified minds receive at the same time the consciousness that it is the cause of all things; and this is what incites them to express it in the affirmative terms of some of the attributes that can be considered to be causes of the qualities of the world. With this apophatic experience, therefore, everything is given: the experience of the operations of God; the consciousness of his being as one which transcends all approach to it; the impossibility of any fully adequate expression of these operations; the evidence that they are the causes of things and, as such, may be expressed in terms analogous to those used in describing the qualities of created things; and, simultaneously, the necessity of correcting these affirmative intellectual expressions by denying them.

In any case, in the experience of the operations of God (an experience that transcends understanding) there is also given an experience of them as causes of the things of creation and, hence, the necessity of expressing what is experienced in both affirmative and negative terms, together with the consciousness that the operations themselves transcend these terms. By themselves the negative terms are just as inadequate as the affirmative ones. A synthesis between them must always be realized. At the basis of this synthesis, however, lies an experience which transcends both the terms of affirmation and of negation that express it. God possesses in himself both what corresponds to the terms of affirmation and what corresponds to the terms of negation, but he possesses these in a way which is absolutely superior to the terms themselves. And this is a matter of experience, not of mere speculation. "Since it is the Cause of all beings, we should posit and ascribe to it all the affirmations we make in regard to beings, and, more appropriately, we should negate all these affirmations, since it surpasses all being. Now we should not conclude that the negations are simply the opposites of the affirmations, but rather that the cause of all is considerably prior to this, beyond privations, beyond every denial, beyond every assertion."[28]

The fact that both intellectual affirmations and negations have a basis in the experience of God's operations in the world diminishes, in the case of Dionysios as well as in that of the other Church Fathers, the too rigid distinction between the intellectual and the apophatic knowledge of God. The intellectual knowledge of the Logos is participation in his activity which gives and sustains reason. If Roman Catholic theology reduces all the knowledge of God to knowledge from a distance, Eastern theology reduces it to a theology of participation in various degrees which are ascended through purification.

Although Dionysios affirms on the one hand that negations are more suitable to God than affirmations, he affirms on the other hand that God transcends the negations far more than the affirmations. This must be understood to mean that in himself God is the most positive reality. But his supreme positivity transcends all affirmations. And this is one more reason not to give up speaking about God in affirmative terms.

Much stress has been laid on the fact that Dionysios names God "darkness," as being the one totally unknown. But Dionysios says that the term "darkness" is likewise unsuitable to God. He is beyond darkness and beyond light, not in a privative sense, but as transcending them. He is the super-luminous darkness. "The divine darkness is that 'unapproachable light' where God is said to live. And if it is invisible because of a superabundant clarity, if it cannot be approached because of the outpouring of its transcendent gift of light, yet it is here that is found everyone worthy to know God and to look upon him. And such a one, precisely because he neither sees him nor knows him, truly arrives at that which is beyond all seeing and all knowledge. Knowing exactly this, that he is beyond everything perceived and conceived . . ." [29]

God is not knowable, and yet the one who believes can experience him in a sensible and conscious manner. This is the positive fact. Man is submersed in the incomprehensible, indefinable and inexpressible ocean of God; nevertheless, he is aware of this. God is the positive reality beyond what we know of as positive; yet in comparison with the created world he is a negative reality beyond what we know of as negative. Dionysios asserts this too in his paradoxical characterization of God, although the paradox does not imply that each part cancels out the other, but rather that both parts are transcended: "this supra-existent Being. Mind beyond mind, word beyond speech . . ."³⁰

Saint Symeon the New Theologian says more of the vision of God on the part of those who are purified, and speaks of it as light that shines through all things. He continuously remarks, however, that this light is above all understanding and because of its infinite character holds open the prospect of an endless progress within itself. At the same time, Saint Symeon experiences God as person and sees him in his quality as cause of all goods. In fact, the light has in itself a meaning and it gives meaning to all things:

> and he will shine more than the rays of the visible sun;
> just as my Lord shone in His Resurrection
> and behold the men, standing near the One who glorified them,
> will remain dumbfounded, by excess of the glory
> and the incessant increase of divine splendor,
> the progress in fact will be endless, in the course of the centuries,
> because the cessation of the growth towards this infinite end
> would be nothing else but the seizure of the unseizable
> and that the one who can satisfy no one
> would become the object of satiety:
> on the contrary, to be filled by Him and to be glorified in His light
> will dig a bottomless progress and an unlimited beginning;
> in the same way as, while possessing Christ who was formed within them,
> they abide near the One who shines with an inaccessible light,
> so even in them the end becomes the beginning of glory,
> and — to explain my thought more clearly to you —
> they will have the beginning in the end, and the end in the beginning.[31]

The one who shines forth for those who, through purification, have attained the perfection of love is Christ as person. Only from a person does an inexhaustible light well up, a continuous newness of meanings and love:

> You, oh Christ, are the Kingdom of Heaven; You, the land promised to the gentle; You the grazing lands of paradise; You, the hall of the celestial banquet; . . .
> And Your grace, grace of the Spirit of all sanctity, will shine like

the sun in all the saints; and You, inaccessible sun, will shine
in their midst and all will shine brightly, to the degree of their
faith, their asceticism, their hope and their love, their purification
and their illumination by Your Spirit.[32]

He is the cause of all things, but he himself is not one of them.
The affirmative and negative terms complete one another, but all
are the expression of an apophatic experience, not of speculative reflection
carried out from a distance.

Indeed, You are none of these creatures, but superior to
all creatures, for You are the cause of all creatures, in
so far as You are Creator of all
and that is why You are apart from them all,
very lofty, for our mind, above all creatures,
invisible, inaccessible, unseizable, intangible,
escaping all comprehension, You remain without change,
You are simplicity itself and yet You are all diversity —
and our mind is totally incapable of fathoming
the diversity of Your glory and the splendor of Your beauty.[33]

Saint Gregory Palamas has given a final precision to the patristic
tradition regarding the knowledge of God. He does not deny that the
natural mind is able to know God, but he holds that philosophers
have deviated from the normal use of that knowledge.[34] Speaking of
natural knowledge guided by reason that has not been diverted from
its natural use, he says: "The vision and the knowledge of God through
creatures is called natural law. That is why, even before the patriarchs
and the prophets and the written law, this natural law called and
brought back to God the human race and showed forth the creator
to those who did not go astray from natural knowledge, like the Greek
philosophers. For who, by possessing mind and perceiving so many
distinctions of substances, the balanced impulses of the movements
opposite to one another . . . , will not know God as from an image
and from what is caused? . . . he will also have the knowledge of God
through negation. Thus the knowledge of creatures brought the human
race back to God before the law [was given]. . . . "[35]

Of course, once the Son of God had come in the flesh the faith
that he brought raised us up to a higher knowledge. Anyone, moreover,

who refuses this knowledge is to be condemned. Even in the Old Testament there existed a faith which transcended reason, and through the Incarnation of the Word that faith has been further strengthened. "In fact this faith is a vision beyond mind. And the possession of what is believed is a vision beyond that vision which is beyond mind. But what is seen and possessed through this latter vision, being beyond sensible and intelligible things, is not the essence of God . . . "[36]

Whoever has risen to this state knows God as the very cause of all, not so much through his own reason as through an experience of God's power.

The vision of God in light is higher not only than rational knowledge but also than the knowledge that comes through faith. Thus it is also more sublime than knowledge that comes through negation. For its apophaticism is vision transcending every kind of knowledge, even negative knowledge. This apophaticism makes use of negative words in order to express its vision, but the vision itself transcends these words. Addressing himself to Barlaam, who maintained that the highest knowledge of God is that through rational negation, St. Gregory Palamas says: "The vision (contemplation), my dear man, is one thing and theology is another, because it is not the same to say something about God as it is to gain and see God. For negative theology is also a word. But visions (contemplations) are above words . . . "[37]

The vision and the experience of God are expressed, however, in negative words as well, not because this vision is not a real vision of him, but because it transcends everything that the words express. God is expressed as "darkness" not because he is not seen at all, but in a transcendent sense; that this darkness is God, however, is something that is known. Palamas interprets in this way the words of Dionysios from the Epistle to Dorotheos: "The divine darkness is that 'unapproachable light' where God is said to live. And . . . if it cannot be approached because of the outpouring of its transcendent gift of light, yet it is here that is found everyone worthy to know God and to look upon him. And such a one, precisely because he neither sees him nor knows him, truly arrives at that which is beyond all seeing and all knowledge. Knowing exactly this, that he is beyond everything perceived and conceived . . . "[38]

Commenting on these words Palamas says: "Here he says that the same thing is both darkness and light, that he sees and does not see, that he knows and does not know. Therefore, how is this light darkness? 'Because of the outpouring of its transcendent gift of light' he says. Therefore, in a proper sense, it is light, and in a transcendent sense (καθ' ὑπεροχήν) it is darkness, since it is invisible to those who would want to approach and see it through the works of senses and of mind." And the capacity to enter into that darkness belongs to those who are purified of egoistic passions, like Moses who lived only for God and for the fulfillment of his will towards the people of Israel. "Theology through negation, though, is proper to every worshipper of God.... But the one who has attained that light sees, he says, and does not see. How is it that in seeing he does not see? Because, he says, he sees beyond vision. Therefore he knows and sees in a proper sense and he does not see in a transcendent sense (οὐχ ὁρᾷ ὑπεροχικῶς), since he does not see through some operation of the mind and of the senses, for he has transcended every operation of knowledge, reaching beyond vision and knowledge, that is to say he sees and knows at a higher level than we do, as the one who has attained to a stage higher than man and is God already by grace; and by being united with God, he sees God through god."[39]

We could sum up the patristic tradition about the knowledge of God in the following points:

a. There is a natural capacity for a rational knowledge of God which is both affirmative and negative, but apart from supernatural revelation and grace this capacity can hardly be maintained at all. This same capacity also owes its existence to a certain self-evidence of God in the world.

b. Knowledge through faith based on supernatural revelation is superior to natural knowledge from reason and strengthens, clarifies, and expands the latter. This knowledge contains within itself a certain conscious experience of God, like that of a pressure exerted upon the human persons by God's personal presence. This experience is superior to that which comes from natural knowledge, and, as such, is something which transcends rational knowledge both affirmative and negative, although it has recourse to affirmative and negative terms in order to give itself a certain expression.

c. Through purification from passions knowledge that comes from faith develops into a participation in things communicated to us by God who is above knowledge. This knowledge might rather be termed ignorance, or apophatic knowledge of a level higher than that of the apophatic knowledge through faith mentioned above, because it transcends everything that we are able to know through senses and through mind, and involves more than the mere pressure exerted by the presence of God as person. It does not exclude a knowledge of God as cause or the necessity of expressing God even here in affirmative and negative terms, although the content of what is known transcends the content of such terms to a much greater extent than the knowledge of him through simple faith.

d. One who has this vision or experience of God is simultaneously aware that, in his essence, God transcends the vision or experience. This is the most intense experience of the relationship with God as person, who as such cannot be defined, being totally apophatic.

e. In general, the apophatic experience of God is a characteristic that gives definition to Orthodoxy in its liturgy, sacraments, and sacramentals and is superior to Western experience which is either rational or sentimental or both at once. The apophatic experience is equivalent to a sense of mystery that excludes neither reason nor sentiment, but it is more profound than these.

Knowledge of God in the Concrete Circumstances of Life

If intellectual knowledge, both affirmative and negative, is more the product of theoretical reflection while it is in apophatic knowledge that people grow spiritually, then this latter knowledge is essential for all Christians in their practical life.

Every Christian knows God in his providential action by which the Christian is led in the particular circumstances of his own life, sometimes having good things for his lot, at other times — as a kind of training — being deprived of them. This latter form of guidance Saint Maximos calls leading through judgment. Everyone knows God through the appeal that he makes to him, placing the person in various circumstances and in contact with various people who demand that he fulfill certain duties and who test his patience in difficult ways. Everyone knows God in the qualms of conscience he feels for the wrongs he has committed and, finally, every one knows him in his own troubles and failure — temporary or lasting — in his own illness or that of those close to him that results from certain evils done or as means of moral perfection and spiritual strengthening; but every one also knows God in the help that he receives from him in overcoming these and all the other barriers and difficulties that stand in his way. This knowledge helps in leading each man on his own way of perfection.

It is a thrilling, burdensome, painful and joyful knowledge; it wakens within us our ability to respond; it gives fervor to prayer, and it causes our being to draw closer to God.

In this knowledge, our being experiences in practice the goodness, power, justice and wisdom of God, his attentive care for us, and God's special plan in its regard. In this connection the human person experiences a relation of particular intimacy with God as supreme Personal reality. In this knowledge I no longer see God only as the creator and the providential guide of all things, or as the mystery which makes himself visible to all, filling all with a joy which is to a greater or lesser extent the same in all cases; but I know him in his special care in regard to me, in his intimate relations with me, in his plan whereby, through the particular suffering, demands, and direction that he addresses to me in life, he leads me in a special way to the common goal. This intimate relationship which God has with me certainly does not remove me from solidarity with others or from the obligations I have towards others, towards family, nation, my home, my age, and the contemporary world. But God makes himself known to me through the appeals that he addresses to me especially, so as to stir me up to fulfill my duties, or through the remorse that I feel when I have not fulfilled my own special duties.

This thrilling character of the knowledge of God, imbued as it is with fear and trembling, was brought out forcefully by Saint John Chrysostom. In the conception of Chrysostom, it results to a great extent from the general experience of the terrible mystery of God. But this mystery is experienced especially in those states of responsibility, consciousness of sinfulness, need of repentance, and in the insurmountable difficulties of life. The psalms of the Old Testament give particular expression to this knowledge of God. All these circumstances produce a sensibility and refinement in our very being that lead it to perceive the realities beyond the world and to search for their meaning. In such circumstances especially, the knowledge of God is accompanied by responsibility, fear, and trembling. They make the soul more sensitive to the presence of God, or to the presence of the God who wants something special for me, for it is his special plan for me that produces them. It is not within a state of indifference that God is known. He does not wish to be known in such a state, for indifference does not help me towards perfection. That is why God puts me in circumstances like those described, and through them makes himself transparent on account of the interest he takes in me. It is especially with this purpose in mind that he is the *mysterium tremendum*.

The difficult circumstances which pierce our being like nails urge us towards more deeply felt prayer. And during this kind of prayer the presence of God is more evident to us. In general it is a good thing to pray in all circumstances, because in itself prayer is a means of making the soul sensitive to the presence of God and of deepening our own self-knowledge before God. Saint John Chrysostom says: "Prayer stands in the first place; then comes the word of instruction. And that is what the apostles said: 'Let us devote ourselves to prayer and the ministry of the word' (Acts 6.4). Paul does this when he prays at the beginnings of his epistles so that, like the light of a lamp, the light of prayer may prepare the way for the word. If you accustom yourselves to pray fervently, you will not need instruction from your fellow servants because God himself, with no intermediary, enlightens your mind."[40]

The state of prayer is a condition in which through an increase of sensibility we apprehend God as a "Thou" who is present. It is precisely for this reason that in prayer we speak directly to God, while, during the time of his own reflection, the believer feels himself to be alone and outside a direct relationship with God.

In this state of direct relationship with God the power of God is also felt directly, especially when one who believes asks for help from him in the awareness that such help can come from him alone. If there are different degrees to the presence a person has before us, he has the most intense degree of that presence when he stands before us as a second person and when we talk with him. Moreover, this presence achieves an even greater intensity when we feel that that person is open to our appeal to him. That is why God, whom we address in prayer in the conviction that he hears us and is committed to helping us, is felt to be most intensely present before us.

Saint John Chrysostom interprets this in the following way: "I am not talking of a prayer lightly and carelessly offered but of one made in earnest, which comes from an afflicted soul and from a contrite heart. This is the kind of prayer which mounts up to heaven.... So it is, too, with the human mind. As long as it enjoys full freedom from fear, it is relaxed and spreads itself far and wide. But when the pressure of affairs on earth has cramped its course so that it is indeed afflicted and bruised, it sends upward to heaven prayers which are pure and strong. So that you may know that the prayers which are uttered in time of affliction would have the best chance of being heard, hear what the prophet says: 'In my affliction I cried to the Lord, and he listened to me' (Ps 119.1). Therefore, let us stir up our conscience to fervor, let us afflict our soul with the memory of our sins, not so that it is crushed by anxiety, but so that we may make it ready to be heard, so that we make it live in sobriety and watchfulness and ready to attain heaven itself. Nothing puts carelessness and negligence to flight the way grief and affliction do. They bring together our thoughts from every side and make our mind turn back to ponder itself."[41] Then we appeal directly to the ultimate source of all powers, which is experienced as person, unable to remain indifferent. And this source of all powers wishes that you address yourself to it with all your power. Full relationship between person and person is a relationship of power in the good sense of the word, a relationship of feeling which is quite the opposite of indifference and negligence.

God makes himself known to us in all our difficulties if we strive to see our trespasses which are their foundations. Most often these difficulties arise because we have forgotten to see everything we have as gifts from God and, as a direct consequence, to use them ourselves as gifts vis-à-vis others. For God wants to make us too distributors of his gifts, so that we may increase our love towards others as we act in this way. Symeon Metaphrastes says that when those who were praising you have abandoned you, and slander and persecute you, you should think that "these things have come upon you from the righteous judgment and commandment of the God who loves mankind, because you have shown yourself ungrateful to him. For the things you have given your benefactor are the very things you have taken back. The measure you have used for giving will be the measure used when you receive and righteous is God's judgment accomplished in your case, ungrateful and thankless soul that you are, because you have forgotten the blessings of God. For you have forgotten the great and rich gifts that your benefactor gave to you."[42] When things go well with us, therefore, and also when they go badly, we should think of the responsibility we have for our brothers before God. In both situations this keeps the thought of the Personal reality of God vigilant in our conscience, preserves us in relation with him and makes us direct our thought to him. This thought, moreover, deepens our consciousness of him. In the first situation, when God gives us good things, he invites us to unite ourselves in love with him and with others. In the other situation he admonishes us precisely because we have not been doing this, and advises us to repent and to do in the future what we have not done in the past. In both cases God is speaking to us, calling upon us to respond to him by our works.

God addresses himself to us and awakens our reponsibility in an extremely penetrating way through the faces of the needy. He himself has said this (Mt 25.31-46). God emphasizes man's incommensurable value as man before him; this value is so great that God directly identifies himself with man's cause. In such cases we must consider that just as God asks us to help others so he asks others to help us when we are in need of help. "Oh my soul, help the one who suffers injustice, so you can escape from the hand of one who wrongs you. Do not delay in coming to his aid so that God too may help you be freed from the hands of those who trouble you."[43]

In everyone who is poor, oppressed, or sick, it is Christ who encounters us, asking — through this abasement — for our help. In the outstretched hand of the poor is the outstretched hand of Christ; in the faintness of his voice we hear the faint voice of Christ; because of the want and submission in which we hold him fast, his suffering is Christ's suffering on the Cross which we are prolonging. In all things God comes down to us and reveals himself to us. It is this very descent that makes plain his mystery that passes all understanding, and makes plain his love that surpasses all loves in the world. All the circumstances and persons through whom God speaks to us are appeals from him, living and transparent images of him; the God who is simple descends to us in a multitude of forms and situations, indeed in all the situations and forms of our life. And yet, though known to us through all these things, his mystery nevertheless remains beyond all understanding. In the suffering of the just, God shows that the love for him and for neighbor must pass through the fiery test of suffering.

In his explanation of the vision which the prophet Isaiah had of the seraphim who covered their faces when looking at God (Is 6.3), Saint John Chrysostom says: "And so, when the prophet says that they could not endure to look upon God, even though God was condescending and accommodating himself to their weakness, he means just this: they cannot endure to comprehend him with a pure and perfect knowledge; they dare not look fixedly at his essence pure and entire; they dare not look at him even after he has accommodated himself to them."[44]

This existential experience of God is combined with the apophatic experience of him, although it places more emphasis upon the moving, personal character of God in his relationship with us than does the apophatic experience which sees the light of God in the overwhelming of the world. Existential experience also combines with the knowledge of God as creator and providential guide of the world (cataphatic knowledge). As a result it makes God known in these capacities in a way that is more intimate for man, while at the same time existential experience is broadened by means of cataphatic knowledge. The combination of these three kinds of knowledge can be seen in the case of Job or in a host of places in the Psalms. To Job, who wishes to understand why God has sent him his suffering, God displays his wonders of nature so that Job might accept the mystery of his acts which transcend all understanding. The Psalmist too, knowing from so many circumstances in his life the presence of God which transcends understanding, praises him at the same time for the greatness of his acts in nature.

Through these three kinds of knowledge the personal interest God shows towards man, together with his mystery and greatness that are beyond understanding, come into relief. Through all three, God is known as lover according to the measure of our love for him and for our neighbor.

NOTES

1. The Greek theologian Christos Yannaras also notices the distinction between Western and Eastern negative theologies, and he includes both the negative and affirmative theologies of the West under the general framework of Western rational theology. Yannaras, however, attributes no value to affirmative theology, while we acknowledge that it has a certain necessity for expressing apophatic experience, although we are always aware of its insufficiency. Yannaras says: "It is evident here that the apophatic attitude cannot be identified with the theology of negations. Historically this identification was achieved in Western apophaticism. It has as its presupposition natural-affirmative knowledge and its simultaneous negation. . . ." *De l'absence et de l'inconnaissance de Dieu (Paris 1971), pp. 87-88.*

2. *Oration* 28.6, PG 36.32C-33A; ET E. R. Hardy/C. Richardson, *Christology of the Later Fathers, LCC* 3 (Philadelphia 1954), pp. 139-40.

3. *Oration* 28.3, PG 36.29A-B; ET Hardy/Richardson, pp. 137-38.

4. *Oration* 38.7, PG 36.317B-C; ET C. G. Browne/J. E. Swallow, *NPNF* 2nd Series, vol. 7, p. 346.

5. *Oration* 28.2, PG 36.28A-B; ET Hardy/Richardson, pp. 136-37.
6. *Oration* 38.7, PG 36.317C-D; ET Browne/Swallow, pp. 346-47
7. *Gnostic Chapters* 1.48-49, PG 90.1100C—D.
8. Both Lossky and Yannaras have explained Eastern apophatic theology from the starting point of the personal character of God. What distinguishes our position from theirs is that we do not hold exclusively to a knowledge of God which is apophatic, but see it as a combination of the apophatic and the cataphatic. The problem runs through the whole of Yannaras, *De l'absence et de la connaissance de Dieu,* and cf. Lossky, *The Mystical Theology,* pp. 23-43.
9. *Great Catechetical Oration* 3, PG 45.17C-D; ET W. Moore/H. A. Wilson, *NPNF* 2nd Series, vol. 5, p. 477.
10. *The Life of Moses,* PG 44.380A; ET Malherbe/Ferguson [= 169], pp. 96-97.
11. Ibid. PG 44.377A; ET Malherbe/Ferguson [= 163], p. 95.
12. Ibid. PG 44.381A-D; ET Malherbe/Ferguson [= 174-77], pp. 98-99.
13. Ibid. PG 44.380A; ET Malherbe/Ferguson [= 169], pp. 96-97.
14. Ibid. PG 44.377C-D; ET Malherbe/Ferguson [= 167], p. 96.
15. Ibid. PG 44.377A; ET Malherbe/Ferguson [= 163], p. 95.
16. Ibid. PG 44.377A-B; ET Malherbe/Ferguson [= 164-65], pp.95-96.
17. *Letter* 9.1, PG 3.1104B-C; ET Colm Luibheid/Paul Rorem, *Pseudo-Dionysius The Complete Works* (NY/Mahwah, 1987), p.281.
18. Dionysios the Areopagite, *The Divine Names* 2.8, PG 3.645C; ET Luibheid/Rorem, p. 64: "for the caused carry within themselves only such images of their originating sources as are possible for them...."
19. John Chrysostom, *The Incomprehensible Nature of God* 1.5, PG 48.706; ET Harkins [= 1.30-31], p. 64.
20. *The Life of Moses,* PG 44.401A-B; ET Malherbe/Ferguson [= 224-26], p. 113.
21. Ibid. PG 44.401D-404A; ET Malherbe/Ferguson [= 231-32], pp. 114-15.
22. Ibid. PG 44.404A-B; ET Malherbe/Ferguson [= 234-36], p. 115.
23. Ibid. PG 44.404C-D; ET Malherb/Ferguson [= 238-39], p. 116.
24. M. J. Le Guillou, "Réflexions sur la théologie trinitaire à propos de quelques livres anciens et récents," *Istina* 17 (1972) p. 460.
25. *The Divine Names* 1.5, PG 3.593C-D; ET Luibheid/Rorem, p. 54.
26. Ibid. 4.7, PG 3.701C; ET Lubheid/Rorem, p. 76.
27. Ibid. 1.2, PG 3.588C-D; ET Luibheid/Rorem, p. 50.
28. *The Mystical Theology* 1.2, PG 3.1000B, ET Luibheid/Rorem, p. 265
29. *Letter* 5, PG 3.1073A; ET Luibheid/Rorem, p. 265.
30. *The Divine Names* 1.1, PG 3.588B; ET Luibheid/Rorem, p.50.
31. Symeon the New Theologian, *Hymn* 1.175-190, ed. J. Koder, SC 156, pp. 170/172; ET George A. Maloney, *Hymns of Divine Love by Saint Symeon the New Theologian* (Denville, NJ, 1976), p. 15.
32. Symeon the New Theologian, *Hymn* 1.132-133, 141-146, ed. Koder, p. 168; ET Maloney, p. 14.
33. Symeon the New Theologian, *Hymn* 15.71-79. ed. Koder, p. 282; ET Maloney, pp. 52-53.
34. *Defence of the Holy Hesychasts* 1.1.19-20, ed. P. Christou, Γρηγορίου τοῦ Παλαμᾶ. Συγγράμματα, vol. 1 (Thessalonike, 1962), pp. 382.20-384.24; ET J. Meyendorff/N. Gendle, *Gregory Palamas. The Triads* (NY/Mahwah, 1983), pp. 27-28.
35. *Defence of the Holy Hesychasts* 2.3.44, ed. Christou, vol. 1, p. 578.4-11, 19-20, 21-24.
36. *Defence of the Holy Hesychasts* 2.3.41, ed. Christou, vol. 1, p. 574.25-29.

37. *Defence of the Holy Hesychasts* 2.3.49, ed. Christou, vol. 1, p. 582.3-6.
38. *Letter 5*, PG 3.1073A.
39. *Defence of the Holy Hesychasts* 2.3.51-52, ed. Christou, vol. 1, pp. 583.31-584.4, 14-23.
40. *The Incomprehensible Nature of God* 3.6, PG 48.725-726; ET Harkins [= 3.35], p. 11.
41. Ibid. 5.6, PG 48.744; ET Harkins [=5.46-47], p. 157.
42. Symeon Metaphrastes, Κατάνυξις (Athens, 1875), p. 381.
43. Ibid. p. 150.

Chapter Seven

The Being of God and His Uncreated Operations

The Relation of Being and Operation in God

The Eastern Fathers have made a distinction between the being and the operations of God. Saint Gregory Palamas did nothing more than hold fast to this distinction between the being of God and the uncreated operations flowing from it. Nevertheless, while speaking of the variety of the divine works, we can sometimes forget to observe that, through each of these operations, it is the God, who is one in being, who is at work. We must always keep in mind, however, the paradoxical fact that, although God effects something on each occasion through a particular operation, yet he is wholly within each operation. On the other hand, through each operation God produces or sustains a certain aspect of reality; consequently this aspect of reality has its cause in something corresponding to it, though in an incomprehensible way, within God himself. The operations which produce the attributes of the world are, therefore, bearers of certain attributes found in God in a simple and incomprehensible way. The operations, therefore, are nothing other than the attributes of God in motion — or God himself, the simple One, in a motion which is, on every occasion, specific, or again, in a number of different kinds of motion, specified and united among themselves. God himself is in each of these operations or energies, simultaneously whole, active, and beyond operation or movement. Thus his operations are what makes God's qualities visible in creatures, creating these with qualities analogous, but infinitely inferior, to God himself, and then imparting his uncreated operations or energies to them in higher and higher degrees.[1]

That is why Dionysios the Areopagite sees God as above any name and yet at the same time indicated wholly through many names: "This surely is the wonderful 'name which is above every name.' ... These same wise writers, when praising the Cause of everything that is, use names drawn from all the things caused: good, beautiful, wise, beloved,

God of gods, Lord of Lords, Holy of Holies, eternal, existent, Cause of the ages. They call him source of life, wisdom, mind, word, knower, possessor beforehand of all the treasures of knowledge, power, powerful. . . ."[2] He sees God in his entirety in all the actions directed toward the world. But he also sees him as beyond all these operations.

All those names have reference to the "beneficent processions" from the source of divinization, not to these qualities.[3]

We only know the attributes of God in their dynamism and to the extent to which we participate in them. This does not mean, however, that God himself remains passive in his simplicity and in the diverse motion we project upon him. It is from God himself that the operations originate which are productive of new and various qualities in the world. But we only know them through the prism of the effect they produce in the world. God himself changes for our sake in his operations, remaining simple as the source of these operations and being wholly present in each one of them. "For the truth is that everything divine and even everything revealed to us is known only by way of whatever share of them is granted. Their actual nature, what they are ultimately in their own source and ground, is beyond all intellect and all being and all knowledge. When for instance, we give the name of 'God' to that transcendent hiddenness, when we call it 'life' or 'being' or 'light' or 'Word,' what our minds lay hold of is in fact nothing other than certain activities apparent to us, activities which deify, cause being, bear life, and give wisdom."[4]

We experience nothing from God, in content, other than his varied operations that have to do with the world, which is to say, in relation to us. Beyond this we know that at their basis is the personally subsistent essence, but how it is, we do not know, for it is an essence beyond all essences. All we know in God is his dynamism experienced in relation to the world or through the prism that we ourselves are, a dynamism not subject to any necessity at all, that is, not subject to passion and totally free.

In fact, the human person itself — as subsistence of a being, which, as such maintains the being as an inexhaustible source of acts — does not have a name by which it can be characterized in itself. The names we give to persons (John, Paul, etc.) are conventional. They do not tell what the person is. All other names by which we wish to characterize the person refer to its modes of manifestation. That is why the person himself uses a pronoun — something that takes the

The Being of God and His Uncreated Operations

place of a name — ("I") in order to indicate himself. And in intimate relation with the other, it calls the other "Thou." How much less, then, is it possible for the supreme subject to have a name. The name does not indicate the content of the person, instead it limits and governs. But the person cannot be limited and governed by knowledge; in a general way and *par excellence* the person is apophatic. It transcends existence that can be perceived directly. It is perceived through its acts. It exists on another plane, one which transcends existence. How much more, then, is this true of supreme Person. Moreover, the attributes themselves cannot be contained in names. They have a dynamic character and, through different acts, they activate their effectiveness, or rather the inexhaustible simplicity itself of the divine essence is activated under the form of certain varied qualities through its acts.

The qualities of God, as we know them, disclose their richness gradually as we develop the capacity to participate in them. Yet, as a personally subsisting being, God remains always above them, although in a certain manner he is their source. therefore, we do not err if we consider them in their totality as existent in his being in a manner beyond all understanding and in an inexhaustible simplicity. Thus, as dynamic manifestations of God, they are "around his being", and are not identical with his being itself.

We know the God who is for us, but this knowledge does not show him to us as if this God were to be opposed to God understood in himself.

In his descent to us, God communicates to us in modes adapted to our condition something of what he is in fact, leading us to stages which correspond more and more to himself. In a rational manner, under the form of the attributes, we know, understand, and express him very schematically and generally. But in his operations we know God more concretely, more intensely. Yet, the expression always remains inadequate, and mostly makes use of symbols and images.

In the varied and gradual communication of his inexhaustible content, in the gradual and varied disclosure of the content of his attributes, the infinite richness itself of God's uncreated operations is revealed. Through a new operation or energy we receive an added element or a nuance of his content imparted to us. An attribute, in this sense, appears as the expression of various multiple operations that impart to us a divine good which is, to a certain extent, common to them and which we experience. If, in attributes, the divine being gives us the appearance of having come down to the level of our understanding under a certain number of aspects, the operations make these aspect or attributes even more specific and innumerable. Frequently they make God known to us through experience both in the general aspects under which God has descended to meet us and also in the innumerable, more specific ways in which they are imparted to us at every moment.

On the other hand, the same God in his entirety makes himself known to us and, frequently enough, causes us to experience him through each operation and, through them, the same God in his entirety makes himself known to us as bearer of a number of general attributes. God is good. But how many nuances does this goodness of his not have as we see it shown to us in innumerable operations that correspond to the needs we have at each moment and to the needs of all? Through his attributes God makes something of his being evident to us, but this something is made specific within one vast and uninterrupted symphony of continually new acts that guide creation and each element of it separately towards the final goal of full union with him. Through all of these God pursues the fulfillment of this plan.

Thus the operations of God do not appear to us as grouped only according to the attributes which they actuate and impart to us, but also according to the various sections of the plan God follows in creation. Through some of these operations new periods are inaugurated which come about through more climactic acts anticipated and prolonged through operations connected with them. The creation of the world is an operation or a sum of operations followed by the operations culminating in the incarnation and resurrection of the Son of God. Salvation has its subsequent application through a succession of other operations that derive from these. The entire dynamism or movement of creation towards deification has its cause in the dynamism of the divine operations which aim at leading creation towards deification. The power for these acts which proceed from God, and through which creation is led to him, is to be found in God. These acts neither enrich nor change God himself, for he is above all his acts and above all the divine attributes which he manifests through them.

The words which have reference to divine operations can also serve as names of God's being, for it is the being that produces the operations. They can also be new, moreover, inasmuch as the operations

The Being of God and His Uncreated Operations

are new; nevertheless, some fundamental words still remain at the basis of the new words because in the new operations it is the same divine attributes that are imparted to the world, though these display an ever greater profoundity, richness and subtlety. But the mystery of the personal reality of God is experienced, properly speaking, through the renunciation of all the words that point to the attributes and operations of God directed towards us.

Dionysios the Areopagite holds that, inasmuch as we possess the various aspects of our existence through a participation in the participable qualities of God, these aspects can be thought of as being "of themselves." Yet they have a support which transcends any quality or attribute of God that is "of/in itself." Dionysios places "existence in itself" above all the other attributes of this kind, however, and seems to identify this existence with God's essence (*esse* — *essentia*). But inasmuch as the essence is only really given in a subject, or hypostasis, it could be said that what supports all the attributes of God, in which creatures participate, or the very support of existence itself, is the hypostatic reality or the threefold divine hypostatic reality. "Being in itself is more revered than the being of Life itself and Wisdom itself and Likeness to divinity itself. Whatever beings participate in these things must, before all else, participate in Being."[5] "[The Preexistent] is not a facet of being. Rather, being is a facet of him. He does not possess being, but being possesses him."[6] "The God who is transcends everything by virtue of his power. He is the substantive Cause and maker of being, subsistence, of existence, of substance, and of nature.... He is being for whatever is.... For God is not some kind of being. No. But in a way that is simple and indefinable he gathers into himself and anticipates every existence."[7]

As personal reality, God is the undetermined source of all the qualities which are determined in some way through their procession from him. The personal divine reality is undetermined in an eminent way because it is the hypostatizing of the superessence from which every created essence receives its existence. God can be said to be the tripersonal superessence, or the superessential tripersonality. What this superessence is, we do not know. But it exists of itself; like any essence, however, it is not real except by the fact that it subsists hypostatically, in persons.

As superessential hypostatic existence, however, God is not encompassed by the category of existence as this is known or imagined by us, but transcends it. For all the things that we know as existing have their existence from something else and, in their existence, they depend on a system of references. This points to a relativity or a weakness of existences. He who exists of himself, however, has an existence free of all relativity. He is not integrated within a system of references and he has no weakness at all. He is existence not only in the highest sense, but he is also a superexistent existence. As such, he does not sustain existence passively, nor is he subject to any passion or suffering. This is the meaning of the Greek word ἀπαθής applied to God; it does not have the meaning "indifferent."[8] The entire life of God is act or power. All his attributes he has of himself, hence not through participation in some other source. That is why he possesses them all in a mode incomparably superior to that of creatures, for all these possess their attributes through participation in the attributes of God, through his operations.

Very life itself, very existence itself, very wisdom itself cannot exist as general attributes belonging to a multitude of entities which themselves depend on one another. In such a case these attributes would not be experienced concretely by any of the entities as *per se* attributes. Their very existence would be an abstraction. Since, in reality, the world exists as a sum of dependent entities, it cannot be — taken as a whole — an independent reality.

These attributes can only have existence as attributes of a unique personal reality. In fact only supreme person — in his own right and in all that belongs to him — can be *per se*/"of himself."

Even the human person, as image of the superexisting Personal reality, has in some fashion this quality of being *per se*/"of himself." The person is the ultimate forum that decides on his deeds, his thoughts and his words. Many actions are brought to bear upon him, but he stops them and alone decides whether he wishes to transmit them. The person is not just a part of a system of gears through which a movement passes that began somewhere else. He does not exist for the sake of the general system of which he is somehow a part, but he exists of himself, and, in a certain way, he can transcend the system. The person considers how an action which is being brought to bear upon him might be useful to him, and thus it is far more a question of requesting his adherence than of passing through him without asking. The person does not exist for the sake of anything else, but all things exist for him. However, our human person is brought into existence by another factor and, to be enriched, stands in need of connections with elements of a system, even though the person may use these connections the way he wants. The human person develops through the totality of the acts he produces and by his relations with the things that surround him. But even these latter always exist in function of the person. Indeed, in some way the person does not come into existence through an act of making, but springs into existence in response to a call from God.

Thus, even the human person does not entirely belong to that system of references within which nature, through its strict laws, is totally integrated. Hence, only a reality of its own kind, though incomparably superior, can have the capacity of not belonging — even in the slightest degree — to a system of references. In nature's system of references all things end in death so that other things might appear. Our human being can exist as a person who is not included integrally within the system of references only because of the fact that a supreme Personal reality of this kind does exist. The relation to supreme Person is not identical to belonging to a system of involuntary references. In relation to supreme Person, as indeed in its relation to any person, our human person is free. In fact it is precisely that supreme Personal reality who gives our human person the possibility of freedom over against the system of references, just as, to a certain extent, the person of our neighbor does also. Any other person with whom the human person is in relation makes appeals to the person in order to accomplish certain acts; he does not use the person as a simple point through which his own movements pass.

Thus, even our human person is "of himself"/*per se*, or, in a certain sense, absolute, since the person himself decides upon all those acts of his which have an effect within himself and upon the reality outside.

The supreme Personal reality is "of himself"/*per se*, however, in the supreme sense of the word, for in fact he exists from no one and all things exist from him: his own acts and the realities which they produce. He does not merely effect modifications within the realities outside himself; he also creates them. Very existence itself (*per se*), as an existence which is real and not just an object of thought (whoever might be the thinker), is subsistent; it is hypostatic, the absolute hypostatic existence. This means that all things have their origin in his power and will. This means in turn that his being is of an order entirely different from that of created being. He is superessential, superexistential, the transcendence of creation as a whole. The reality of supreme Person is totally free of any system of reference; in the most complete way, it is the ultimate forum of all his acts, and, hence, of all other existences too. Only this explains the existence of our human persons and can assure these a certain freedom over against the system of references in which they find themselves.

Only as supreme Person is God "of himself"/*per se* and are all his attributes from himself; he can give to the human person too the possibility of participating in this quality of being *per se* which belongs to him and to his acts.

In this way the attributes — life, existence, wisdom — cannot exist of themselves, but only if they belong to supreme Person. In fact, only in relation with such Personal reality do we also feel ourselves overwhelmed by his powers which we feel no longer as coming from somewhere else or as merely relative. This is so because we do not experience these attributes or operations as lacking all support, as having their being "of themselves" in their own right, or as themselves constituting the ultimate essence. If that were true, they would overwhelm us in a way that was total, impersonal, and involuntary but simultaneously self-exhausting or destructive of us. In themselves they would not be an incommunicable reserve, truly infinite, from which we could receive according to the measure of our own voluntary growth in love towards God. Hence Dionysios the Areopagite declares that even when we add to these attributes the modifier "self" (αὐτο-*per se*) we think of what it is that supports them. It is through this support that they are of themselves (*per se*) and it is through its will that they are communicated to us according to our capacity.

That is why the names "self-existence," "self-life," etc., indicate on the one hand the support they have in God as supreme reality and, on the other hand, the fact that from him they all have existence, life, and so forth. By our sharing in these attributes we enter into a relationship with the one who is above relationship. The support they have is the very one who possesses them "of himself," the one who explains them. "In a letter to me you once asked what I meant by being itself, life itself, and wisdom itself. You said you failed to understand why I sometimes call God 'life itself' and sometimes 'subsistence of life itself.' Therefore, sacred man of God, I have thought it necessary to solve your problem ... to call God 'life itself' and 'power itself' and then 'subsistence of life itself,' 'subsistence of power itself,' involves no contradiction. The former names are derived from beings, especially the primary beings, and they are given to God because he is the cause of all beings. The latter names are put up because he is transcendentally superior to everything, including the primary beings. 'But,' you may say, 'what is meant when we talk of being itself, life itself, and all those other things to which we ascribe an absolute and primary existence derived ultimately from God?' My answer is this. "This is not something oblique, but is in fact quite straightforward, and there is a simple explanation for it. The absolute being underlying individual manifestations of being as their cause is not a divine or an angelic being, for only transcendent being itself can be the source, the being, and the cause of the being of beings. Nor have we to do with some other life producing divinity distinct from that supra-divine life which is the originating Cause of all livings and life itself. Nor, in summary, is God to be thought of as identical with those originating and creative beings and substances which men stupidly describe as certain gods or creators of the world. Such men, and their fathers before them, had no genuine or proper knowledge of beings of this kind. Indeed, there are no such beings. What I am trying to express is something quite different. 'Being itself,' 'life itself,' 'divinity itself,' are names signifying source, divinity, and cause, and these are applied to the one transcendent cause and source beyond source of all things. But we use the same terms in a derivative fashion and we apply them to the provident acts of power which come forth from God in whom nothing at all participates. I am talking here of being itself, of life, of divinity itself which shapes things in a way that each creature, according to capacity, has his share of these. From the fact of such sharing come the qualities and the names 'existing,' 'living,' 'possessed by divinity,' and suchlike."[9]

Even the infinity experienced by us has its support in superexistent apophatic Person who, therefore, is superior to it and "moves far beyond infinity."[10]

St. Maximos the Confessor says the same when he declares that God is not subject to the category of existence, for everything that falls under the category of existence also falls under a 'how' of existence and as such is limited, for any kind of 'how' excludes other kinds of how. Moreover, on this how of the existence also depend a 'when' and 'where,' that is, a time and a place which likewise provide limits in the process of individuation. "God is not accessible to any reason or any understanding, and because of this we do not categorize His existence *as* existence. For all existence is from Him, but He Himself is not existence. For He is beyond existence itself whether expressed or conceived simply or in any particular mode."[11]

But God would have nothing to do with self-existence, however, if he had no possibility at all of receiving it or of communicating it. Both sides of this paradox are satisfied by supernatural revelation in its teaching on the holy Trinity. God has existence of himself, and yet he is alive, for he receives and communicates existence within himself. This latter fact completes the character of person for this is not only reality "of itself"/*per se* but also communion. The divine persons are interior one to the other — and, hence, receive nothing from outside — but they are not confused with one another since they find themselves within a movement and communion of being and love. The total interpersonal communion intensifies the personal character of God to the highest degree.

The Apophatic Character of God

The divine Personal reality (as transcendent of whatever of its attributes which can be defined, though not received from anyone else) is the apophatic reality *par excellence*. If everything that comes under the ray of knowledge and everything that is participable belongs to the category of existence, the personal subject is superexistent. We have seen that, as image of God, even our human person somehow possesses in this respect a superexistential, apophatic character.

The reason why God cannot be defined lies in his superexistentiality. For all words are of the order of existence and this order is definable.

As self-existent, that is, as not entering into any system of references at all and thus being superexistent or person in a preeminent way, God is *par excellence* apophatic, indefinable. Inasmuch as existence is not given to God from without, but he himself is the source of existence and hence the supreme personal reality, neither is God himself defined or named except through personal pronouns, or else he is identified with existence *par excellence* or with the source of existence that transcends existence.

To Moses' question about his name, God answers, "I am who I am" (Ex 3.14).

As he who is truly existent (because he is of himself or it is he who supports existence *per se* and as such is superexistence and transcendent of being), God is the supreme personal reality. Only the supreme personal reality is totally apophatic because only this reality is, in an eminent way, superexistent. And as the subsistence of the divine being, it is clearly superexistent or apophatic *par excellence,* since God is the hypostatization of the divine superexistent being.

From God's character as supreme personal reality, Paul Evdokimov has drawn the conclusion that there can be no rational proof of God: "The insufficiency of the proofs for the existence of God is explained by the fundamental fact that God alone is the criterion of His truth, God alone is the argument for His being. God can never be subject to logical demonstrations nor enclosed in the causal chain. . . . This means that faith is not invented; it is a *gift* . . . faith is given to all so that God might bring about His presence in every human soul."[12] God is confessed as the one who has produced faith in the soul. God talks with us as person to person. Faith is the experience of this communication.

This is true. But it is also true that once someone has this experience, all things become proofs for the existence and activity of God. The eyes of one who believes open up and they see God in all things. Then to believe becomes something that is totally rational, and not to believe, something irrational. But through reason one does not experience God in his inner reality but only in his capacity as cause. Even in our reason, on the other hand, — if it is not perverted by sin — there exists a capacity of seeing God as cause. For our reason has as its ultimate support the reason of a Personal reality who created it.

Thus God indicates himself as the truly or existent or superexistent one and manifests himself as personal reality: "I." He is "I" *par excellence.* Self-existence can only have a personal character. Impersonal essence is not superexistent; in all respects it would fall within a system of references. An essence not subsisting in a hypostasis is not found anywhere, while the most complete existence is possessed by essence subsisting as person, and perfect existence by the essence which exists as supreme personal reality. The supreme essence is self-subsistent; it is personal. The essence which is subject to a system of references does not subsist by itself, either in its form or in its reality. It enters into the order of existence determined by the superexistent subject.

It is because it subsists as supreme personal reality that the divine superessence can be *of itself* (*per se*), since it is also only in this way that it exists *for itself.* An essence or a nature subsisting as object exists for a subject distinct from itself, that is, for a person, and on the basis of this fact it receives, in relation to the human person, its form from the latter, while in relation to divine Person, it receives its very substance from him. Reality which is *for* the other receives even its existence or its form from that other. It is inferior to the person and, as such, is not superessence but essence purely and simply and falls within the system of references. Only a person exists for himself, and only the hypostasis is superessential *par excellence*.

It is only because there exists a personal reality as supreme, superexistent support for self-existence (existence *per se*), that existence is given universally. Because existence on the accessible plane is produced voluntarily by the superexistential personal reality, it cannot be either its own cause or the ultimate cause of any universal existence. Only the superexistent personal reality, as support of the existence *per se,* can produce existence on all accessible planes, without exhausting itself.

Existence on the accessible plane is an argument for its source within the superexistent or self-existent Personal reality. Put another way, the latter cannot be known or understood except through the mediation of existence on the accessible, sensible, and intelligible plane. But the reverse is also true. Our experience and direct knowledge, moreover, can reach only as far as the existence-giving, sustaining, and fulfilling operations of the superexistent personal reality and as far as participation in the attributes manifested within those operations.

The threefold supreme hypostasis creates, sustains, and perfects all things through its inexhaustible acts, because it is the threefold hypostasis of the superessence. Our reality as subject is the hypostatization of a nature whose fundamental part is the spirit, and among all the essences created by God the spirit is the image of the superessence hypostatized by the trinitarian persons. Only for this reason can our reality as subject have the character of being person and for this reason is it endowed with an eternal stability which other essences do not have, though the angels too are similar essences. It is only for this reason, moreover, that the human subject is also apophatic and is not exhausted by its acts, for its acts (or its energies) are not one with its essence, as is true in the case of objects. Only as hypostasis of a nature which has as its basis an essence in the image of the divine essence — and hence is permanent like the divine —

can the human subject rise again with the body. The fixed character we have, as hypostases of an essence made in the image of the divine superessence, makes us apt for sharing an inexhaustible and therefore eternal communion with the threefold divine hypostasis.

All the attributes or operations of God are infinite, because he never exhausts himself in bestowing them, nor will creatures ever reach the end of their participation in them, nor will they themselves ever cease to shine forth from their hypostatic support that transcends all being. Nevertheless, this hypostatic or multi-hypostatic support transcends — as its source — the infinity of these attributes or operations.

The divine apophatic personal reality from which proceed all those operations that confer being and deification is experienced within a relation that has been willed by this reality. We cannot grasp or define this reality in the way we grasp, define, or experience all the degrees and modes of existence. We are not going to praise "the absolutely transcendent . . . being. . . . What I have to say is concerned with the benevolent Providence made known to us, and my speech of praise is for the transcendentally good Cause of all good things, for that Being and Life and Wisdom, for that Cause of existence and life and wisdom among those creatures with their own share in being, life, intelligence, expression, and perception. I do not think of the Good as one thing, Being as another, Life and Wisdom as yet another, and I do not claim that there are numerous causes. . . . But I hold that there is one God for all those good processions and that he is the possessor of the divine names of which I speak. . . . "[13]

It is not only definable existence which has its explanation exclusively in a supreme and super-existent personal reality, but human persons too, who share to a certain degree in its super-existence, in its absolute nature and in its apophatic quality.

According to our faith, if a *super-existent Personal reality*, one not enclosed within nature's system of references, did not exist, then the human person (itself super-existent in a certain fashion) would not be able to exist either, as one capable of an existence not totally enclosed within nature's system of references — or rather included within it by one arm, so to speak, in order to imbue that system with its own personal character — and as one called to communion with a perfect and eternal existence of this kind, that is, in free relation with supreme Person. Only the transcendence of the divine Personal reality assures the existence of human persons who are not totally enclosed within nature's system of references (once God secures for them this liberty). Otherwise everything would fall under the rule of the meaningless laws of nature and of death.

Moreover, apart from the existence of human persons, the world as creation would seem to have no purpose or be a simple demonstration of God's unilateral and, hence, limited power on his own behalf. A God who would have need of that kind of demonstration of power would bear his own weakness within himself. The world of nature is created for human subjects, not so that they might have the possibility to manifest through it a creative power of their own similar to God's, but that the world might be a means of communication between themselves and divine Person and, through human persons, be included within the plane of divine-human personal relations.

On the other hand, the supreme Personal reality, as existence, that is, absolute or *self-existence* (*existence per se*) is not mono-personal, but a *personal community*. For this reality is fullness of life, and fullness of life is experienced in personal community. It is a personal community, self-existent, super-existent, transcending all being and ablolute. It decides all its own acts in communion. It is the common source of all existing acts and realities.

NOTES

*The Romanian word *lucrare* is translated here as "operation" to suggest its active, verbal quality, but "operation" should not be taken as pointing to a philosophical-theological context dependent on Western scholastic tradition. *Lucrare* as used by the author is much closer to "energy" in the Byzantine context of the essence-energies distinction, but because the explicit word for "energy" is also used in the text, it has seemed better to adopt a less technical approach to the translation of the many uses of *lucrare*. [Trans. note.]

1. Dionysios the Aeropagite, *The Divine Names* 9.9, PG 3.916C; ET Luibheid/Rorem, p. 118: "And yet what do the theologians mean when they assert that the unstirring God moves and goes out into everything? This is surely something which has to be understood in a way befitting God, and out of our reverence for him, we must assume that this motion of his does not in any way signify a change of place, a variation, an alteration, a turning, a movement in space either straight or in a circular fashion or in a way compounded of both. Nor is this motion to be imagined as occurring in the mind, in the soul, or in respect of the nature of God. What is signified, rather, is that God brings everything into being, that he sustains them, that he exercises all manner of providence over them, that he is present to all of them, that he embraces all of them in a way which no mind can grasp, and that, from him, providing for everything, arise countless processions and activities."

2. *The Divine Names* 1.6, PG 3.596A-B; ET Luibheid/Rorem, pp. 54, 55.
3. Ibid. 1.4, PG 3.589D; ET Luibheid/Rorem, p. 51.
4. Ibid. 2.7, PG 3.645A; ET Luibheid/Rorem, pp. 63-64.
5. Ibid. 5.5, PG 3.820A; ET Luibheid/Rorem, p. 99.
6. Ibid. 5.8, PG 3.824A; ET Luibheid/Rorem, p. 101.
7. Ibid. 5.4, PG 3.817C-D; ET Luibheid/Rorem, p. 98.
8. This is what Dionysios the Aeropagite and Saint Maximos the Confessor call ἄσχετος: *The Divine Names* 5.8, PG 3.824B; *The Ambigua*, PG 91.1153C. The same thing is expressed by the Fathers through the term ἐξῃρημένος (detached from everything): *The Divine Names* 2.8; 9.10, PG 3.645C-D, 917A.
9. *The Divine Names* 11.6, PG 3.953B-956A; ET Luibheid/Rorem, pp. 124-25.
10. Ibid. 9.2, PG 3.909C; ET Luibheid/Rorem, p. 115.
11. *The Ambigua*, PG 91.1180D.
12. *Les âges de la vie spirituelle* (Paris, 1980^3), p. 46.
13. *The Divine Names* 5.2, PG 3.816C-817A; ET Luibheid/Rorem, p. 97.

Chapter Eight

The Super-Essential Attributes of God

Infinity

The super-essence or super-existence of God, totally unknown with respect to what it is in itself, manifests itself by entering into relation with us and making itself known to us in a series of dynamic attributes. In comparison with these attributes, the world and our own being manifest certain attributes that correspond to their created and finite character. For as the finite essence of creation cannot be explained apart from the super-essence of God and its connection with that essence, neither can its own attributes be explained apart from the dynamic attributes of God and their own relation with these. Moreover, the finite essence of the world and the various essences which form, as it were, branches of the world's essence are arranged so as to reach up, through grace, towards an ever greater participation in the divine attributes.

One of the attributes of the divine super-essence is *infinity*. This manifests itself in the endless operations of God in regard to the world, and its maintenance, guidance, and perfection. To eternity God will never cease to deify the world. But in general the world is surrounded and permeated by the divine infinity and cannot exist apart from its relationship to that infinity. To this attribute there corresponds — as an attribute of our created essence — finitude. Our finitude can only exist, however, within the framework, the bosom, of the divine infinity, as the result of the power of the latter, and sustained by it (otherwise, it would disappear), arranged so that it might participate directly in that power and be penetrated by it, yet without ceasing to be a natural attribute of the created world. Always — beyond any limit — there is something more, without which our finitude can neither exist nor be conceived. There is no possible addition which can make the creature infinite. Infinity is transcendent to it, but at the same time the creature is conditioned by infinity, and participation in this infinity is given to the creature through grace.

The Fathers affirm the infinity of God and the finitude of creation just as they also affirm that creation has been destined to reach direct participation in God's infinity through grace.

The divine super-essence is the source of infinity; moreover, the divine essence is hypostatized, though hypostatized in a trinitarian mode. Thus its infinity belongs to this triadic personal character of the divine super-essence. The triadic community could not be satisfied if its content were limited in character.

The person of a finite essence is also finite, for its spirit moves within the framework of certain finite powers and is linked to the reality of a world of objects. Even the communion between created persons is finite, although it expands the content of the life of each of them very greatly.

But even this limited content of created realities cannot exist apart from the power and the presence of the triadic infinity. Existing, as it does, from the beginning by means of participation in that infinity, creation is called to achieve an ever more developed participation in that infinity. This explains how the ambiguity can arise that creation may be considered as both a finite and an infinite reality.

The meaning of genuine infinity was made clear by Saint Maximos the Confessor who asserted that this infinity is not a matter of intervening distances which we might strive to bridge so as to reach their border, beyond which further intervening distances would begin. In infinity fullness is given and possessed in a way that is real, not just as a continuous aspiration. Hence there is no time in infinity. Everything is possessed in a continuous present. We are called to reach the experience of this fullness by passing beyond the borders which succeed one another in the face of the efforts we make in the course of our earthly life. The longing for this infinity sustains our movement within the finite order. In this sense we live even now in the horizon of infinity or see infinity looming before our eyes. "The nature of created things, . . . after the natural passing over times and ages, will come to rest in God who is one in nature and without any limit, for in God there is no interval [no distance]."[1]

Without going so far as to identify ourselves with God, we will rise to the greatest possible relationship he has with us — represented by infinity — and surpass the human pole of this relationship represented by limitation.

Growth into the divine infinity through grace or the good will of God who enters into direct communication with us means at heart a maximal communion with him as subject, one that goes beyond that kind of approach which is accustomed to treat all things as objects and simply passes from one side of them to another. In general when we are intimately related with a subject, we always remain within him. How much more so in our relation with the divine subject. This implies a simple but complete experience of the infinite life of the divine subject, or better of the direct manifestation of him through that life for the sake of his communion with us.

"When all meanings of things that have been thought, whether sensible or intelligible, pass away, then at the same time with all these meanings all understanding and relation with sensible and intelligible things will cease.... Then the soul will be united with God beyond mind and reason and knowledge, in an incomprehensible, unknown, and unutterable manner, through a simple contact, no longer understanding and no longer reasoning about God.... Then it will be free from any kind of change.... For any circling movement of existing things will come to an end in the infinity around God in whom all things that move receive their stability. For infinity is around God, but it is not God, for he is incomparably above even this."[2]

Saint Maximos knows the mystery of the hypostatic super-essence of God, his dynamic attributes, among which are infinity and the forms in which creatures capable of participation have participated: "God is infinitely beyond all things that exist, both those things which participate and those things in which they participate."[3]

Infinity is God's ambiance and through it he makes himself accessible or communicates himself to creatures which have reached union with him as supreme subject. God as supreme subject or as trinitarian communion of subjects, trancends infinity inasmuch as he is its support and source. It is only by belonging to the divine Person or to the divine personal community that this infinity is not an ambiguous, monotonous infinity of which the human person could grow weary, as in Platonist and Origenist theory. Only divine Person or the communion of divine persons is genuinely inexhaustible and offers to the human person the possibility of enjoying its inexhaustible richness. Moreover it is only in communion with God as person or as a community of persons that — without losing its own natural boundary — our human being can make its own that experience of the infinity of God which it realizes in part within interpersonal communion. Absorbing in itself the ambiance of the divine infinity, this infinity irradiates also from our human being. Through the divine operation which becomes proper to it, our human being expands beyond its own boundaries into the infinite.

Even in the course of his earthly life, the believer can have a foretaste of the experience of luminous communion with God in whom he sees no boundary nor does he feel any monotony or boredom, but has the continuous sensation of being at the very beginning: as they are powerless to find the perfection of light, the purification is incomplete for them. Indeed, the more I shall be purified and illumined, unhappy one, the more will appear the Spirit who purifies me, and, it seems to me, I begin to be purified and to see more each day. In a limitless abyss, in a measureless height, who will be able to find a middle or an end?[4]

In Christ, after the resurrection, his humanity was raised to the supreme participation in the divine infinity; it understood the Godhead that is beyond understanding and fully enjoyed the divine energies imprinted on its human energies. And in union with Christ all those who believe are raised to this same participation in the divine infinity: that God "may grant you . . . that Christ may dwell in your hearts . . . and to know the love of Christ which surpasses knowledge, that you may be filled with all the fulness of God" (Eph 3.16-19).

Simplicity

At the beginning of his exposition concerning the divine attributes, Dionysios the Areopagite situates the unity of God, a God who simultaneously also contains within himself the trinitarian distinction from which proceed those operations that create, sustain, and perfect the world.

Yet, according to Dionysios, these distinctions introduce no composition into God, for the persons are united in the Father as their unique source, while the beneficent processions towards creatures are united in the unique being of the three hypostases. The distinctions among these processions appear when the divine being has reference to ourselves, while the mode whereby the threeness of the hypostases does not contradict the unity of the divine super-essence is beyond our understanding.

> For the truth is that everything divine and even everything revealed to us is known only by way of whatever share of them

is granted. Their actual nature, what they are ultimately in their own source and ground, is beyond all intellect and all being and all knowledge. When, for instance, we give the name of 'God' to that transcendent hiddenness, when we call it 'life' or 'being' or 'light' or 'Word,' what our minds lay hold of is in fact nothing other than certain activities apparent to us, activities which deify, cause being, bear life, and give wisdom. For our part, as we consider that hiddenness and struggle to break free of all the working of our minds, we find ourselves witnessing no divinization, no life, no being which bears any real likeness to the absolutely transcendent Cause of all things. Or, again, we learn from the sacred scriptures that the Father is the originating source of the Godhead and that the Son and the Spirit are, so to speak, divine offshoots, the flowering of the transcendent lights of the divinity. But we can neither say nor understand how this could be so.[5]

Just as our own reality as subject is simple in itself, but from it spring up endless thoughts, feelings, and acts, so in a way that is similar but infinitely more exalted, the threefold and common divine subjectivity is simple in itself, but from its unfailing abyss acts spring up endlessly and through these it makes itself known in a multitude of attributes.

Inasmuch as the things created by the threefold divine subjectivity are many, they form a composite world. Even more is every individual entity in the world constituted of identical or various elements, and thus is composite, for each element within an individual entity has at its origin an eternal reason and a special divine operation, and the reasons of all things as well as the operations that underlie them are united in a reason and an operation that are common and at the same time very complex for the purpose of creating, sustaining, and bringing to perfection each partial reality of the world, and more generally, the unity of the world as a whole.

Only the human subject — leaving aside here the angelic one — is simple in its spiritual foundation. But for its fullness it too has need of a body composed of numerous elements, identical and various, just as it also needs the world out of which the elements of its body are brought together and which is its medium of thought and activity. Thus each element of the world, and each divine operation in reference to it, has at its basis a thought and a unitary operation of God, while the composition of the world has simultaneously an underlying unity, preserved, as it is, in its mysterious unity by a simultaneously unitary and diverse operation of God who is one in his essence, the unitary source of all his thoughts and operations.

Saint Maximos the Confessor sees the whole of creation prefigured in the totality of God's eternal reasons which, in the work of creating and perfecting the world, branch out from their unity and then return to it or, more precisely, lead the whole world toward an eternal unity in God through the very work of perfecting its individual component parts as a kind of dynamic matrix for the world. By the fact that God is above all, he can neither be understood, nor expressed, nor participated in by created things. But by the fact that from him all have their origin, "the one reason is [in fact] many, and the many reasons are [in fact] one. Through the beneficent, creative, and sustaining procession of the one reason to creatures, the one reason is many, while through its relation to them and its providence towards them, it turns them around and leads them towards the source that controls all things, towards the center of the streams that spring forth from it, which holds their beginnings from of old and gathers together all the many which are one."[6]

The ontological unity of the world in God is shown first of all in the fact that all the individual entities existing within its framework are in relation among themselves and with the creator and Pantokrator who, on the other hand, transcends any relation which might determine or differentiate him. The unity of the world is demonstrated subsequently in the fact that all things differentiated among themselves are united through the existing identities among them and, in the last analysis, through the general efficient reason of the created world, for the general reason of the world is not divided because of the genera that come from it. Nor is the reason of any single genus divided because of its species, or the reason of any single species divided because of the individual of the species. There exists, therefore, a general reason of the world, despite the variety of genera, a unity of each genus despite the variety of subordinate species, and a unity of each species despite the variety of individuals belonging to it; but there exists also a unity of the individual despite the variety of component elements and accidents. Moreover, the strongest and most mysterious unity is that of the human subject through its fundamentally spiritual character.[7]

This unity in itself and this relationship with all things fits man to be the genuine connecting link, the true given center of the world, but also the center which leads the world towards an ever greater unity. On the other hand, as one who is himself in union with God, man brings the world more into union with God to the extent that he himself grows in that union. If God were not an absolutely simple unity and at the same time the source of so many reasons and acts which create and perfect the world, the world would neither be diverse nor would it have its own unity or grow in that unity. "The last one introduced among creatures is man, as a natural connecting link between all, as the one who, through his parts, mediates between extremities and in himself brings into unity those things which are separated a great distance from one another by nature." Starting "from the separation which exists between them," and proceeding in good order, man's work of unification "ends in God in whom there is no separation."[8] Man has the capacity to unite all things among themselves and also with God, because within his thought all things meet and through his will he can achieve a unity in himself, a harmony with all others and with God. Hence man can be called "the great world" (macrocosm) because he is able to contain and master all things spiritually.[9]

The one who reestablished and perfected the unity in himself and between all things and God was Christ precisely because he was both God and man. Since man had not moved toward the perfection of his unity with God and with all things, God became man so that, in the humanity he assumed, he might heal the "rents" which had appeared because of sin and recapitulate all things in himself and reconcile us with God. He made the whole of creation one and at the end "through love he united created nature with the uncreated nature in order . . . to show it as one and the same through its aptitude for grace." In Christ, man "in his entirety has interpenetrated integrally with God and become everything that God is, apart from identity of nature."[10] And in the power of Christ, men too can bring about this work of unification.

The believer is unified first in his own self, overcoming the separation between soul and body and between his various tendencies. This is brought about through the strengthening of the spirit which is equivalent to the liberation of the body and the spirit from the passions which weaken man and cause separation within himself as well as in his relations with his fellow men and with God.

Man strengthens his spirit by subjecting all his movements to the movement towards God.[11] The simplicity of the divine monad, which too has within itself a dynamism with respect to creation as it imprints itself on man, liberates him from the whole variety of movements and desires, or imposes upon all these the movement towards God and the desire for him. By refusing to direct his thoughts towards various finite objects viewed in themselves, man, in a kind of knowledge which is above knowledge concentrates the power of his spirit — through these very same objects — towards him who is above all composition. "For in lack of knowledge God makes himself known. Do not understand the lack of knowledge as ignorance (for this is darkness for the soul) nor as that which yet knows him (for the unknown one is not known), because this latter is only a species of knowledge. But understand that lack of knowledge as that through which we become simple, stretching out beyond understanding and suprassing any meaning that refers to God."[12] But in this understanding we contribute the entire simplified richness of the knowledge of those many things and of the experience of life, just as, in the drop of honey, a bee contributes the pollen gathered from all the flowers.

By acquiring the unity or simplicity which is in God, the composition of creation overcomes the force of decomposition and corruptibility. Hence through the resurrection of Christ bodies acquire incorruptibility. Corruptibility is overwhelmed by the unitary force of the spirit. In hell there occurs, on the contrary, an extreme split between soul and body, indeed even between the tendencies of the soul and of the body, just as there is division among men and between man and the world.

Through his effort, man extends that unity, which he realizes within himself and with God in Christ, into his relations with his fellow men. The lines followed by men are linked with each other in a continuous and ever closer communication which ascends towards the same source and goal.[13] In the divine simplicity all men will come to a supreme simplification and unity. And this is equivalent to the supreme fullness. God and all created things will possess a unique simplicity and fullness.

The fullness towards which we strive transcends the duality between present and future, between virtue and knowledge, between good and truth. As we have everything in God, we will no longer seek another goal. We will be above even the distinction between the human and the divine, says Saint Maximos the Confessor. For the believer who has reached God is no longer distinguished from God, although by nature creatures remain distinct from God and distinct among themselves. But through grace and through habituation of the will to good they form a unique monad with God "who is simple and undivided, of a single form and power, and they become one with the Trinity that is simple and undivided according to nature."[14]

At bottom, this teaching expresses the faith in the perfect eternal communion of our multi-personal subjectivity with the tri-personal divine subjectivity. In this communion the universe of objects will be brought within the sphere of the subject. We will no longer feel any separation between our person and objects, or between our person and other human persons. Things sharpen the separate reality in respect to the person when, through them, a person opposes other persons or they are snatched away by other persons.

For this reason some people can travel backwards along the road towards greater and greater interior division and separation from God and from their fellow men. Pride, greed, anger, measureless desire — all are factors in these divisions and rents within human nature, and obstacles in the way towards open and full communicability among men. They also increase a false complexity of problems, ideas, and tendencies within men and among them. The complexity is false because it moves with the same essential monotony as that of the passions which thereby reveal a dissatisfaction with what is finite, or what might be better called an "infinity" of the finite. Often the interminable psychological analyses — which seem to be detecting more and more of the varying spiritual states and propensities they themselves determine, together with the many and various relationships among human beings — move within this infinity of the finite and of identical essential monotony. And all of this inside a labyrinth whose infinite twisting paths turn back in the same limitation and give rise to a language which is more and more complicated, nuanced, and diverse, but complicated and nuanced within the confines of a dead end, projecting no light from beyond itself. This is that hell which is closed within monotonous composition and deepens this composition into splintering divisions and "infinite" complexity. It resembles a body that is, on the one hand, indestructible, but is being macerated *ad infinitum* on the other. Man cannot abandon the passion for infinity even when he is totally enclosed within the finite.

Eternity

Two conceptions of God have stood out in Christianity. One comes from the Bible and is proper to Christian life; the other comes from Greek philosophy and is put forward in manuals of dogmatic theology, especially those influenced by scholasticism. The first conception presents us with a God who is living and full of understanding for men; the second an immutable, impassible God who seems to have no place in religious life.

The Eastern Fathers have succeeded in achieving a synthesis of the two concepts: the changelessness of God, and his life and activity in regard to creation. This synthesis found its most pregnant formulation in the Palamite doctrine of the uncreated energies which do change although they come forth from the essence of God which remains unchanged. This doctrine — actually a more precise formulation of the thought of the Fathers — took seriously the fact that God has a personal character and as such can, like every person, live on more than one plane, or, better, on two principal planes: the plane of existence in oneself and the plane of activity for the other. A mother, for example, can play with her child, bringing herself down to his level, yet at same time she preserves her mature consciousness as mother. God in himself, who is above time, meets with the creatures of time through his energies.

The eternity of God is contained in the inexhaustible fount of his own self-existence. Existence cannot normally be born out of nothingness. Self-existence, existence *per se*, moreover, can only be a personal existence, and it is the supreme personal existence which, inexhaustible in itself, constitutes the ultimate source of all acts that manifest its life. Properly speaking, God, who is beyond all determination, the super-existent one, also transcends eternity. In comparison to ourselves we experience him as eternal inasmuch as he has deigned to enter into relationship with us.

Eternity cannot be the quality of an immutable substance (even if we conceive this immutability as an eternal act of composition/decomposition), nor can it be the quality of an eternally valid law existing in itself. This kind of susbstance, as exterior object, lacks the most essential dimension of the inexhaustible character: that of interiority. And a law of that sort, as object of reason, cannot exist in itself apart from a substance or a reason which, from the same eternity, might be able to conceive it. Eternity cannot be lacking that most essential dimension of the inexhaustible character, a dimension which must simultaneously be a dimension of life in its fullness. An eternity devoid of free and conscious life would be, at best an ambiguous eternity, lacking the fullness of existence, hence, at bottom a false eternity. Even the eternity that belongs to pure reason would be killing in its monotony and thus limited.

Genuine eternity must be the quality of a perfect subjectivity, for only this is wholly incorruptible and possesses the most essential dimensions of inexhaustibility and infinite freshness of manifestation, namely, interiority and free will. Only the subject is totally without composition, inexhaustible in its possibilities and free.

But where there is no communion, true life does not exist. The fullness of life can only subsist in the perfect communion between perfect subjects.

According to Christian teaching the eternity of an unchangeable substance is as much a false eternity as that of a continuous becoming. Above these two false eternities of a Parmenidean or Hegelian type stands the true eternity of the Holy Trinty. The Trinity of the perfect persons is the fullness; in fact it explains everything, and remains eternally unchanged in its love; but love is life.

Eternity is life and life is motion: not an identical motion, however, going around in a circle, for as a modality, this is monotonous and finite; nor is it a motion of someone exteriorly towards the other. But it is a motion above all motion (κίνησις ὑπὲρ πᾶσαν κίνησιν). Karl Barth has rightly said: "the pure *immobile* is — death. If, then, the pure *immobile* is God, death is God. That is, death is posited as absolute and explained as the first and last and only real. It is said to have no limit and no end, to be omnipotent, so that there is no conqueror of death and for us no hope triumphant over death."[15]

But whatever is found to move in an identical and automatic way is also dead. It is only in the perfect communion between inexhaustible subjects and in the reciprocal interiority of their infinity that inexhaustible, unlimited, and eternal life is to be found. And one who participates in this kind of divine interpersonal communion himself receives eternal life. "And this is eternal life, that they know thee the only true God, and Jesus Christ whom thou hast sent" (Jn 17.3).

The unfailing life of subjectivity cannot consist in a passage from preoccupation with one thing to preoccupation with another. The eternal life of subjectivity cannot depend on finite objects even if these objects are conceived by it and are infinite in their number. Such a life, even if it were infinite, would be made up of finite moments or composed of finite thoughts. In these circumstances God would have to give thought to finite things in order to have life. His life would depend on what is finite, limited, and transitory. A continuous passage would be occurring even within the divine life and thus the latter would not be a true eternity.

The life of the eternal subjectivity must be a fullness which in all respects is not a transitory one; it must consist in a love for another subjectivity and in a perfect union between itself and that subjectivity which has the same fullness, so as to be, simultaneously, unfailing life. The life of the eternal subjectivity is an infinite reference to its subjectivity contemplated within another "I" so as to be truly love, eternal, unfailing love; it is reference to another "I" who is himself also the bearer of his own infinite subjectivity and responds with that same eternal, unfailing love. A divine "I" loves with an eternally inexhaustible love — a thing proper to the divine — or with its fullness (which is like that of another "I") and this occurs in reciprocity. This is divine life, and it exists together with immutable fullness. It is the same infinite existence of love, the love of an infinite person, directed towards a person worthy of infinite love (and vice versa) but within the interiority of the same subjectivity. In any other circumstances, eternity would be either an unbearable boredom, if it were the prerogative of a single consciousness, or else an absurdity, if it were the prerogative of a substance or a law that was aimless.

The divine life is an infinite fullness that is continuously present but is not sensed, even as continuity, for where continuity is sensed, the passage from one thing to another is also sensed and the future is awaited. In the divine life there is neither past — for through the past is measured the distance travelled towards perfection — nor future, for through the future an advancement in perfection is hoped for which is not possessed in the present. In the divine life there is a present with no reference to past or future, because life is lived always in fullness.

God is eternal because within God there is no movement beyond the communion already realized towards a more perfect one. Such a movement beyond is possible only where being is limited yet simultaneously capable of growth. Thus only the human being is capable of such "movement beyond" and this is true because it is not completely subject to nature's laws of repetition and because it can grow within a truly infinite existence. If this were not true, and if there were no supreme (and therefore eternal and infinite) personal existence, the capacity of the human being for growth could only develop from a beginning to an end, and would thus not satisfy its thirst to reach infinity and eternity.

But the divine life is not a fossilized condition that has beginning or end; it is a living communion between the supreme subjects. God transcends every mode of determined existence which, by the very fact of being determined, proves that in itself it does not have everything. Dionysios the Areopagite says: "For God is not some kind of being. No. But in a way that is simple and indefinable he gathers into himself and anticipates every existence. So he is called 'King of the ages,' for in him and around him all being is and subsists. He was not. He will not be. He did not come to be. He is not in the midst of becoming. He will not come to be. No. He is not."[16] The eternity of God derives from his fullness and from the fact that God is not part of any system of references, that he transcends existence.

Only because he is in himself the fullness that transcends all determination and becoming, all increase and decrease, could God have created a world destined to participate in his eternity, understood as fullness of interpersonal communion. For the creating of the world could have no other point. Moreover, a world existing by itself as an impersonal eternity, increasing and decreasing continually within a closed circle, would have no reason and would be entirely inexplicable.

God is the true eternity — or has the true eternity — because he is perfect communion of supreme persons and beyond all limitation. Only this kind of eternity makes possible the understanding of time and the relation of time to eternity. Eternity in this true sense can be considered no longer as irreconcilable with time or identical with it. Time is neither something contrary to eternity, a falling away from eternity, nor is it eternity unfolding. The divine eternity, as life in fullness, as dialogue of eternal perfect love between subjects who are perfectly interior one to the other, carries within itself the possibility of time, while time carries within itself the possibility of participating in eternity, a fact that can be made actual in communion with God through grace. For since God is eternal interpersonal communion, he can enter into loving relation with temporal beings. Saint Maximos the Confessor says that "the reasons of time are in God."[17]

God created the world so as to make it a sharer in his eternity or communion, not by reason of its own nature but through grace and participation in it. For eternity, as transcending temporal creation, cannot come in the form of temporal additions, but as a gift from another plane.

Even during their earthly life the saints share in a foretaste of the eternity of God. Saint Maximos the Confessor says of Melchizedek, whom the Scripture presents as being "without father or mother" and as one who "has neither beginning of days nor end of life" (Heb 7.3) that "he has raised himself above time and nature and became worthy to be likened to the Son of God, becoming as far as is possible through habit — that is through grace — what we believe the giver of grace to be by nature." For the saints in general, "uniting themselves wholly with the whole God to the extent possible for the natural power existing in them have had this quality of his imprinted so much in them that, as in faultless mirrors, they are only recognized now from him — having God's image which can be seen in them and showing themselves in an unchanged way through his features. For there remained in them not a single one of the old features which displayed their humanity, but all these yielded to the stronger, as light fills the air mixed with it."[18]

Saint Gregory Palamas, quoting Saint Maximos, also says that one who has been deified becomes "without beginning" and "without end."[19] He also quotes Saint Basil the Great who says that "one shares in the grace of Christ ... shares in his eternal glory";[20] and Saint Gregory of Nyssa who observes that the man who participates in grace "transcends his own nature, he who was subject to corruption in his mortality, becomes immune from it in his immortality, eternal from being fixed in time — in a word, a god from a man."[21]

But if during the course of this temporal life only the saints, at certain moments, become partakers of eternity, at the end of this life — in the eschatological plane — all who have believed and striven to live according to the will of God will be sharers in eternity because they will share in the communion of the uncreated God.

In this we see that God created man and the world for eternity. But eternity is won through a movement towards God which comes about in time. Thus time is the medium through which the eternal God leads creatures towards rest in his eternity.

This movement and, therefore, time as well, were defended by Saint Maximos the Confessor at some length in his work *The Ambigua* against the Platonist/Origenist theory that held motion to be a sinful fall of spiritual beings away from their unity in God, the reason behind their confinement in bodies as a direct punishment. While, according to this theory, souls confined within bodies seek to free themselves as soon as possible from temporal movement and from the world and rise up into the divine eternity, Saint Maximos considers that God himself has stamped motion on the rational creatures he created, as the one means by which they can advance towards final rest in the divine eternity. The Origenist theory viewed created things within the following scheme: movement (through the fall), creation, final stability. Saint Maximos reverses the first two elements of this triad: creation, movement, blessed rest in the eternity of God.

Created beings could not have possessed eternity from the beginning, for this would have meant that they were eternal through their own nature; but a contradiction exists between the quality of being "creature" and the attribute of having "eternity by nature." They had to attain to eternity through an effort of their own, helped by divine grace. From this results the positive necessity of motion and time. Movement in time is thus used by the divine eternity in order to attract the created beings within itself. A mother puts her child at a certain distance from herself and then calls the child to her so that it may strengthen itself through the exercise of the movement that it makes towards her, attracted by its desire for her. "The creation of all things sensible and intelligible has to precede movement in their conception. For it is not possible for motion to exist prior to creation."[22] "Hence if all rational beings are created, they are certainly also set in motion and, from their beginning, move through the agency of the will towards the good existence according to nature, because of the fact that they exist. Now the end of the movement is existence in the one who is the good eternal existence, just as their beginning is existence itself of God the giver of existence and bestower of the good existence, the beginning and the end."[23]

The motion which rational beings use to pass from existence, through good existence, to the eternal blessed existence in God, is a movement brought about through the agency of the will and so comes to be called "work" or "operation." It is through work, through operations, that these beings advance towards God, inasmuch as they purify themselves from passions, acquire the virtues (among which the foremost is love), and thus, freed from passions, come to know the divine reasons of things, that is, they see the meanings of these in God or see God in all things. This is a road of ethical perfection and enrichment in knowledge and at the end of this road God appears to rational beings or they enter into direct loving communion with him. "The eighth and the first day, or more exactly, the one and eternal day is the all-pure and wholly luminous appearance of God which occurs after all that moves has come to a halt. In those who, through their will, have made use of the natural reason of existence, he comes in his entirety and offers them the eternal good existence through participation in himself as the one who is the only existent, eternally existent, and blessedly existent."[24]

The Fathers stress that rest in the divine eternity is the result of the human being's effort to rise to the culminating love of God: "Thus everyone who has mortified his earthly limbs (that is, his tendencies towards what is earthly) and has quenched all his carnal thoughts and rid himself of all affection for the flesh — through which he divides up that love of his which he owes only to God . . . so as to be able to say like the blessed Paul: 'Who shall separate us from the love of Christ' (Rom 8.35) — has become without father, without mother and without genealogy like Melchizedek the great, held back from union with the Spirit no more either by the body or by nature."[25]

The Fathers emphasize that one who has come to belong wholly to God will participate fully in the eternity of God, for in this case God also has become wholly his. But this means a total love between man and God. This state is attained, however, through effort and in time. Yet love comes from God as an offer, and he makes this offer continuously. Man's love is only a response to this offer and it could not occur if this offer did not exist — an offer which is simultaneously a power given to man to respond to God. This means that the eternity of God holds the time of creation bound to itself, or that the time of creation is continuously bound up with the eternity of God. Moreover, God's eternity is present in the time of man through the offer of his love which provokes and helps man to respond.

Saint Maximos the Confessor says: "When it ceases its motion, time is aeon, and when the aeon is measured, it is time carried by motion. Thus the aeon is, to put it briefly, time without movement, and time is the aeon measured through movement."[26] He also says: "Deification, expressed briefly, is the concentration and the end of all times and all ages and of all that exists in time and ages."[27]

This means that the eternity which will be put in place at the end of time, will be a concentration of the entirety of time together with the efforts made by men, a concentration penetrated by the divine eternity with which man has entered into full communion.

In other words, the aeon becomes time when creation appears with its motion, and time becomes aeon when creation ceases from its motion in the God who is above motion, as the one who, "from all ages and unto all ages," has everything in himself. The aeon preexists as a potentiality of time in the bosom of the divine eternity — though without becoming confused with it — and as a reason (or inner principle) of time linked to the reason of the cosmos (Acts 17.26).

God gives real being to created things and sustains their development through his uncreated energies. In this sense he too is present in them with his eternity.

Time began, without doubt, simultaneously with the created world. However, without a preexistent eternity, it could not have begun. Nor is time, however, merely a simple period among the endless periods that have been and will be. Eternity before time and eternity after time is something other than time. Yet eternity explains time which comes from it and has its end in it. Time was in eternity as potential aeon and will have its end as aeon made actual and eternal with all the realities that were experienced as unfolded time. Eternity is time's foundation. As the unfolding of the aeon, time is a kind of ladder extended by eternity (or by one of the operations of eternity) towards the created world. It is the ladder extended by the eternity of God placed at my disposal, according to my own measure, through one of the operations God carried out on my level. For I cannot yet experience eternity as such.

Time does not belong to the being of the creature, as Saint Maximos the Confessor remarks. This is so because in the life to come time is no longer experienced in its unfolding. But Maximos also says that in its earthly existence creation cannot be conceived apart from time. Time as such does not remain exterior to the creature but, from the outset, becomes a condition of its ascent. It is just as true, however, that the creature has been made to transcend movement and time. It could be said, therefore, that time is the condition of its ascent. It is just as true, however, that the creature has been made to transcend movement and time. It could be said, therefore, that time is the condition of the dymamic relation of the creature (which has not yet attained to God) with the eternal God. Once it attained fully to God, the creature, together with its time become aeon once again, takes its place in his eternity. Then the relationship of God to the creature which has arrived at union with himself has achieved its maximum intimacy. This demonstrates at bottom how much the creature is made for God, how much it is linked with the eternity of God.

Since the most sublime relationship between divine Person and the human person can only be a relationship of love and can have no other aim than union in a perfect love, the vision of this intimate link between eternity and time destined to become aeon imbued with eternity can be transcribed in terms drawn from that relationship.

We have said that the eternity of God can be conceived as present in our time through the offer of his love which provokes and helps our response.

Love is the self-offering of one "I" to another "I" and a waiting upon the latter's offering as response to the offering of the former. It is only in the immediate and full response of the one to whom love is offered that every period of waiting, every interval is eliminated, as immediate union becomes real. God has offered us his love from the moment of our creation. But our response to God's gift of self does not have the character of a self-offering that cannot be any more complete, that is, a response which removes the waiting for and hoping for some fuller self-offering. As creatures we are limited, yet at the same time we are capable of transcending ourselves and our tendency is towards that transcendence. This introduces time, which is to say, the past with its discontent with what we have been and with the extent of our self-offering, and the future with its tendency for us to be something more and to offer more of ourselves.

In relation to us the eternal God is placed in a position of expectant waiting. Hence there appears the relation between himself and time, and from this it can be seen that God holds time bound up with his own eternity. Eternity accepts time within itself, that is, God accepts the creature, who lives in time, into his eternity although time also represents a spiritual distance between created persons and God. Eternity is thus as much in time as it is above time. A distance remains between ourselves and God, but at the same time this distance has its place within the framework of love and hence of God's eternity. The distance is time understood both as the expectant waiting for an eternity that is directed towards creatures and the hope of the creature directed towards eternity.

This distance will be overcome only in the full final union between us and God. Saint Maximos the Confessor says: "The mystery of Pentecost is, therefore, the direct union with providence of those who are cared for by providence, that is, the union of the created nature with the Word through the operation of providence, a union in which there no longer appears either time or becoming."[28]

In God the duration of this expectant waiting is reduced to nothing for the love between the divine subjects is simultaneous in all its perfection. Not being able to grow any further, nor to fall away from this simultaneity and perfection, the divine love persists, as offering and as response, in a bi-lateral (or tri-lateral) eternal act.

The partners whom God created for the sake of that love which is to exist among themselves and with God himself, since, unlike God, they could not be by nature and of themslves the bearers of his infinite subjectivity in all respects — hence also of love — had to reach perfect relation in love, and hence eternity, through the power of will. These partners cannot reach eternity except through unlimited response to the unlimited self-offering of the eternal God, for only in this way do they open themselves to God's eternity and are able to participate in it.

The divine persons do not receive eternity from outside themselves, because they do not receive fullness of life from without by response to the love of a superior being. Beings created with an existence that is limited, and who must respond to God's love so as to open themselves to him, can only make that response gradually. This means growth and effort. Their response could not be from the outset, therefore, a self-offering and, consequently, a love which was equivalent to that of the divine offer, namely, one characterized by simultaneity of promptness and the perfection of fullness. For this reason, God in his turn offers them his love gradually and according to the measure of their own growth and capacity for response. Thus their complete response will only occur when God gives himself totally to them, after they have grown in this direction. In his relations with them God makes his energies actual in a gradual fashion; he does not communicate with created beings through his integral essence, as he communicates in the interior life of the Holy Trinity.

But, on this road of ours towards eternity, God himself experiences together with us the expectant waiting (and hence time) on the plane of his energies and of his relations with us. And this is so because he himself voluntarily lives out the limitation of the offering of his love. See, for example, the history of revelation and of its full actualization. God experiences simultaneously his eternity in the inter-trinitarian relations and his temporal relation with created spiritual beings; or indeed in his very relations with creatures he experiences both eternity and time.

This is a kenosis voluntarily accepted by God for the sake of creation, a condescension (κατάβασις) in relation to the world, lived out simultaneously along with the eternity of his trinitarian life. God experiences both of them through the fact that he causes the offer of his eternal love to be felt even in our temporality but also that eternity which is the source of this offer, even despite the fact that we hesitate or refuse to respond.

God waits "with enduring patience" for our return to him, for our awakening to the love he offers us. But at the same time as he waits, God also rejoices in non-temporality, in the absence of any interval in that reciprocal manifestation of love between the trinitarian subjects. But what makes the paradox even greater is that the joy of the inter-trinitarian love co-exists along with expectant waiting for the response of human persons and with sadness for its delay: "Behold, I stand at the door and knock; if any one hears my voice and opens the door, I will come in to him . . . " (Rev 3.20). For God, time means the duration of the expectant waiting between his knocking on the door and our act of opening it. He does not force his entrance into the hearts of men. Time in this sense implies both the freedom and the respect accorded by God to conscious creatures. Union with God in love cannot come about without the free response of man to the offer of his love. But God, expectantly waiting, experiences time without forgetting or stepping outside his own eternity, while we, when we do not hear his voice, experience a time that has no consciousness of eternity.

The vision of God in our regard extends through the whole of the future and so he awaits with enduring patience and is content with less than we are. God is, therefore, in expectant waiting, in time, and also, beyond all waiting, in eternity.

Since the acts of God in offering his love take into account the levels we have reached in our capacity to respond, we can talk of a "history" of revelation and of God's action in his relations with us; we can speak of him advancing with us in the course of our own becoming. But inasmuch as through our process of becoming we not only reduce the duration that separates us from full union with God, but also secure a continuous advancement within the loving atmosphere of his Person, our time can be said to fill up gradually with an eternity that we sense more and more. And God, waiting expectantly with hope and living our continual approach to him, likewise has eternity present during the time of his expectant waiting.

But the duration between God's offering and our response is not necessarily being reduced in a gradual fashion. We could respond more quickly if we wanted to participate more quickly in God through grace. And in fact some do respond more quickly, while others disappoint God's expectant waiting: "O Jerusalem, Jerusalem! . . . How often would I have gathered your children together as a hen gathers her brood under her wings, and you would not!" (Mt 23.37)

God announces the future through prophets. He announces his future blessings or punishments. This means both the conditioning of his acts by time and the anticipated embrace of time. Our time is a reality for God too, yet he is also above time. He is above it by the very fact that man is moved in his interiority by God's offering, his appeal, and by the fact that the eternal love offered by God moves us to a response. In the action manifested by this continuous appeal, God resembles a bow which is stretched over the interval between his offer and our response, between eternity and time. Only when we become totally insensible of this offer, when we are in no way preoccupied to respond, then we no longer hang on God's operation nor are held up by it any longer within a movement that leads towards eternity. Thus God makes his eternity effective in the fact that we are led on to transcend the duration between the offer of his love and our response, and are led, therefore, to the transcending of time. This occurs by the power of his inter-trinitarian love, and thus thanks to the eternity of God, to his love and to his life above time.

This meaning of time can also be seen in the fact that we are always stretching out to what lies before us, that we are not enclosed in what we are, and that we have not reached what we want or what our existence asks us to be, that we are incessantly on the way — we are travellers. Time is the expression of the fact that we do not remain and cannot remain in what we are, but also that we have not definitively reached that fullness in which we can rest, that we are suspended over the abyss of nothingness. This is also visible in the fact that we are always seeking a more satisfactory meaning for what we are and for what is around us.

Thus it is the quest which is within us, the tendency towards the future, the leaving behind of what we are and the reaching out towards another goal (Phil 3.14; the *epektaseis* of Saint Gregory of Nyssa). This proves that at no point in time do we ever have within us all that could be desired of our existence, that we are made for eternity. A definite or prolonged rest in the present moment is not possible as long as we still live in a life that is insufficient, that is, as long as we live in time. The present moment is a moment extended towards the future; it is not exclusively a present moment. Properly speaking, we do not have a present because we do not have within us a perfected infinite life. Only God, the fullness of existence, is an eternal present. And only in him can we find rest because in him we have life without limitations. This does not mean that we must not be at work in every moment. But every act, although it is immediate, is for the future; it extends towards the future, and we are alive only inasmuch as we extend ourselves towards the future through the present act. If we wish to remain in what we are, we are dead, we exist in a life which is consumed in a moment.

Through time we hurry towards a more satisfactory response to God's appeal, to the offer of his love, and God himself attracts us towards this, he attracts us into himself as into the genuine existence. For the response already given no longer keeps us in existence, since God sends out towards us and in us an offer, hence a more advanced energy that corresponds to what follows upon the state we have reached. Therefore, we have to make ourselves dead to the present moment so that we may act in the present for the future, in order to find in the future our true existence. We have to leave behind what is, for the sake of something that is not yet, because what now is is on the way to becoming dead.

Time as duration is always interval, or the movement in the interval between two ends of a bridge. We cannot bear to remain in the interval.

There is something ambiguous about time. Time is, and it is not. So it was viewed by Saint Basil the Great. It is the launching out from a state on its way to becoming dead, over nothingness and towards fullness. It is the flight from Egypt through the desert of Sinai towards the promised land. To remain in the same place means to die. We have to launch ourselves out relinquishing a state threatened by death, in the sure faith that we will discover fullness. It is the leaving behind of the present, as a life only apparent and threatened by death, to pass over that nothingness which leads to life, to pass in a certain sense through the cross. The cross is situated within each moment, and after each cross the next moment comes to us as a gift of God. This movement over the void we make out of hope in God and listening in faith to God's appeal so that we may reach the promised land.

In fact, this means to live no longer for yourself but for the one whom you have not yet found, or not fully found: to die to yourself. And this means to accept the death of what seems to be life in order to find the true life. It means to overcome death by death. To live in time means to live out of God's grace, or to be dying and forever obtaining life from the hand of God.

But it is only inasmuch as this acceptance of death to yourself means that you accept to live from God that this death brings the true life. Otherwise, against your will, you are dying in the face of every moment that has passed, and without obtaining life. "He who finds [seeks to gain] his life will lose it," [for he cannot hold on to the moment that has passed] "and he who loses his life for my sake, will find it" (Mt 10.39; cf. Lk 17.33). According to Saint Cyril of Alexandria, there can be no entry before God except in a state of sacrifice, that is, in a state of death which you have willed in regard to yourself, in a total offering to God.[29]

Time thus implies within itself the greatest freedom of the creature. Without this freedom time would have no meaning. If the creature were fixed in good, as God is, he would be eternal. If he moved around monotonously in a circle, the purpose of movement and of time would not be seen. If God were to bear creation towards himself without its freedom, we could ask why he did not lead it to himself from the beginning. Time without freedom loses its meaning. In that case eternity too would be devoid of freedom. It would be an impersonal eternity, an eternity of relativity. Time presupposes the communion of the supreme persons, a communion that has brought free created persons into existence.

Clearly, time does not exist in the communion of the supreme persons, but it finds its explanation from that communion, a communion which seeks to attract within itself other persons too who do not exist from eternity but who are created for this pupose. In the course of time the freedom that created persons have is made clear, along with their capacity for ambivalent decisions in respect of communion with other persons and, in the last analysis, in respect of communion with the supreme persons or in respect of the definitive enclosure of the created conscious being within itself. Time comes to an end either in perfect communion with the communion of the supreme persons, that is, in the infinite fullness of communion, or in isolation within one's own emptiness. These are the two eternities, the two cessations of time. In the eternity of perfect communion there is complete freedom and a unique and supreme feeling for all things, and a movement that transcends all motion; in the eternity of solipsism there is the impossibility of any movement and hence of any freedom.

One who makes use of time as a way towards the eternity of hell, rather than using it to transcend himself more and more, moves forward from the present state into a state more heavily characterized by domination. Such a person thereby moves forward into death because he does not come forth from himself in any real way and for this reason does not allow himself to launch out into that real interval which leads him to another subject and finally to the divine subject. He does not experience time as death in his own regard and as a leap into eternity; that is why he is continually afraid of biological death. He makes use of time to move further into himself, to strengthen his selfish ego, to become stuck in time. This is the time that leads a being further into death, into emptiness, and it leaves him in emptiness. One who experiences only this time and fights merely in this sense against the advance of biological weakness is spiritually dead and will not be able to arise from death to life. For the spirit, this kind of time cannot properly be called time at all because it is not an interval between persons, between the human person and divine Person. It is already, even before it ends in hell, a time in appearance only or an interval in appearance only, because the person does not really come out of himself nor does he achieve any increase of life or gain anything truly new; and because the person does not move beyond himself, he does not move within the temporal interval so as to overcome it through his own self-offering to the other and, ultimately, to God. Time which is merely an interval between a person and those things he wishes to accumulate, or between a person

The Super-Essential Attributes of God   165

and other persons who are treated as things to be dominated and exploited — this is not a real interval properly speaking, but only an apparent one, an advance into the desert of self leading to total death. For such an "I" the successive moments are no longer a free gift of God which make possible his advance towards God, but rather a curse which pulls him deeper and deeper into definitive death. He is afraid of time and does not see its total value.

Only as interval and, therefore, as a link between persons and, in the final analysis, between the human persons and divine Person, is time real and hence positive, progressive, and creative — the progress of the person in uniting his life with the life of others and with the infinite life of God. Time is real, therefore, as the real movement of the human person beyond himself in order to transcend the interval, not to escape from it.

Only by transcending time as real interval, not by avoiding it, do we attain to eternity, because it is only through transcending the real interval that we unite ourselves with supreme Person in love. For as long as a residue of selfishness persists in us, that is, as long as we have not transcended this interval by passing over it, the supreme subject does not bestow himself fully upon us; and this, either because the leap I make out of myself is not total and represents no sacrifice, no total gift of my being, or because after a momentary leap I withdraw again into myself.

Obviously, the overcoming of the interval that exists between ourselves and between ourselves and God always remains inadequate during our earthly life and, even though we do make some progress, is always being hampered by sin and selfishness. On the other hand, if I do not seek the supreme subject through the subject of my neighbor, I am condemned also to finding my neighbor only partially. I do not find in him the continuously essential "novelty" which takes me out of myself, gives me life and saves me from death as, in relation to him, the interval is largely overcome. It must be noted that this transcending of time does not remove man from the inter-personal reality, as with the Platonic conception of eternity. Quite the reverse is true.

In my stretching out beyond myself towards the other, I likewise wish to discover him as a self-offering gift. The person of the other is the most precious gift of all and fills me with life, provided only that at the same time he remains person, that is, he offers himself freely or is not laid hold of as if he were an object. Only the person can be this kind of free gift of self, for only the person can offer himself freely and it is only this gift that fills me with life. But the other gives himself to me only inasmuch as I give myself to him. My going out of myself is, from another point of view, the bestowing of myself. In going out of myself, I am no longer my own, but belong to the other towards whom I go out. I can give myself to the other completely or infinitely, however, only if through him I see the infinite God.

On the other hand, we do not have power to give ourselves completely to one another and to God if we have not received from someone above us the impulse to bestow ourselves as gift in this way. This is the meaning of the statement by Saint Cyril of Alexandria that there can be no entry before the Father except in a state of sacrifice, and that we are raised to that state only if Christ takes us into himself in his own state of sacrifice or if he dwells in us.[30]

The very impulse which Christ stamps upon us so that we might bestow ourselves as gift — an impulse given through the holy sacraments — does not cause us to bestow this gift without interruption, but instead our self-offering is followed by withdrawal within ourselves, that is, we do not overcome the interval, we do not transcend time totally and definitively. All these delays in our giving the gift of ourselves to God reveal the delays we make in giving ourselves to others. We do thirst for a perfect and absolute correspondence between the appeal and the response to love, but this correspondence can only occur from God and in God through total trust in him and through the fulfilment of his command to love one another fully by loving him fully.

Through his experience of the interval between our response and his appeal as well as the appeal to love of our neighbors, God lives all the pains which grow up between partners who have not yet reached the fullness of love.

Thus God shares man's sufferings in a certain way. We are used to saying that God suffers if man does not respond to his love.[31] But God suffers not because he himself would have need of our love, but he suffers for all the sufferings which appear in us owing to our refusal to respond to his love and to our reciprocal appeal for a complete and unhesitating love. The blessings of God come to us in the form of his love and of the love among ourselves. If we refuse this love or its fullness by refusing our own complete and unhesitating response, then we are refusing God's blessings and God himself. God's suffering for our sake comes from the sufferings we bury ourselves in through this course of action. His suffering derives from the fact that he cannot make us participate in his blessings because of our refusal to accept his love.

The interval between the offer of God's love and our response is also prolonged by the necessity we are under of growing spiritually through our own free effort. Men mature in a gradual fashion. Unless a certain amount of time has first passed, we are unable to respond continuously in the most adequate way to the demands being made upon us. Here we see the importance of the teachings of past generations, of dialogue between human beings, of the experiences on which these are based, and of the reflections made by each individual. God directs his claims and communicates the gifts of his love to men according to their spiritual level. Historical time forms a whole, an unfolding aeon in which some are influenced by others both for good and for evil. That is why we will be judged as a whole, and, in the case of the judgement of each one, the influences he has undergone from others as well as those he has exerted upon all others, upon the whole, will be taken into account.

As long as we preserve a spiritual mobility, time persists with its double possibility that matches the ambivalent capacity of our own freedom: it can provide the occasion for rising or falling; it can be a road leading towards the bright or the dark eternity. Time will cease simultaneously with this ambiguous quality that is proper to it, when God deems that he can make it possible that we respond to love simultaneously with the appeal addressed to us, or when we are definitively and totally locked up within our own solitude; when the appeal and the response of the dialogue correspond to one another completely, or when there is no more appeal or response at all; when there is no longer any appeal because there will be no response to it, and no more response is produced because the appeal is no longer heard. A continuous refusal to respond to love and to offer oneself will fix the spiritual creature within a total absence of any possibility of communication. Then there will be no more expectant waiting, no more hope.

Because in this state there will be nothing new, it can be said that then there will no longer be, properly speaking, any time, because time will contain nothing of eternity (understood here as the genuine eternity) and so will be empty of all content. This is time become insignificant and useless through its own total emptiness and the absence of any motion, direction, or goal. This eternity will be a miserable one, inferior to time itself. Saint Maximos too speaks of this eternity as inferior to time.

Emptiness in its endless monotony and fullness represent the two radically different forms of eternity: the former is dead eternity, the latter is living. Time which is able to move forward towards the fullness of the genuine eternity is creative.[32] It absorbs life from the infinite divine energies and tranfers it to the created plane. Time which has fallen completely away from the stream of eternity and descended into a fixed and unchangeable monotony no longer has anything even of the character of time left in it, and is an eternity opposed to the genuine one. Properly speaking, it is no longer time because it is no longer a succession of continuously new states stimulated by the hope of reaching always farther into eternity. Instead, it is an eternity of monotony and of emptiness where neither hope, nor expectation, nor fulfillment is possible. This is time devoid of substance or of meaningful succession, since there nothing is expected, nothing happens within it; it is no longer attracted by eternity. It is a unique state with no end, experienced as a curse, as petrification, as conscious death. It is the impossiblity of the dark eternity of hell, the most exterior darkness of existence, the absence of life, but an absence experienced as torment.

The changelessness of God — a quality that he causes those who are increasing in love to share in — is changelessness in the fullness of the life of love, and there can be nothing else higher than this. The changelessness of hell is the total emptiness of life. Those in this state have cut themselves off completely from the dialogue of love that kept them linked with eternity. Their life can no longer be called life, their existence no longer existence. Time coincides with becoming because it tends towards full communion with God, towards eternity. In God there is no becoming, nor is there any becoming in hell. To admit a process of becoming in God is to view him no longer in the fullness of life and no longer to acknowledge fullness in the Creator. There will be no more time in heaven or in hell. It will no longer exist in heaven because those who are there have God as fullness, and it will no longer exist in hell because in hell there can be no more tending towards God (Rev 12.12). But this will not be rest, because emptiness without hope is torment. "Their worm does not die" (Is 66.24; Mk 9.44, 46, 48). Time is a grace given for the sake of repentance (Rev 2.21), and it is a hope. But those in hell will no longer have this grace. "Now to those who, through their wills, have made use of the reason of nature against nature, God will give eternal unhappy existence instead of eternal happy existence, since he who is eternally happy will not be a good for those whose dispositions have been opposed to him nor will they any longer have any motion of their own towards the appearance of him who appeared, through which he helps those who seek him."[33]

If God offered his love beforehand to conscious creatures through the things of creation and through his uncreated energies, in Christ he gives himself to them as hypostasis. In Christ the divine hypostasis is accessible to us on our own human level for the sake of full communion. Christ overcomes in himself the interval between divinity and humanity, and between himself as God and ourselves. This state is made real for us at present, however, only potentially and, as it were, through a process of maturation.

The human will of Christ responds fully to his divine will, but through this the distinction between them is not suppressed. The divine will always remains as that which offers, calls, seeks a response, and imposes a responsibility. The human will remains that which responds.

On the other hand, the fact that the human will of Christ responds on behalf of men and asks on their behalf means that it continues to be in relationship with their temporality, their aspirations, and their difficulties. And this causes Christ to experience these relations with time-bound humanity also as God. So long as we are not all together within the perfection of human response to the offer of the divine love, Christ also will remain — and even more than was true of him in his reality as God before his incarnation — linked to our temporality, although, on the other hand, as a subject of eternity he has also brought into this temporality the power to make a more complete human response to the divine offer.

The incarnation of the divine Word, and the fact that in him the transcending of the temporal interval between man and God coexists with God's relation to time-bound men, show of themselves the inner link between divine eternity and human temporality.

The Son of God became man in order that, through our own movement, he might help us overcome the temporal interval that separates us from full communion with God. In some fashion he performs this movement together with us and because of this he finds himself within this interval still, although on the other hand he is above it.

Relying on the affirmation of St. Paul in Hebrews 11.39-40, Origen made the following remarkable commentary to Jesus' words: "I shall not drink again of this fruit of the vine until that day when I drink it new with you in my Father's kingdom" (Mt 26.29). "He waits, therefore, so we may return, so we may imitate his example, so we may follow his footprints and he may rejoice with us and drink the wine with us in his Father's kingdom. For now, since he is a merciful and gracious Lord, with greater emotion than his own apostle he weeps with those who weep and wishes to rejoice with those who rejoice. (Rom 12.15) . . . as he draws near the Father and stands at the altar and offers his sacrifice for us; that is to say that as he approaches the altar, he does not drink the wine of joy, for he still suffers the bitterness of our sins."[34]

Notice the simultaneity between the complete offering of Christ to the Father through sacrifice, (namely the overcoming of the temporal interval) and the link with those who suffer in time, since it is precisely for them that he gives himself.

"How long will he wait? Until, he says, I have accomplished your work. When will this work be accomplished? When he has made me complete and perfect — I who am the last and greatest of all sinners . . . Finally so long as I am not yet subjected to the Father, neither can he be said to be subjected to the Father. Not that he lacks for himself submission to the Father, but for my sake in whom he has not yet accomplished his work, he himself is said not to be subject."[35] Christ will not receive the fullness of joy until his whole body receives it: " . . . since we are all called his body and members of him, as long as there are some among us who are not yet made subject with a perfect subjection, he himself is said not yet to be subject."[36] Neither will the departed saints have full joy "while they are weeping for our sins."[37] This means that as long as I have not overcome the temporal interval in my love for all, time remains as an objective reality.

Origen certainly believed that this return to the Father through Jesus would be universal and is not for all eternity. Those are errors of his own. The idea, however, that Jesus himself has not received the fullness of joy nor complete rest in eternity apart from those who struggle in time will be taken up by Saint John Chrysostom, Saint Maximos the Confessor, and finally by Pascal, who gave it the impressive formulation: "Jésus sera en agonie jusqu'à la fin du monde."[38]

Eternity is in solidarity with time without being confused with it. Eternity is the origin of time and its prospect; it is the force moving time forward towards itself. At the end, eternity will overwhelm time and confer upon it its own quality. Then time will no longer exist (cf. Rev 10.6), for we will possess nothing but love. Saint Maximos the Confessor says that through love "we will be able to have not only one nature, as it were, but also one deliberative will with God and one another, having no interval (διάστασις) between us and God or between one another. . . . "[39] Then God will wipe away the tears of those who will be fully with and in him (Rev 21.4).

Supraspatiality

Inasmuch as space sets limits, God is above space. At the same time, however, he is present in all space, although the parts of space do not inscribe corresponding parts in God. God transcends space as he trancends time; he is above a "when" and a "where" just as he is above every "how," since all these would limit, determine, and define him.[40] He transcends all these because as one who is superexistent or apophatic, God is beyond every system of references. Yet he is in all things in a mode which is not spatial or temporal, for all things receive their existence through him. He is in all things, for he is in all his acts which have reference to us, creating, sustaining and perfecting acts through which he enters our system of references, or enters into the plane of existence, as the one who produces and determines these acts and through them makes himself accessible.

As an apophatic subject beyond composition, God is supraspatial. But a perfect subject can only be in perfect communion with the other infinite supreme subjects. Precisely for this reason the possibility of space arises in God, for it is in the distinction of the divine persons that the possibility of the otherness of finite persons arises who are to be attracted into communion with him. Finite persons are not from the outset in perfect communion among themselves or between themselves and God; hence the distance which separates them from perfect communion takes the form of space just as it also takes the form of temporal duration. Thus space is the form of the relation between God — the supraspatial and infinite one — and finite persons, the form which makes possible their movement between one another, and thereby also towards God, for God cannot be found apart from communion with other persons.

Certainly, there also exist created subjects who, like the angels, only have the interval of duration as interval between themselves and God or between one another. But God is not monotonous in his creative action. He also creates subjects clothed in material bodies, in order to make material forms a means of spirituality and, consequently, images of a visible beauty. As subjects clothed in material bodies, they need an adjacent existence; and so they need a space. Moreover, they have need of a large space that will provide free movement, for just as time is given for the freedom of created subjects, so space is given so that they may have the freedom to draw near or to move away, or to preserve the distances that separate them. A time and a space are given in order to foster the "yearning" or the "desire" between them while they also give them the possibility of distancing themselves when they do not love one another.

The Trinity cannot show forth its visible image except in created persons who are situated in a space that is common. Space in this sense, that is, as a medium common to human persons, stands in relation to the holy Trinity. But just as the Trinitarian persons are interior to each other, so are human persons spiritually interior to one another in part and are capable of growing in this mutual interiority. Once this has occurred, human persons are in a certain fashion present in all space or transcend space.

In the holy Trinity, through the distinction of human persons and the union among themselves, both the origin of space and its unity are given. Each human person has in himself the whole of space, or is linked to the whole of space, for the body of the person is developed out of all that exists in space and the soul of the person has a content which has been gathered together from the whole of space. Persons who are united among one another carry the whole of space together with them. Space is a single reality borne by each person and borne in common by all human persons; space is transcended by them, however, in a unity which is theirs beyond space.

The quality that human persons have of being bearers of the image of God can also be seen in this respect, the God who is one in essence and threefold in persons, existing as an unconfused unity among all human persons.

It is impossible to understand space in a purely individualistic perspective while it is correct that each human person considers himself in a certain way to be the center of space, the same person nevertheless gravitates towards other persons, and achieves a balance between himself as center of space and other persons as centers of the same space. A single human person would have no need of space and would feel alien in it or consider it unreal.

When we say that God has conceived and created space, we must also have regard, in a corresponding fashion, to God in Trinity. A unipersonal God would provide no sufficient basis for the creation of space. Space is closely connected with interpersonal communion. Space acquires and maintains a surer reality when it has reference not only to myself but to other persons as well, when I can and must say: from me to such a one the distance is this. Space, like time, is an interpersonal relation. It distinguishes and unites us, and indicates the perspective of a still greater nearness. Thus space proves itself an existential reality. It is not a theory or a form of intuition, just as time is neither of these things (Kant). Space depends on the other "I" too, or the overcoming of distance depends also on him, just as the overcoming of temporal duration depends on love with the other becoming a reality. For if it is only I who want to go to him, while he runs away, the distance remains. But it remains because I know about him. Space can thus be both a tormenting reality — if it is used to avoid communion — and a positive reality — when it serves as a means of manifesting a communion which is not the blending or submerging of individuals. Space, like time, can also lend itself to an ambiguous use, but this use is always as a form of relation. Space makes it possible for a man either to withdraw from the gaze of the other or to draw near to him. Space, like time, is given as an interval but also as a link between man and man. We can preserve this interval and make it wider, but we are also able to reduce and overcome it entirely, just as we can with the interval of time.

As a reality for the world, space is given, however, so that it might be overcome by the bringing about of a perfect communion between ourselves and God and between one another after the likeness of the holy Trinity. Thus space, like time, has its origin and end in the holy Trinity.

As those who are ontologically above space, we must overcome it in a certain degree through our own will and through grace. If time is duration between God's appeal to love and our response, space is the distance linked to this duration. The interval between God's appeal to love and the perfect response of human beings to this appeal is made up of duration and distance. Both represent a certain distance of the world from God, but at the same time they are both given by God as a distance which is meant to be overcome. Both of them are given as distance between one man and another, as an interval between the appeal to love of the one and the response of the other, yet always as an interval that must be overcome. The interval of time is called duration and the interval of space is called distance, in the strict sense. But both are distance or interval in a broader sense.

On both of these sides of the interval God is found with his eternity and omnipresence like a bridge and a force that attracts people and urges them towards one another and towards God. Spatial distance also represents a temporal duration. In order to overcome the former I must overcome the latter. But I can be very close to someone in space, and yet at the same time at a huge spiritual distance which is equivalent to a long temporal duration that I must cover. The overcoming of spatial distance vis-à-vis a person does not mean that the temporal duration has been overcome in respect to that person. The temporal duration is itself a distance and tends to produce its own spatial distance. Moreover, once temporal duration between two persons is overcome, the spatial distance between them almost does not seem to matter, or in any case is easier to overcome. Once spiritual distance or temporal duration is overcome, spatial distance loses its tormenting character, or at least the overcoming of the former easily leads to the overcoming of the latter. This underscores the fact that the spirit vanquishes space and that space no longer matters for those who are united in spirit. What distances more profoundly is temporal duration. God as Spirit is everywhere with us. To overcome our distance from him is a matter of time, not of space.

This opens a perspective with regard to the final transcending of space which differs from that regarding the final overcoming of time. Time as duration will cease, whereas space will not cease but will be overwhelmed. One who will respond immediately and fully to the appeal for love that comes from God and from other human persons, will be with them everywhere, yet without his distinctiveness ceasing to be everywhere. God will be transparent and felt in his energies through all things. Each human being will likewise be present to everyone in his energies, permeated by the divine energy, through all things. Even during this life the saints see and act at a distance.

The overcoming of time as duration between the appeal for love and the response to this appeal is more difficult than the overcoming of spatial distance, for the former is always a matter of spiritual effort while the latter is a matter of physical effort.

It is paradoxical that the more time someone has for others, the more he vanquishes time and simultaneously space as well.

But duration is vanquished through the spirit. Once duration is overcome, so too, through the spirit, is space.

If we try to vanquish time in an exterior manner through speed, we remain enclosed within it; we remain in duration empty of communion. Even if the moments of duration are passed through quickly, the plane of duration is not overcome. If we complete quickly the road that leads towards the proposed goal, we always discover other goals, or we remain within the tormenting duration of solitude. Exterior speed can lead us rapidly to someone, but if we have not vanquished the interior distance, we slip quickly past the person we have reached.

Time is overcome only if we stay with another person for a long period. For then each person will have time for the other, and there will be no person who is not accompanied by some other who has time for him. Space is overcome only by passing through it spiritually and remaining a long time within exterior space, not flying over the top of it. Through using a great deal of time for various persons and through much perseverance in travelling spiritually through spatial distances, we grow practiced at discovering in all things both their variety and their eternity and infinity as well. The eternity and the infinity that we discover will be rich in character, not abstract and monotonous.

Time and space are given to us as an inevitable path towards the eternity and infinity of life in God; as gifts of God we cannot, therefore, dispense with them. In the moments of total communion, in the absorbing loving contemplation of the mystery of the other — a mystery which is above space, undefined, and inexhaustible — space is overwhelmed, swallowed up, and left behind. For a child the experience of his mother is the original experience, as Heribert Mühlen says; in it the concentrated experience of things and of space is included.[41] Ordinarily, in the loving relationship between persons space is transfigured, overwhelmed by the subjectivity of that person. From the beloved person there radiates out over space a transfiguring light that causes the space around him to be filled with his soul, filled with the person himself, and made personal. This is an overwhelming of space by means of the interior light of the person, an overwhelming that can have various degrees right down to the swallowing up of space for the sake of our own experience. Love songs have always brought out this reality.

Saint Symeon the New Theologian repeats continually that when Christ reveals himself to him in light, Symeon does not know whether this takes place within space or outside of space. On the contrary, when no one loves you, you do not feel anything except space, the tedium in space devours you. And when a person hates you all the space around him becomes unpleasant, unbearable so that you do not know where to flee in order to escape from the spreading reflection of his unbearable presence.[42] Even when a person is missing from the space where we were accustomed to see him, his absence is felt as a special absence, or the space seems somehow to have been amputated by that absence. He is present even in absence.[43] Somehow the person continues to be present through the special energy of his subjectivity. But this presence is not full and therefore it stirs up even more the longing for his full presence. This "absent presence" brings forth with particular power the "longing" that the place be filled by the person in question. This shows that space was not made to be on its own. The absence of persons from space somehow renders it lifeless, dead. Space does not contain full meaning in itself, or only for the sake of the isolated "I." It is the ambiance of another person in relationship with me. Space was made to be filled with the fullness of communion so as to be the context and the means of communion, the place of encounter and of interpersonal relation, the medium of reciprocal revelation; it fulfills its purpose completely when it is transfigured and overwhelmed by interpersonal communion.

Space exists through the relationship between us; it is "ours," not mine. Space which was for me alone would be meaningless and tormenting.

But space receives its full meaning only if we see it as means of God's communion with us. Our human communion has need of space but has not been able to create it itself, although it can transfigure space and bring it into the sphere of the subject. This means that only a communion of supreme persons has been able to create it, not only for the sake of that communion but for our sake too who are created for communion in the image of the supreme communion. And if space is really to be brought into the sphere of the subject, this can only be realized in full communion with that supreme communion.

God gave existence to space out of an inner possibility included in his Trinitarian life so that, after the pattern of the Trinitarian communion in which we are to grow, it might be for us a means of communion between him and us and, among ourselves, between one another. God put space as an interval to be overcome that separates his communion without interval from our communion among ourselves and with him — a communion which, inasmuch as it is not yet perfect, has an interval within itself and between it and the Trinitarian communion. Space is the form of our communion in movement towards perfect communion, towards the overcoming of that interval which it represents. Through this means we must ascend towards perfect communion with God and among ourselves, after the likeness of the Trinitarian communion. But we cannot do this unless the Trinitarian communion descends to us through grace. God is omnipresent in space as loving Trinity and as source of our own love for him and for one another, and he causes our union with him and among ourselves to grow without the loss of our reality as individual persons. Through the omnipresence of God in Trinity, there is given from the beginning an ontological unity of all things in diversity in the same diversified space as well as in the diverse unity of our beings which are striving towards a greater and greater unity. Just as time will be overwhelmed in the interiority of reciprocal and perfect communion, so will space also be overwhelmed in the interiority of the same reciprocal and perfect communion, in the perfect human intersubjectivity that comes about when it is raised up into the divine intersubjectivity.

This ascent has many stages. Through his energies God in Trinity is brought down on each occasion to the level attained by conscious creatures in their communion with one another and in the communion between themselves and God. Through this descent to us, God wishes to lead us to the goal of perfect communion, the goal of overcoming the interval of time and space that separates us from it, by coming down in a different way in the case of each of us, for we find ourselves at different distances one from the other. In each human being God comes to us at various temporal and spatial distances. And each human being is found at a different temporal and spatial distance from him. When we have reached the goal of perfect communion with him and among ourselves, there will no longer be a variety of distances, but God will be close and intimate to everyone in the same way, in every place and time, so that there will no longer be a distinction, properly speaking, between here and there, between now and then. We will find ourselves purely and simply within the divine eternity and infinity having neither past nor future, neither here not there.

But it may happen the other way; by overcoming spatial distances people can find themselves at insurmountable spiritual distances. It can happen that people convert diminished external distances, or a physical proximity that has been imposed on them, into vast internal distances which are insumountable. In fact, the experience we are undergoing today shows us as a probable, indeed almost certain, prospect that distances can be diminished until they virtually disappear while enormous gulfs between men are effectively being opened up. The prospect of a "fixed chasm" (Lk 16.26) that can no longer be removed from its place appears more and more possible. The exterior distance between "here" and "there" can become minimal or unimportant, while a hardening of spiritual distance is taking place that no longer provides one person with the motivation or the possibility of moving towards another. In such a case God himself, together with his uncreated energies, has withdrawn as linking bridge and as longing and attraction between men. Thus solitude will have a supratemporal and supraspatial character in the bad sense of the term, which might better be described as subtemporal and subspatial. The way for this has been paved even here on earth by the fact that the selfish man "does not have time" for others so that space might be overcome; hence he has no "longing" for others since he no longer feels the need to travel over the distance between them, or else he covers that distance not in order to reach someone, but only to pass further beyond. This selfish speed overcomes time and space not for the purpose of drawing near others, but of passing them by.

In the end not only will time be vanquished by a twofold immobility, but space also. Time will be overcome either by stability in the infinity of our communion with God and among ourselves who are united with God, or else by the impossibility of advancing towards God or towards our neighbors. Space will similarly be overcome either

The Super-Essential Attributes of God

by the transparency of God and of each neighbor in the whole of space — that is, by the accentuated seal stamped on space by the personal reality of God and of our neighbors — or else by the impossibility of advancing any longer towards communion with God and with our neighbors that arises from the hostile transparency in the whole of space held by the evil angels and our neighbors who are enemies to us. Their presence will crowd in upon us so much, or space itself will be so much marked by them, that, strictly speaking, we will have no more apprehension of space, just as those in perfect communion with God and their neighbors will have no apprehension of it. It is clear that the oppressive harassment of someone who is in hell, a harassment which comes from the hostile faces of the evil angels and of his neighbors who are there, does not contradict the reality of a terrible loneliness. The "ugly" face produces in you tediousness, in the sense of loneliness.[44] When loneliness means the indifference of everyone, it is less tormenting than when it means the enmity of everyone. In the former case you are alone in a space which you know you can overcome. The tedium can be remedied. In the latter case, you no longer have any space around you where you can still meet someone interested in you. The tedium in this case is definitive.

But just as all experience gathered together over time will be accumulated in the supratemporal stability of blessedness, in the same way all the experience of what was accomplished in space will be accumulated in supraspatial existence. The supratemporality of creation will be the aeon in which time will be wrapped up and filled with the eternity of God, while the supraspatial character of creation will have the whole of space wrapped up within itself. In the light of the face of Christ and the faces of all those who will meet us, the good we have done will be reflected and in the terrifying face of Satan and in the hostility of those in hell, the evil we have done and the torment of our conscience will be reflected. The time and space in which we lived do not perish without a trace; they remain either as joy or torment.

The dynamic factor behind the growing unification of the world and its increasing unification with God, that is, behind the overcoming of space, is man. From the outset man is the point where the parts of the world and of space are linked together. He is called to gather all these parts within himself in the closest possible embrace. That is why, rather than "microcosm," Saint Maximos the Confessor prefers to call man the true "macrocosm." According to our faith man is the unifying factor of the world because through the various parts of man, and especially through his reason, he is linked with all the parts of the world. For the world as a whole is a system of materialized reasons or inner principles which human reason gradually gathers within itself through the collaboration of its various subjects.

Man becomes, or becomes again, the unifying factor of the world only to the extent to which he frees himself from the passions that separate people from one another. The potential union of all things is gradually made actual within man and progresses upwards, that is, man leads all things towards their union with God. The believer, freed from passions, overcomes his separation from his neighbors, then the separation that divides him from the sensible world which he gathers and spiritualizes in himself, then the separation between earth and paradise, then the separation between himself and the angels, and finally the separation between God and creation, as he gathers creation together in himself.

But this union of men with the world and with God was first brought about fully in Christ as the divine Logos who re-established human reason within an activity that was entirely passionless. The Son of God became man because man is the unifying link of the world.[45] At the end, Christ, "having united the created nature with the uncreated one through love... will show it as being one and the same according to the habit of grace, himself as a whole wholly interpenetrating the whole of God, becoming everything that God is except for the identity of essence. . . . "[46]

When, in the life to come, we achieve full union with God through love, we will have transcended time and space, for in God there is no interval to be overcome. "The world is a limited space and a limited stability, and time is a circumscribed movement. . . . When nature passes, however, with its operation and thought beyond space and time, namely beyond those things without which there is nothing, or above limited stability and movement, and is united directly with providence, it will discover providence as a reason which is by nature simple and stable and has no limit and hence no movement."[47] After the natural passage through time and the ages, "the nature of created things will come to rest in God who is one in nature, and no longer have any limit [which anyone might either reach or pass beyond] for in God there is no longer any interval."[48]

In Christ, God has also accepted a kenosis in the realm of space. Properly speaking, it was through Christ that God came to man in the closest possible proximity, although with his being God did not cease to be present everywhere. This kenosis is best described as consisting in the fact that, through the humanity he assumed, through the body which occupied a place in space, he made himself accessible and able to be grasped as God in the highest degree.

To support this approach towards understanding such a fact, Eastern tradition has taken account of four points: the accessibility of God is revealed through the divine energies; what is human is capable, through the purification from passions, of becoming the medium for manifesting what is divine; in Christ the human has been raised to the highest level of deification or of penetration by the divine, yet without ceasing to be human; the divine is such that it can be manifested through the human, when the latter has been purified.

The Son of God, transcending all things, has taken our nature within his divine hypostasis and, more than any other man, he has been able, through this nature, to be open to humanity as a whole and more than anyone else he has been able to gather the whole of creation into himself.

An Orthodox theologian says: "It is within the framework of this Cyrillian thought that one understands what Leontios of Jerusalem meant when he spoke of the common hypostasis of Christ: a hypostasis that, instead of being another isolated and individualized hypostasis among all the hypostases that constitute the human nature, is the hypostatic archetype of the whole of mankind, in whom 'recapitulated' mankind, and not merely an individual, recovers union with God. This is possible only if Christ's manhood is not the human nature of a mere man (ἀνθρώπου ψιλοῦ or γυμνοῦ) but that of a hypostasis independent of the limitations of created nature."[49] In Christ human nature is deified not only through the uncreated energies but also through the divine hypostasis who bears it and is manifested through it. The divine energies which radiate through his human nature do not radiate outwards from the starting point of an alien hypostasis, therefore, but from the hypostasis belonging to that nature who is at the same time the hypostasis of the divine nature, that is, Christ who, as man, is linked with us through his humanity which is organically connected with us, and embraces us also as one who is God of all. By making himself the hypostasis of a human nature which is not closed up within a human hypostasis, the Son of God is a kind of foundation of all human hypostases. As such he is likewise the foundation of all our operations, both those belonging to our nature and those inspired by grace, and together with him we, as those included in him, embrace the whole of the created world.

In Christ God is in the closest potential proximity to us and, if we make the union with him actual through faith and through liberation from the passions, we can in him be united with all who believe, and we can simultaneously hold the whole of space caught within the range of the divine-human energies of Christ which radiate through us. The distance between us and God and, among ourselves, between one another is thus overcome.

On the other hand, when a number of people actually keep themselves at a spiritual distance from Christ, the incarnate Son of God, then he too is seen, from the point of view of accessibility, as being at a distance. Such people stumble at the idea that God would be accessible to the highest possible degree and they do not believe in Christ. Thus, although in his being, on the plane of transcendence, God is everywhere, in the order of accessibility which he assumed in Christ this paradox exists: on the one hand, in Christ God is in the closest possible proximity to all; on the other hand, God allows himself to be kept at a distance, to have to be sought out (or not) by men, to yearn himself to draw near to them. That is, in Christ, God accepts space, though obviously only in order to overcome it and embrace it with our help, as he embraces us without confusing us with himself and without doing away with the space which is bound up with human beings.

The distance between ourselves and God is overcome in Christ not only because God has come down to us, but also because we are raised up to God. In Christ all of us have potentially overcome the distance separating us from God and from one another. But this has not yet happened in act. Only Christ has overcome — as man too — the distance from God both potentially and actually. Yet, in respect of the human race, even he has not actually overcome the distance separating him from everyone, since some force him to remain at a distance. But it is only in Christ that we can actually overcome the distance keeping us away from God and from one another. In him our eschatological goal has been reached: the conquering of time and space; and we too can reach it. These are conquered not only as something that lies between us and God but also as something that lies between ourselves as human beings, for as those who have been recapitulated in Christ, distance no longer exists even between us.

In Christ God is here alongside everyone, not only with his being, but also with his energy, ready to enter into action. But God does not use force to do away with the distance between him and us or the distance separating us from one another. He invites our free love to help in the overcoming of this distance, or better, he invites our response to the offer of his love, an offer which has been made in so evident and impressive a fashion through the incarnation and the cross he accepted on our behalf. The overcoming of the distance is a matter of freedom and spirituality. But when we do not make use of our freedom and spirituality to overcome the distance that separates us from Christ-God, then we are not using them to overcome the distance keeping us from our neighbor either, and this is to our own loss. For the recognition of God in Christ would mean the recognition of the whole of our own value as this has been shown to us by God through the fact that he himself became man. But Christ does not wish to extract this recognition from men by force, and by his refusal to use force in overcoming this distance, God accepts in Christ another kenosis.

On the path towards the overcoming of this distance the cross is inevitable. The very acceptance of the human face as his own face is for God a cross. Only through the cross is nearness achieved, yet at the same time it leaves our being with freedom and with the consequent risk of not recognizing God in the image of man. In this, paradoxically, there is hidden a misunderstanding of the value of man on the part of those who do not accept God. But the drawing closer to us through the cross is a force which does not cease to be active in overcoming the distance.

After the incarnation of his Son, the presence or omnipresence of God has, in general, entered into a dynamic phase through which it exercises its power of attraction over us and helps us in a much more active way than before to overcome the distance separating us from God and from one another. God's presence is not static, that is, permanently and everywhere the same, because it is a presence that is actualized between persons and comes from a Personal reality accessible to human persons. Moreover, it is a new omnipresence, belonging, that is, to the incarnate hypostasis (though not to the body itself) and hence it is found on the plane of human accessibility which has been initiated through the personal will of God who is threefold in persons.

This new, accessible, and active presence of God in Christ extends in the Church its actualization for the sake of men. From a potential omnipresence it strains to become an actual one. On the eschatological plane it will become an actual and visible omnipresence. Right now it is an actual presence within the Church, inasmuch as her members recognize through faith that Christ stands in the closest possible objective proximity to men and that owing to this proximity he can become through their faith an actual presence for them. But this presence increases in intensity with each person according to the measure of that person's effort to grow in spiritual sensibility.

Omnipotence

Just as in himself God is supratemporal and supraspatial yet makes himself present within time and present everywhere in space by coming down into relationship with created beings who are both temporal and spatial, so in the same way God transcends omnipotence, yet makes himself omnipotent by coming down into relationship with all who, through their participation in him, possess a certain power. It is in this sense that Dionysios the Areopagite says that God is above all power as the creature understands or experiences it, for he is able to bring about anything in the created order (ἡ θεαρχία πάσης ἐξῄρηται . . . δυνάμεως).[50]

God surpasses every power (πᾶσαν δύναμιν . . . ὑπερέχων).[51] Yet the one who has in himself the source of all power or omnipotence and is its cause, is not thereby lacking in power, but transcends it in a positive sense.[52] This also implies his character as person, for only the person is more than the power he manifests or would wish to manifest; and only divine Person is above the power he manifests or would wish to manifest and is always unlimited in his source, producing "all things through his power which is total and unthwarted."[53]

It could be argued that nature, as conceived by pantheism, is also inexhaustible in the manifestation of its power; it stays within a cyclic repetition and dissolves existing individuations in order to create others which are identical. The newness in its various manifestations is insignificant. On the contrary, the person is always new in his manifestations. As creature, the human person is new on the same unique plane of the created order. The person is only the image of that infinite newness of divine Person on the plane which surpasses the limited created order. If creatures were to present themselves only within individuations which benefit from a created power, then the existence of God as one distinct from nature and enjoying a real omnipotence could be disputed. But creation participates in the power of God not only in its created form, but also in its uncreated form. This is equivalent to direct, always new, and infinite participation in God as person. Only participation in God through grace proves his existence as something distinct from nature. Here lies the importance of the participation of the creature in the uncreated energies of God.

All the forms and stages of existence have come into being, continue in being, and develop through participation in the power of God, a participation which is offered to them freely and in limitless variety, either as the foundation of natural powers or in the direct form of the uncreated energies. "This inexhaustible Power ... guides the powers which keep each creature in being. It establishes the unshakable remaining of the world. To those made godike it grants the power for deification itself."[54]

In this the possibility is also given for the power of creation to grow towards the infinite through participation in the infinite power of God which transcends the limits of creation's own created power.

But from another point of view, omnipotence is implied in God's character as absolute Person. A reality with the character of an object, or an impersonal force cannot be omnipotent, that is, powerful from all points of view, because it has no power over its own movements (whether these change it in some essential manner or do not change it at all), but, in regard to these movements, it is subjected to a system of laws. The reality which is not free with regard to its own motion or absence of motion has, to put is plainly, no power at all. Such a reality is the support of a certain power and, at the same time, is powerless, not even taking into account the fact that this kind of power is in one way strictly limited. The explanation for a power like this which is subject to certain laws can only lie in a will, and the will that produces the power simultaneously provides it with particular laws as limits. Only an absolute will has true omnipotence.

The formal definition of omnipotence is: the power of a person to do whatever he wants. This definition does not have in view a will that limits itself in its acts, in function of what the subject knows he can do. That would no longer be omnipotence. The power of that person would be limited.

If a power without will, such as that of impersonal or involuntary movements, is not a true power, then the will that is limited in its manifestations by a power lesser than its own sphere would indicate a subject — not an absolute subject, however, but one similar to the human subject which is unable to overcome every obstacle, or do whatever it wants. In both cases omnipotence is lacking. In both cases a limited power is given which seeks its own explanation; the explanation is only to be found, however, in an unlimited power, that is, in a personal will which can do anything it wants.

In God no act is performed independently of his will. And the divine will does not choose its objectives either in function of the consciousness of a limited power, or in an arbitrary manner; it chooses in function of the good, and the good is one with the being of God. For God is "essential Good" (ὡς οὐσιῶδες ἀγαθόν) as Dionysios the Areopagite says.[55] Or, as Saint John of Damascus says, in God "the good is concomitant to his essence."[56] Because of his infinity, no objective that God might choose in an arbitrary fashion could move outside the order of his being or outside its dependence on that being. Not to be able to work against his will means not to be able to work against his being. And if the omnipotence of the divine being is in solidarity with its infinity, then the possibility of working against it implies a decline from omnipotence. Thus one thing only God cannot do: he cannot decline to the state of not being able to do all that he wants.

Dionysios the Areopagite treats as a sorcerer or conjurer whoever asks: " 'If God is all-powerful, how then is it possible for your theologian to declare that there are some things he cannot do?' " Dionysios observes: "He is here criticizing the divine Paul for stating that God 'cannot deny himself' " (2 Tim 2.13). Then he explains: "Denial of the true self is a falling away from truth. Now truth is a being and a falling away from truth is a falling away from being. If the truth is a being and if a denial of the truth is a falling away from being, God cannot fall from being. One might say that he is not lacking in being, that he is not able to lack power, that he does not know how to lack knowledge."[57]

But the good *par excellence*, or the absolute good, coincides with perfect being or with God himself for the further reason that the good cannot be an abstract good, the object of pure thought, but must be a subsistent good which, as such, is a reference of one person to another. A good which does not refer in a conscious manner, and hence personally, to someone else who perceives it consciously, hence to another person, is not itself good. The absolute good is thus the perfect relationship or love between absolute persons who form the greatest unity that can achieved without having persons confused with each other. And since, in God, the good is eternal, this good is nothing other than the greatest, eternal, and unconfused unity among the three divine persons. The eternal good is the holy Trinity.

All God's acts of power directed outside himself, as having to be in conformity with his being as interpersonal communion, that is, with the good, also reach out as foundation and perfection of the communion of other persons with himself and among themselves, just as in the case of the personal Trinitarian communion. This extension of the good as personal communion cannot consist in a multiplication of the divine persons. The divine persons cannot multiply in time. In that case they would no longer be divine persons. Moreover, a multiplicity of eternal persons, produced on the basis of some internal necessity, could not be numbered and this would render the perfection of communion between them impossible. And if God were not able to bring into existence persons who, though not divine, were capable of communion, he would be enclosed within himself and could not show forth his omnipotence voluntarily.

By deciding, therefore, to act outside himself in conformity with his being, which is to say, as the good that is eternal interpersonal communion, God makes use of his power to create persons who are to move towards the perfection of communion with him and among themselves. This movement is to come from themselves on the one hand, while on the other hand created persons are to be placed within this movement by God himself through his coming to meet them. For this purpose he both implants in them a natural power of movement towards himself and also strengthens this natural created power of theirs with the uncreated power of his benevolence which comes to meet them.

There can be no other purpose for the manifestation of God's power outside himself, that is, for the movement which he sustains through the created power implanted in creatures and the uncreated power offered to them.

In his work *The Ambigua* Saint Maximos undertook (against a

Platonizing Origenism) a vast and profound defense of the movement of creatures. While Origenistic thought held movement to be a result of sin or of the will of certain spirits to quit their pre-existent unity in God, and considered bodies and the material world as a prison created by God for the punishment of these spirits, Saint Maximos treats movement as a means given to creatures by God from the moment of their creation for the purpose of achieving their full union with him; it is, therefore, a movement that passes from *existence bestowed as gift to good existence,* which is acquired through the contribution their own will makes in actualizing their power of movement to go forward in a real way towards God, and finally to *eternal good existence* in God. During the entire course of this movement and particularly at its end-point in God, created beings enjoy the uncreated energies of God, that is, the perfection of their being and power through participation in the fullness of divine life. The power given us by God has as its purpose that we put into real operation those natural powers of ours which have also been given us by God; this process of putting them into real operation is nothing other than the movement stamped upon us and guided towards God, as towards the good proper to us, by our own will and consciousness.

"The whole reason (meaning) of the entire creation of the rational beings has three modes: that of existence, that of good existence, and that of eternal existence. The first, namely existence alone, is that which was given to those who exist through being; the second, or the good existence, was given to them through their deliberative will as the ones who are in movement by nature; and the third, or the eternal good existence, was given through the generosity of grace. Through the first mode, power is offered to them, through the second, activity, through the third, the ceasing of activity. The reason of the existence which by nature has only the power for activity cannot have a full activity without a deliberative will. And the reason of the good existence, having, through the deliberative will, only the activity of natural power, does not have this activity fully without nature. And that of the blessed eternal existence, circumscribing the former ones, that is, the power of the first reason and the activity of the second, is neither intrinsic to beings as a power, nor does it necessarily follow the deliberative will . . . but it is their end, making stable the nature with regard to power, and the will with regard to activity . . . . Therefore, if activity makes no use of nature's power

— either in conformity with nature or contrary to it — it will receive as an end either happiness or unhappiness, that is, the eternal existence in which the souls rest and all movement will cease. And the eighth or the first day, or better, the unique and infinite day, is the unshadowed and all-shining presence of God who will appear after the cessation of everything that moves. By coming then in his entirety into the entire being of those who, through freedom, have used well the reason of existence, he will provide them with the blessed eternal existence through the participation in him as the only one who is properly existent, existent as good, and eternally existent. And to those who have used, through freedom, the reason of existence contrary to nature he will give instead of the blessed eternal existence, unhappy eternal existence."[58]

If God manifests his power outwardly in order to raise up other persons to communion with him (or to the good), he is putting into operation, from within his omnipotence, both the power to create persons limited in being and in their own natural power, as well as the gradual bestowal of his uncreated power in degrees corresponding to the measure of their capability to make use of it and so as not to be overwhelmed by it. This is the kenosis or condescension of God in the manifestation of his power. On the other hand, the created beings are wonderful, for they are capable of receiving God wholly within themselves. God has created a being capable of becoming god through grace, a nature capable of being, with this end in view, the nature of a divine hypostasis.

Thus in his manifestations God descends and exalts himself freely (that is, in a way that is not constrained either by an internal law or by an external one), so that he might give created subjects the possibility of their own free manifestations, their free acceptance of communion with himself. For communion is conditional on the freedom of those who bring it about. The kenosis of God is thus the condition for extending his interior communion as the Good with persons other than the divine persons. Yet, in one way, even this benevolent descent which seeks to extend the good, to extend communion, is itself the sign of his freedom and absolute power. For, according to our faith, only absolute Person can bring persons into existence out of nothing, persons who, although created, are themselves absolute too, and are even able to set themselves freely in opposition to God. Consequently, by creating such persons who are in a certain sense absolute, God's trust in his omnipotence is manifested, that is, his certainty that these persons will not endanger his omnipotence, given the fact of the absoluteness that is God's through his own being, as distinct from these persons who are absolute through their participation in him, on the basis of his will.[59]

In another way, however, the kenosis accepted by God is not an identical, definitive state. God descends to creatures in order to raise them ever higher towards himself, and hence in some fashion he too rises up to the bestowing of certain ever higher degrees of power, hence of the manifestation of his own power. The eternal reserve of these ever more exalted bestowals of gifts is his omnipotence. Thus the power given to creation by God and which has as its purpose the ascent of creation to direct participation in God's uncreated power — his energies — is itself, as solidary with time and space, a condition for the relation of God's omnipotence with creation.

As source of the ever more exalted movement of the creature towards the infinite God, limited power will find its fulfillment (a fulfillment it cannot reach in itself — as is true also of time and space within which this movement is effected) when God himself bestows the gift of himself wholly upon his creature in a way that transcends its own movement. Then the creature will participate in the life, and thus in the unlimited power, of God without being confused with him and conscious always of enjoying God as much as this is possible for a creature, which is to say through participation, not through being.

As one who manifests his power in the form and degree adopted to leading creation towards full communion with himself, God is, by preference, given the title *Pantokrator*[60] in the tradition of Eastern Christianity. From the infinite reserve of his omnipotence or supra—omnipotence God manifests as much as is necessary for the conservation, salvation, and the guidance of creation towards the perfection of communion with himself. He does not manifest his omnipotence in a capricious manner. The term *Pantokrator* preferred in the Eastern Church seeks to emphasize that God's omnipotence, in its relation to the world, has emerged from the state of indetermination and defined itself voluntarily and out of love for the world as a power that acts on a level which the world can bear and acts for the benefit of the world, not against it.

In the Churches of the West the term "omnipotent" has been maintained in connection with the idea that the operation of God

The Super-Essential Attributes of God 191

could also work against the world, if not for its destruction, at least for its continual limitation and domination, so that the world's consciousness of its own nothingness might continuously be preserved within it. If in Eastern Christian doctrine the omnipotence of God is the source of the deification of creation, and hence of the communication of the divine power to creatures, in the West omnipotence has been conceived more as a means of defending God against creation. From this Catholicism has drawn its conclusions about the domination of states and human society by the Church, while Protestantism has drawn its affirmation of the exclusiveness of God's effective power over against any such effective power in human beings which is always regarded as sin (*Allein-wirklichkeit und Allein-wirksamkeit Gottes*). Salvation itself is seen as a satisfaction offered to the honor of God to make up for the offending of that honor by man, or as a softening of God's wrath.

In the Church of the East God is glorified for the gifts he gives man for the purpose of man's deification. The Orthodox East, which continues the thought of the Fathers, has placed emphasis on the sustaining, protecting, and helping goodness of God (God as refuge, as shelter), on encouraging the fulfillment of human aspirations and potentialities, on the trust which is to be placed in these, and on respect for human freedom. Salvation is seen as a new descent of the divine life among men, as the opening of the prospect of their full participation in God through resurrection and deification.

Thus while Western Christianity has represented more a mistrustful brake on humanity's path towards progress, the Orthodox Churches have always supported the peoples' aspirations for progress. In the Christian East the idea of an energetic and gift-giving God has been thrown into relief, a God who communicates continually more exalted energies to men according to the measure of their growth in order to lead them on to those stages which are higher still and thus benefit the world and lead it to its perfection. The Christian East has put more emphasis on God's love for the world in his will to lead it towards full communion with himself in love, while Western Christianity has emphasized more the omnipotence of God who wants to have the world hold him in respect. In the East the lordship of Christ has never been separated from his goodness. It has been viewed paradoxically as the lordship of "the Lamb who was slain" (Rev 5.12-13), just as the term *Pantokratōr* has been associated with that

"Father," good, kind, and intimate.

Paul Evdokimov infers this parental relationship of God with the world from his relation as Father to his Son. Thus the world is explained through the love within the holy Trinity. He says: "The word *God* makes us think spontaneously of a being who holds all powers, and this brings its omnipotence to the fore; but this is never an omnipotence pure and simple, without object. . . . 'I believe in God, the Father almighty, Creator of heaven and earth.' The divine omnipotence is qualified immediately as *paternal*. Before everything else, and essentially, God is Father and only after is He Creator, Judge — and what lies at the heart of the Christian hope: Savior and Comforter. And He is all these because He is Father. Thus, if at the center of the vision of God there is placed the divine paternity, the eternal communion between the Father and the Son, at the center of revelation there corresponds to this the communion between God the Father and man, His child. The essential theme of salvation is that of adoption — sonship."[61]

In Eastern Christianity the sense of salvation is also determined by the intertrinitarian love of God. Christ became man in order to raise man to the communion of Trinitarian love, to deify him; moreover, this communion is not brought about through some external force which exists to frighten man, but through condescending love.

In solidarity with this approach the Eastern Church has considered spiritual power as a greater and more direct power of God than physical power or power over the world. Spiritual power is accompanied by kenosis in respect of external power. Saint Paul the Apostle says: "[The Lord] said to me, 'My grace is sufficient for you, for my power is made perfect in weakness.' I will all the more gladly boast of my weaknesses, that the power of Christ may rest upon me" (2 Cor 12.9). The spiritual power is so great in comparison with the physical one that it can overwhelm the latter, and because it is direct divine power, it produces effects which physical power cannot produce. Thus the miracles produced by this power are called simply "powers," as being the effects of a higher power or of the direct power of God, while physical power is only an indirect result of the other. "Then he began to upbraid the cities where most of his mighty works had been done" (Mt 11.20; Lk 10.13; Mt 13.54,58; Mk 6.2,5,14; Mt 14.2; Lk 5.17, 6.19, 9.1; Acts 3.12, 8.13; Gal 3.5).[62]

That is why Saint Maximos the Confessor understands movement (which he considers as a way to God) as the movement whereby man is made spiritual, the movement whereby he grows by strengthening the power of the Spirit over lower tendencies. Its stages are: the purification of passions; a comprehension of the divine meanings or reasons of things not marked by the passions; a comprehension of the divine meanings or reasons of things not marked by the passions; the understanding of God in a simple act which is simultaneously complete union with him. The growth of the human spirit in power is an ethical growth, for due to the fact that no one can approach God as source of power unless he loves him as the good, growth in existence is a growth in the good.

In the life to come this spiritual power, whether of good or of love — and in fact it is not so much the power of man as of God who pours it into whoever has ascended to God through the stages mentioned above — will entirely overwhelm the physical power and will do away with the worldly power which at times has adopted attitudes opposed to God. "Then comes the end, when the Lord delivers the kingdom to God the Father after destroying every rule and every authority and power" (1 Cor 15.24). As time and space will be overwhelmed by eternity and be spiritual supraspatiality, so will the physical and worldly powers be overwhelmed by the power of the divine Spirit which has become man's own. The whole of created being will become bearer of the uncreated energies.

The divine being, as supreme being, unlimited and self-existent, is the ultimate and inexhaustible source of all energies; moreover, it is the source of certain infinite energies and, as such, the cause of any kind of created power.

By the very fact that God brings into existence different hypostatized substances, God also gives them a power of their own. Just as all substances are joined in unity among themselves and with God — as having their origin in the divine essence — in the same way their powers are linked to one another among themselves and also with the divine power, because they have their origin in the power of the divine essence. Dionysios the Areopagite says: "In short, nothing in the world lacks the almighty power of God to support and to surround it, for that which completely lacks power has neither existence, nor individuality, nor even a place in the world."[63]

The infinite energy of the divine essence is spiritual. Hence it is capable of overwhelming any physical power, any created power. But it does this gradually through the agency of the human spirit, gradually strengthening the energy of the latter by means of its own uncreated energy.

If God could have created from nothing any other substance together with its corresponding power, how nuch more can he use his own spiritual power mediated through the human spirit to overwhelm all created substance and its power. Saint Maximos the Confessor insists very much upon the fact that man is the link that unifies the world and joins the world to God.[64] He has this character because in himself, even in his biological dimension, he subjects physical power to the spirit, that is, he spiritualizes it. Through knowledge he holds the universe within his spirit. But man would achieve the genuine spiritualization of nature only when, through the energies of the divine Spirit, he would actualize all the powers of his spirit. In Christ this has been brought about in a climactic way and in the power of Christ those who unite themselves with him through faith and live like him can do the same.

The full victory of the divine spiritual power over nature has been realized in the resurrection of Christ. Karl Rahner has drawn attention to the fact that the resurrection of Christ is the fulfillment of our aspiration that the spirit be victorious over the automatic laws of nature, an aspiration implanted in the human person. Rahner calls this fact "the transcendental basis of the resurrection" or "the transcendental hope of the resurrection." In this transcendental aspiration and capacity for victory over nature through the spirit there is even provided the foundation of a "transcendental christology."[65]

The resurrection of Christ is included in the horizon of our existence, a horizon consisting in the fact that we live within a tension towards perfection. Man is a being who looks to a future which is his fulfillment. The transcendental hope of the resurrection is simultaneously "the horizon of understanding for our experience of faith with respect to the resurrection of Christ."[66]

The resurrection fulfills the expectation implanted in the human being because it makes the human person capable of a perfect and eternal communion with God, the supreme Personal reality, and with his neighbors, and overcomes all the restrictions imposed upon this communion by nature in its earthly state. Thanks to the full spiritualization of matter, the resurrection makes possible an intimacy which is interpersonal, perfect, and eternal.

In Christ, the Son of God becomes bearer of the perfect Trinitarian love for men and also of human love raised up to the capacity of responding perfectly to that love. In the state of resurrection, moreover, the Son extends unobstructedly this perfect divine-human dialogue of love which has been realized in himself, by drawing us also into it. In Christ, man has received the power to love God within a unique love together with the only begotten Son of God, and to love men with the very love of God. In Christ's resurrected state this power is communicated to us too, and we are to appropriate it fully in our own resurrected state.

This love, which has passed through the supreme sacrifice, was the spiritual "power" that raised up Christ and was victorious over the inflexible laws of nature. And this "power" will raise us up too (1 Cor 15.43). Because it is the fruit of love and the realized image of perfect love, the resurrected state is true life. "We shall live with him by the power of God" shown to us (cf. 2 Cor 13.4). A wonderful thing is the power of God radiating from creation. Yet it would remain ambiguous and devoid of any clear meaning if it remained subjected eternally to all the inadequacies that burden it down now. Through the resurrection the power of God shows itself as something infinitely greater, infinitely more full of meaning. God will fill this world with his uncreated glory when he clothes it in immortality and makes of it the transcendent milieu of his own endless depth of life and meanings.

NOTES

1. *Questions to Thalassius* 65, PG 90.757C.
2. Maximos the Confessor, *The Ambigua*, PG 91.1220B-C.
3. *Gnostic Chapters* 1.49, PG 90.1101A.
4. Symeon the New Theologian, *Hymn* 8.39-45, ed. Koder, p. 218; ET Maloney, p. 31.
5. *The Divine Names* 2.7, PG 3.645A-B; ET Luibheid/Rorem, pp. 63-64.
6. *The Ambigua*, PG 91.1081B-C.
7. Ibid., PG 91.1312B-1313B.
8. Ibid., PG 91.1305B-C.
9. Cf. *The Ambigua*, PG 91.1096A.
10. *The Ambigua*, PG 91.1308B.
11. Ibid., PG 91.1196C.
12. Georgios Pachymeres, *Paraphrase of the Divine Names* 2.4, PG 3.664C.

13. Cf. Maximos the Confessor, *The Ambigua*, PG 91.1192D-93C.
14. *The Ambigua*, PG 91.1196B.
15. Karl Barth, *Church Dogmatics*, vol. 2.1, The Doctrine of God, tr. J. L. M. Haire (Edinburgh, 1957) p. 494.
16. *The Divine Names* 5.4, PG 3.817D; ET Luibheid/Rorem, p. 98.
17. *The Ambigua*, PG 91.1164B and cf. Acts 17.26.
18. Ibid., PG 91.1137C-D, 1137B-C.
19. *Third Letter to Akindynos* 17, ed. Christou, vol. 1, p. 308.15-26.
20. *The Holy Spirit* 15.36, PG 32.132B.
21. *The Beatitudes*, Homily 7, PG 44.1280C; ET H. Graef, *St. Gregory of Nyssa. The Lord's Prayer, The Beatitudes*, ACW 18, Westminster MD 1954, p. 156.
22. Maximos the Confessor, *The Ambigua*, PG 91.1072A.
23. *The Ambigua*, PG 91.1073B-C.
24. Ibid., PG 91.1392C-D
25. Ibid., PG 91.1144B.
26. Ibid., PG 91.1164B-C.
27. *Questions to Thalassius* 59, PG 90.609A.
28. Ibid., 65, PG 90.760B.
29. Reference not found but cf. *Adoration and Worship in Spirit and Truth* 1, 9, 12, 15, 16, 17, PG 68.197B-D, 592C-93A, 824A-25A, 985B-D, 1025B, 1113C-16B.
30. Cf. *Adoration and Worship in Spirit and Truth* 9, PG 68.620D-621A.
31. Hans Küng, *Menschwerdung Gottes* (Freiburg etc. 1970) pp. 666-667, citing K. Kitamori and H. Ott, *Wirklichkeit und Glaube*, vol. 1.
32. Cf. Karl Rahner, "Christology within an Evolutionary View of the World," in *Theological Investigations*, vol. 5, tr. K.-H. Krüger (Baltimore/London, 1966) pp. 164-66.
33. *The Ambigua*, PG 91.1392D.
34. *Homilies on Leviticus* 7.2.41-46, 51-54, ed. M. Borret, SC 286, pp. 310/312.
35. Ibid. 7.2.62-66, 68-72, ed. Borret, pp. 312/314.
36. Ibid. 7.2.85-88, ed. Borret, p. 314.
37. Ibid. 7.2.111-112, ed Borret, p. 316.
38. Blaise Pascal, *Pensées*, Section 7, Pensée 553, "Le Mystère de Jésus," ed. M. Autrand (Paris 1981), p. 164. "Jesus will be in agony until the end of the world."
39. *Letter* 2, PG 91.396C.
40. *The Ambigua*, PG 91.1180B-81A. Saint Maximos also says (1181A-B): "And again if the being of all things cannot be infinite inasmuch as all these things are multiple (for being has as its boundary the multiple extent of all things, an extent which circumscribes the inner principle of the existence and of the mode of existence of being — since the essence itself of all things is not free from these), then evidently neither will the hypostasis of each individual thing be free from circumscription, as the hypostases will in principle circumscribe one another with respect to number and substance."
41. *Entsakralisierung* (Paderborn, 1970) p. 120.
42. Cf. Neagoe Basarab, *The Instructions of Neagoe Basarab to His Son Theodosius*, [in Romanian] eds. F. Moisil/D. Zamfirescu/G. Mihaila (Bucharest, 1970) Instructions 2.12, pp. 329.32-332.34.
43. Cf. the theme of Yannaras, *De l'absence et de l'inconnaissance de Dieu* (n. 1 above).
44. Neagoe Basarab, *Instructions* 2.12, eds. Moisil/Zamfirescu/Mihaila, pp. 331.16-332.9, describes Paradise as seeing the face of Christ, and hell as having to look always at the face of Satan.

45. Cf. *The Ambigua*, PG 91.1305B-1308C, 1313B.
46. Ibid. PG 91.1308B.
47. *Questions to Thalassius* 65, PG 90.757D-760A.
48. Ibid. 65, PG 90.757C.
49. John Meyendorff, *Christ in Eastern Christian Thought* (Crestwood, NY 1975) p. 75.
50. *The Divine Names* 8.1, PG 3.889C.
51. Ibid. 8.2, PG 3.889D.
52. Ibid. 8.2, PG 3.889D-892A: "Πᾶσαν δύναμιν ... προέχων ... ὡς πάσης δυνάμεως αἴτιος".
53. Ibid 8.2, PG 3.889D; ET Luibheid/Rorem, p. 111.
54. Ibid 8.5, PG 3.892C-893A; ET Luibheid/Rorem, p. 111-112.
55. Ibid 4.1, PG 3.693B; ET Luibheid/Rorem, p. 71.
56. John of Damascus, *The Orthodox Faith* 1.13, PG 94.853D-856A; ET F. H. Chase, Jr., *Saint John of Damascus. Writings*, FC 37 (NY, 1958) p. 199.
57. *The Divine Names* 8.6. PG 3.893B-C; ET Luibheid/Rorem, p. 112.
58. *The Ambigua*, PG 91.1392A-D.
59. A God who would fear the creature would no longer be God.
60. See the entry on παντοκράτωρ in G. W. H. Lampe, *A Patristic Greek Lexicon* (Oxford, 1961) p. 1005 and also E. Lucchesi Palli, "Christus. Sondertypen. 2) Christus — Pantocrator," in *Lexikon der christlichen Ikonographie*, ed. E. Kirschbaum (Rome etc., 1968) vol. 1, pp. 392-393. [Ed. note.]
61. *La femme et le salut du monde* (Tournai/Paris, 1958), p. 147.
62. For δύναμαι/δύναμις see Lampe, *A Patristic Greek Lexicon*, pp. 388-91 and W. Grundmann in *Theological Dictionary of the New Testament*, ed. G. Kittel (Grand Rapids, 1964) vol. 2, pp. 284-317. [Ed. note.]
63. *The Divine Names* 8.5, PG 3.893A; ET Luibheid/Rorem, p. 112.
64. *The Ambigua*, PG 91.1305B-D.
65. Karl Rahner, "Grundlinien einer systematischen Christologie," in K. Rahner/W. Thüsing, *Christologie — systematisch und exegetisch* (Freiburg etc., 1972) p. 47 and "Resurrection. 1. Resurrection of Christ. A. Preliminary Considerations," in *Sacramentum Mundi*, ed. K. Rahner et al., (NY/London, 1970), vol. 5, pp. 323-324.
66. Rahner, "Grundlinien," pp. 38-39 and "Resurrection," p. 323.

Chapter Nine

The Spiritual Attributes of God

"God is Spirit" (Jn 4.24). The divine essence is spiritual essence. This implies more than just immateriality; it means also that the divine essence is support for spiritual attributes: the support of knowledge, of justice, of purity, and of love.

The attributes connected with the divine existence certainly have a spiritual character, because, as supreme existence, the divine existence is itself a spiritual existence. Those attributes which are directly spiritual, however, illuminate the character of Spirit proper to the divine essence in a particular fashion.

The attributes connected with the spirituality of God are also more difficult to understand, that is, more apophatic, than those connected with his existence. For, if the divine existence and its accompanying attributes can be conceived from a formal point of view — and as distinguishing themselves from the existence of creatures and its accompanying attributes by the fact that they are freed from the aspect of insufficiency and from the formal development which these latter possess — the attributes of the spirituality of God convey a content which is similar to but not identical with that of creatures endowed with spirituality.

But who can penetrate into the infinite richness of the content of the spiritual life of God? And who can define that content when even the content of the spiritual life of creatures endowed with spirituality is so complex and impossible of being defined exactly — especially when it is a matter of a creature knowing not only its own content, but also that of another creature of the same nature?

For spirituality is the content that belongs most of all to the person. And the person is known only to the extent to which he reveals himself and to which he can reveal himself and be understood by others. It is a content under the watch of one's own freedom. "But, as it is written,

> 'What no eye has seen, nor ear heard,
> nor the heart of man conceived,
> what God has prepared for those who love him,'

God has revealed to us through the Spirit. For the Spirit searches everything, even the depths of God. For what person knows a man's thoughts except the spirit of the man which is in him? So also no one comprehends the thoughts of God except the Spirit of God" (1 Cor 2.9-11).

That is why the holy Fathers say that we know in general that God is infinite (a formal attribute of his existence, we would say), but what this infinity is (its spiritual content) we do not know. We even know the attributes connected with the spirituality of God as being infinite, for his existence is infinite in all respects, but we do not know the concrete content of the infinity of these attributes.

Omniscience

We know that God knows everything, but what this everything is and how God knows it, we do not know. Dionysios the Areopagite ascribes to God knowledge of all things and transcendence of all knowledge in a way which combines both: "This, I think, is what scripture means with the declaration, 'He knows all things before their birth.' The divine Mind does not acquire the knowledge of things from things. Rather, of itself and in itself it precontains and comprehends the awareness and understanding and being of everything in terms of their cause. This is not a knowledge of each specific class. What is here is a single embracing causality which knows and contains all things. Take the example of light. In itself it has a prior and causal knowledge of darkness. What it knows about darkness it knows not from another, but from the fact of being light."[1] In this sense God is "Mind beyond mind" and "word beyond speech."[2]

God does not understand as we do, does not think as we do, does not know as we do, but in a manner which is above us. In this sense we deny him these spiritual activities. But he is the cause of these activities of the creature and for this reason we attribute them to him in a sense which transcends their meaning known by us. "Now, if you will, let us give praise to the good and eternal Life for being wise, for being the principle of wisdom, the subsistence of all wisdom, for transcending all wisdom and understanding. It is not simply the case that God is so overflowing with wisdom that 'his understanding is beyond measure' but, rather, he actually transcends all reason, all intelligence and all wisdom."[3] Thus we both participate in the knowledge of God and, through union with him, we also grow from rational knowledge, based on the reasons given by God, to a knowledge similar to his own.

One distinction between the manner in which God knows and the manner in which we ourselves know lies in the fact that he knows all things within his very self, in his quality of being their cause. "The divine Mind, therefore, takes in all things in a total knowledge which is transcendent. Because it is the Cause of all things it has a foreknowledge of everything."[4] "He knows everything else and, if I may put it so, he knows them from the very beginning and therefore brings them into being. . . . The divine Mind does not acquire the knowledge of things from things. Rather, of itself and in itself it precontains and comprehends the awareness and understanding and being of everything in terms of their cause."[5]

Western theology became entangled in discussion of the question as to whether God's knowledge of himself differs from his knowledge of creatures. Karl Barth maintains that God's knowledge in respect of creatures is finite, inasmuch as these themselves are finite, while his knowledge in respect of himself is infinite since he is infinite.[6] Catholic theology, on the contrary, asserts that God's knowledge is infinite both in respect of himself and in respect of creatures, for every act of God is infinite and, therefore, hence also his understanding (*intellectu infinitus*, according to the definition of the 1st Vatican Council).[7] The difficulty for both answers lies in the fact that they make a separation between God's knowledge in respect of creatures and his knowledge in respect of himself.

Dionysios the Areopagite does not separate these two kinds of knowledge. He says: "Consequently, God does not possess a private knowledge of himself and a separate knowledge of all the creatures in common. The universal Cause, by knowing itself, can hardly be ignorant of the things which proceed from it and of which it is the source. This, then, is how God knows all things, not by understanding things, but by understanding himself."[8]

But in knowing the creatures, since he knows himself as their cause, God does not detach the entire content of his existence from his quality of being their cause. Thus the knowledge of his own existence is implied in God's knowledge of created things. For only his entire existence is a sufficient explanation of their meaning. God sees creatures in the entire light of his existence, a light that is incomprehensible to us.

Unlike God we detach the knowledge of things from the knowledge of God. Or, at least, when we begin to unite these two knowledges, we know God only in his character as the cause of things; it is not something of God in himself that we know.⁹ On the superior levels of the spiritual life, however, we too come to know more of God, just as in the life to come we will know him fully (1 Cor 13.12), because we are completely united with him and he is wholly within the whole of us.¹⁰

Thus we cannot know creatures fully in this life — except those of us who have become saints — as God knows them; that is, our knowledge in respect of things is not identical with his own. For by detaching created things from the knowledge of God, or from the whole of his knowledge, we do not even know the things themselves in the fullness of their meaning.

The Eastern Fathers in general declare that full knowledge is the union between the one who knows and the one who is known, just as ignorance causes separation or is the effect of separation. Dionysios the Areopagite says: "If knowledge unites knower and known, while ignorance is always the cause of change and of the inconsistency of the ignorant. . . ."¹¹ Therefore, by knowing God perfectly in the life to come we will also be united permanently with him.

In this sense the knowledge of God possessed by those who — according to Dionysios the Areopagite — have made spiritual progress by going out of themselves, cannot be equated with the conception that God is beyond all possibility of approach within a totally inaccessible transcendence, as Hans Urs von Balthasar affirms.¹² For union means both the accessibility of God and that the person who unites himself with God persists as person. It means only that the human mind must abandon its created powers in order to unite itself with God, for the power to achieve this union comes only from God. Dionysios says: "What we should really consider is this. The human mind has a capacity to think, through which it looks on conceptual things, and a unity which transcends the nature of the mind, through which it is joined to things beyond itself. And this transcending characteristic must be given to the words we use about God. They must not be given the human sense. We should be taken wholly out of ourselves and become wholly of God, since it is better to belong to God rather than to ourselves. Only when we are with God will the divine gifts be poured out onto us."¹³

This conception of knowledge through union, and of our progress in knowledge as a progress in union, stands in solidarity with the understanding of time as a path towards eternity and towards union with God in love. Progress in the love of God is progress in the union with him, and this in turn is progress in the knowledge of God and of creatures until they are fully known within the full union and love that are identical with "eternal life" (Jn 3.16).

We wish to mention first of all that this kind of knowledge which comes about through the sort of union which does not confuse — a knowledge possessed by God in respect of creatures and by creatures in respect of God — implies the personal character of God and of those known by him by the very fact that they too know him. Knowledge of things also presupposes that the one who knows goes out of himself. But this presupposes even more a further going out towards other persons. Thus they come to the point where they, through knowledge, possess things in common. In the case of things, however, no union is brought about to which the things themselves contribute, because they have no free dimension of depth, distinct from their surface dimension, something which they could voluntarily keep hidden; hence, no spiritual progress in love is demanded in order to know such a depth. In the case of a person, however, one person must be united in love with another in order to know that person from within in the same way as he is known by himself, and in order for both of them to be enriched through this knowledge. God is certainly united with things — much more than we are — through the knowledge he has of them as one who is their cause. But he is not united with things through a reciprocal union, but as things that bear our seal upon them, or as the seal of the personal relationship between himself and men. Only because of this are things not lost in God or in men.

The second conclusion that results from the fact that no full knowledge exists outside the union in love between the one who knows and the one who is known — hence, that neither distance from the known personal realities, nor total solitude offers the possibility of a complete knowledge — is that God has a perfect knowledge of himself, inasmuch as he is threefold in persons. Full knowledge is always love also, and as such is directed towards another person. The self-knowledge of another person does not give him the joy of love in respect of what that person knows. Through the Trinity of the fully united divine persons, God fulfills the condition of perfect personal knowledge.

In the final analysis, knowledge is the loving reference of one subject to another subject. Even through reference to an object, the knowing subject has indirect reference to another subject, and it is only through this reference that he knows himself and actualizes himself as subject. This kind of pole of perfect reference is possessed by God within himself. He refers to himself as to other persons and these persons refer one to the other reciprocally and perfectly. In his continuous movement towards the Son who is in him, and in the continuous movement of the Son towards the Father, the Father knows himself in his reference to the Son, knowing the Son and knowing himself in the Son. The perfect knowledge or perfect omniscience of God consists in the fact that each divine person knows the other in himself, but in his quality as another person. Hence each person himself knows and actualizes himself perfectly and eternally. This is due to the dynamic reciprocal interiority of the persons, what is called the *perichôrêsis*. This interiority must not be understood, however, after the likeness of physical interiority. It consists in the fact that each person is intentionally open to the others and directed towards them in a love which is total and infinite, and that each person holds on to nothing for himself, but is given wholly to the others. It is a total and infinite spiritual *perichôrêsis* of conscious love.

Within the reciprocal knowledge of the Trinitarian persons as infinite subjects there is given in God, simultaneously with eternity, the basis for the possibility of the knowledge of other subjects, and hence also of the creation of subjects who are limited in themselves. Through this love which gives him knowledge, God comes down to the interiority found in created limited subjects, yet by means of his love God raises them up at the same time to their interiority in him, thus opening up for them the road towards his knowledge.

Given that the source of this action of God lies in his Trinitarian communion, Saint Isaak the Syrian says: "The sun that shines within him [the man who is pure in soul] is the light of the Holy Trinity."[14]

Nothing is understood apart from the holy Trinity. Thus Saint Gregory of Nazianzos calls God a threefold sun with a single brilliance: "nor are they divided in will or parted in power;... but the Godhead is, to speak concisely, undivided in separate Persons; and there is one mingling of lights, as it were of three suns joined to each other."[15] If there were not three suns, there would be no brilliance. One sun by itself would shine no more: "because if you overthrow any of the three you will have overthrown the whole."[16] If among the created essences some are subsistent "minds" without bodies (angels), while others have bodies, God is the supraessential "Mind" identical with the ocean of light where no darkness exists, or he is the supraessential subject who dwells in light unapproachable to man and is covered with the darkness of transcendence (cf. 1 Tim 6.16).

Dionysios the Areopagite says that the light has its source in the supraexistent and supraessential existence of God. The supraexistence of God implies the light which is a higher degree of the existence that comes from God.[17] For the light unites, brings to perfection and turns all things back to the one who, by existing in a supraexisting manner, is the source of light and fills all things with one and the same unifying light, just as ignorance separates, distorts and weakens existence.[18]

Only this complete Trinitarian unity and knowledge explain the joy God has in knowing and loving other persons too, and the joy these other persons have in knowing God and one another in a union without confusion — their "ecstasy," that is, their going out of themselves. If there were no Trinitarian love, neither would there be knowledge of God or any possibility of knowledge and love between God and created persons. The striving for knowledge comes from interpersonal love, and this comes from the holy Trinity. The etymology of the Latin *cognosco* (*cum* + *gnosco*) shows from of old that human beings have been aware of the interpersonal character of knowledge. The same thing is attested by the Romanian word *con-stiinta* ("consciousness"/"conscience"). I do not know myself apart from a relationship with others. In the last analysis I know or am conscious of myself in relationship with God. The light of my knowledge in respect of things or of myself is projected upon the communitarian human image from the supreme personal community. We are conscious of ourselves only in relationship with the other and, in the final analysis, before God. The "I" by itself would no longer possess consciousness; through consciousness it knows its own spiritual "place" in relationship with others. It grows in self-consciousness simultaneously with its growth in self-knowledge, and its growth in self-knowledge corresponds to its growth in the knowledge of God, of its neighbors, and of created things.

The third element that results from the understanding of knowledge as union is this: the fact that rational creatures must progress along a course until they achieve complete interiority among themselves and in God and until full knowledge of God and of his works is granted in the paradox that while, on the one hand, God is fully united with creatures from the beginning and hence knows them fully in his quality of being their cause, on the other hand, inasmuch as they on their part have not achieved union or reciprocal interiority with him, God is not united with them nor has he thus realized fully on his part the state of reciprocal interiority with them. Consequently, God does not see creatures fully realized as they progress along the road towards this goal.

God sees the complete union of creatures with himself and his union with them in their end which is present for him. But concomitantly with this union and fullness, seen in their end or goal, God also sees a certain distance and their actual absence of fullness. He thereby sees how the image of their fullness and total union with God is found in creatures as a potentiality leading them gradually to the actualization of union with him and of their own final perfection. From the very moment when they recognize him simply as the cause of things, God sees the creatures who have set out on this road — those, therefore, who are found in a certain real union with him and thus are on the road towards their own full actualization and towards total union with him. And this recognition is itself always a faith in him.

The case is different, however, with those who do not accept God in any way at all, not even therefore as cause. They exist in total ignorance and thus in voluntary separation from him. They no longer have, through their will, anything from God, for they are closed off from any communication with him. And yet, as their creating and sustaining cause, God is still present in them or united with them in spite of their will. Therefore, in one way God has knowledge of these too from within himself, as one who is united with them as their cause. Nevertheless, in another way, he does not know them, for he is separated from them by the fact that through their will they are separated from him.

That is why Dionysios the Areopagite affirms — denying that God is known only as exalted beyond creatures and as isolated from them within a total transcendence, as Hans Urs von Balthasar is currently saying — that God can always be known from creatures, but it is possible never to know God from creatures: "God is therefore known in all things and as distinct from all things. He is known through knowledge and through understanding. Of him there is conception, reason, understanding, touch, perception, opinion, imagination, name, and many other things. On the other hand he cannot be understood, words cannot contain him, and no name can lay hold of him. He is not one of the things that are and he cannot be known in any of them. He is all things in all things and he is no thing among things. He is known to all from all things and he is known to no one from anything."[19] God can be known from all things through analogy with all things and through his presence in all things as the one who is their cause. "But again, the most divine knowledge of God, that which comes through unknowing, is achieved in a union far beyond mind."[20]

Having the creatures in himself and, in his quality of being their cause, knowing them infinitely more than we know them, God does not, however, see all of them advancing towards the end of their full union with him, in conformity with the union they have with him through their origin; in this case neither do the creatures see God. He does not know them within the process of actualizing their potential image, nor does he see them in the end of this process, that is, in the total actualization of their union with God and of their being. Nor do they know him, either in the course of life on earth or in the actualization of his love in eternity, because they have not become capable of knowing him.

This may be the meaning of those two kinds of Scriptural expressions: a. God knows all things; b. God does not know those who do not do his will, those who are not his own.

We give first some expressions of the first kind of knowledge. The Psalmist attributes to God the knowledge of our intimate reality and of all things: "[God] knows the secrets of the heart" (Ps 44.22), for he is "he who fashioned the heart of each, he who knows all their works" (Ps 33.15). In the book of Job it says: "For he looks to the ends of the earth and sees everything under the heavens" (Job 28.24), while Saint Paul exclaims: "O the depth of the riches and wisdom and knowledge of God! How unsearchable are his judgments and how inscrutable his ways! 'For who has known the mind of the Lord, or who has been his counselor?' " (Rom 11.33-34).

On the other hand, the holy Scripture speaks of a special knowledge God has with respect to those who love him or open themselves to him or are filled with him. Saint Paul says: "if one loves God, one is known by him" (1 Cor 8.3), or: "The Lord knows those who are his" (2 Tim 2.19; cf. Num 16.5). The Psalmist asks God to look down from heaven and see and to hear the voice of his prayer, a request which gives us to understand that God might not indeed look or might not be willing to hear the voice of a prayer (Ps 34.6,17; 61.1, 64.1 etc.).

In fact our Savior tells those who have not done his will: "'I never knew you; depart from me, you evildoers" (Mt 7.23); or: ". . . you will begin to stand outside and to knock at the door, saying, 'Lord, open to us.' He will answer you, 'I do not know where you come from. . . . depart from me, all you workers of iniquity!' " (Lk 13.25,27).

God no longer sees these people in himself except as those who have been created by him, not as those who continue to stand before his face and who are growing in him along the lines of the being he has given them, and in conformity to an eternal reason of theirs in himself. In the time of their earthly life they have gone astray from him. God has not seen them continuing and advancing in him. That is why he will tell them at the end: I did not know you, I did not see you abiding in me; depart from me completely. "[A] godless man shall not come before him" (Job 13.16) during his life, and so he will come before him no more in the life to come either. This ignorance that God has of those who do not do his will is a kind of forgetfulness, a lack of preoccupation with them on the part of God. God has forgotten the one who has forgotten him, the one who has not persevered before him and has not drawn closer and closer to him. God cannot gather such a one by force into his bosom, God cannot make such a one love him by force. Because he is not able to force a person to love him, God is also unable to see him in that realized state which would have been given him by his love for God. But, when the man begins to suffer because of the condition in which he finds himself, then he begins to draw close to God once more, to make himself seen by him as one walking on the path towards union with God and towards his own realization that corresponds to the reason he has received from God. As the man cries to God in this way, God ceases to leave him any longer in forgetfulness; he sees him anew, come alongside himself and following the lines of ever closer union with himself. The forgetfulness of God in respect to this man ceases, or becomes a forgetfulness of his former trespasses, a forgetting of his forgetfulness of the man. And so, as he turns back to God, man beseeches him to abandon the forgetfulness he has shown towards him: "Why dost thou hide thy face? Why dost thou forget our affliction and oppression?" (Ps 44.24) or: "How long, O Lord? Wilt thou forget me for ever? How long wilt thou hide thy face from me?" (Ps 13.1). And he has the conviction that God will leave his miserable state forgotten and so he asks him to forget his previous unrighteous life. "None of the transgressions committed shall be remembered against him; for the righteousness which he has done he shall live" (Ezek 18.22; cf. 33.16). This is God's forgiveness and his return; it is possible during man's earthly life. But even those who have lived in union with God can be forgotten when they depart from union with him (Ezek 18.24).

This variety of God's knowledge with respect to men shows that it is a knowledge proper to a person and seeks to intensify his relationship with men as persons. It is not a philosophical knowledge, indifferent to the growth of men in relationship with him and indifferent to their salvation.

God has foreknowledge of all these changes in our relationship with him during the course of our earthly life, changes to which will correspond changes in his attitudes towards us. He knows beforehand that through their freedom some rational beings will, on one or many occasions, resume their place within the framework of their reason in himself and of their development along that line.

More difficult is the problem of foreknowledge with reference to those who will remain far from God definitively and whom God will consequently forget forever. The question has been raised: does not this foreknowledge of the permanence of the fact that they will not return in some way make their return impossible? Does not God's foreknowledge in some way close the possiblility of manifesting his freedom towards these people? Does it not in some way close the possibility of manifesting their own freedom?

Saint John of Damascus has provided the answer to this question: ". . . God foreknows all things but. . . he does not predestine them all."[21] That is, in his forknowledge in regard to them God has taken the freedom of creatures into account. He knows beforehand what they will freely do. He has not willed to predetermine them so as to know them beforehand as creatures predestined for happiness or unhappiness. He has also taken account of his own freedom to do everything to help them in case they should wish to return. His foreknowledge has included the fact that whatever he does in the future, they will freely reject their return.

The foreknowledge of God in regard to those who will go to eternal punishment consists only in the fact that he does not see them in their final unity with himself, a unity which for him is present even before it comes about in reality. God sees them in the possibility given to them at the beginning to bring about through their own will that unity which they have potentially through creation. He sees in himself what they could have become had they wished to remain in him and to develop in him. But he does not see them in fact made actual along the lines of their inherent potential, because of their remaining in him. He sees them definitively separated from himself by means of their will. He sees that the freedom he has vis-à-vis these creatures could do nothing to lead them back to himself. In other words, the salvation of each one also depends on his own will, once God's will to save all established in him from the beginning has been entailed potentially in their nature (1 Tim 2.4). Saint John Chrysostom says: "If it were his alone, all men would have been saved and would have come to a knowledge of the truth (1 Tim 2.4). If it were his alone, there would not be differences in honor. For he made all of us and feels concern equally for all."[22]

Anyone who wishes to remain in his first union with God and develop it can do this easily even through that very union granted to him at the beginning as the union with God which is inscribed as a potentiality in the nature of each person. Anyone who wishes to be saved gives proof by that very fact that he is not predestined to eternal punishment. It is only those who do not put to themselves, in any way that is real, the problem of whether they wish to be saved, who will go to eternal punishment — only those who have never once been tormented by the question: am I destined for eternal punishment? Because, were they ever once to feel that torment, they would prove by that very fact that they wanted to be saved and so they would be saved.

In Christ, humanity is at the peak of its realization or perfection: this is true in a potential manner before the general resurrection and in an actual manner after it, for humanity then will be found in complete interiority with God. God knows humanity, therefore, in its fullness, or, as we might say, in its fully actualized form. Because in Christ human nature is at the perfected end of its knowledge of God (and therefore also of self-knowledge), or is beyond any possibility of development because it stands the maximum level at which this nature can be known and can itself know God, then God also knows it in this final and maximal state. In Christ, God knows nature and human nature knows God at a level at which none of us will ever know God, because it loves God at a level corresponding to himself while, in Christ, God tastes the love of human nature and knows it therefore at its maximum level of realization. In Christ, moreover, God knows the humanity of all at its maximum level through its total participation in his life, and God has this knowledge because of his own maximum participation in human life. Perhaps it is in this that the true sense of the communication of properties in Christ consists. Of course, human nature's knowledge of God remains a knowledge which is human in form, while God's knowledge of human nature remains a knowledge which is divine in form. In Christ the process of God and humanity becoming totally and reciprocally interior to one another has been accomplished, and it is a process realized even more than through grace: the interiority has been accomplished within a hypostasis.

In Christ, God knows what is human as he knows himself, for he is also man, and what is human knows God as it knows itself, for this same reality is also God. However, Christ remains both God and man. Because, as man, he knows the divine infinity that has become properly his own, the latter remains his infinity though not properly by nature; and because, as God, he knows the human finitude as properly his own, it remains his finitude though not properly by nature, yet is a finitude through which the divine infinity shines, and a divine infinity which overwhelms the human finitude. Christ does not become infinite as man by the fact that, as one who is God and also man, he knows himself as man, but it is rather that the meanings and the roots of human existence disclose themselves for him in the divine infinity; and as God does not become finite by the fact that, as one who is man and also God, he knows himself as God, but it is rather that for him the abyss of the divine existence discloses itself through the human transparence as well.

In Christ the possibility is given us to advance towards the stage where God knows man as he knows himself and where man knows God as he knows himself. But to achieve this we must advance in union with Christ. Thus our advance is towards the stage where each one of us will know his neighbor as himself, since he will love him as himself. For, as the divine hypostasis of humanity, Christ sets up no barrier for his love towards the whole of humanity which he possesses as his own humanity; and in Christ, as hypostasis open to all, all can love and know each other as themselves. It is only necessary that we too set up no such barrier between ourselves and God. Christ is a kind of hypostasis-head of our own. And this makes it possible that we too might advance in knowing Christ-God as ourselves, as our own hypostasis-head.

The Spiritual Attributes of God

The Fathers do not separate God's knowledge from his wisdom. They speak very often of God's wisdom and very rarely of his knowledge. This corresponds to the language of holy Scripture where, for example, God's knowledge is referred to directly only twice by Saint Paul, and each time together with his wisdom (Rom 11.33; Col 2.3). Yet the wisdom of God is mentioned many times in both the Old and the New Testament (e.g. Prov 3.13,19; 9.1; Is 28.29; Jer 51.15; Lk 11.49; Acts 6.10; Rom 11.33; 1 Cor 1.24; 2.7; Eph 3.10; Jas 3.17).

Holy Scripture, however, speaks of the knowledge of God as an act — God "knows the secrets of the hearts" (Ps 44.21) — and frequent mention is also made of a knowledge that God gives to those whom he loves.

It would not be possible to say that, according to scriptural usage, God's knowledge refers mainly to himself while his wisdom refers to the world. It is correct that the Scripture frequently says that God gives a knowledge that refers to himself, but in the final analysis the wisdom that he gives also has reference to himself. Moreover, the acts of God's knowledge that are mentioned in the Scripture almost always refer to men or to things.

We must certainly admit that there exists a knowledge of God which refers to himself as distinct from creation, but about this we know nothing. To us has been revealed only a knowledge of God that stands in relationship to the world. If God says many things about his knowledge and activity in regard to the world, in respect of himself he says only as much as is necessary for us to understand his relationship with the world. Therefore we could not make the knowledge God has in respect of himself into a separate object of our own knowledge. It is here that apophaticism has its most categorical place.

Everything that God has revealed to us about his knowledge simultaneously possesses an aspect of wisdom and is connected with the world. It could not be said that God's knowledge is theoretical in character while his wisdom is practical. All the acts of God's knowledge in regard to the world are simultaneously practical in character in pursuit of the aim of leading the world towards himself. By means of the very knowledge about himself that he gives us, he pursues the same aim.

The separation between God's knowledge as a theoretical occupation and his wisdom as a practical occupation appeared in the West as the same time as scholasticism, and suffers from an exalting of the value of speculative knowledge in itself, detached from a transforming role that would thus connect it with love.

What has been said so far about the omniscience of God constitutes no exception to this understanding of the transforming purpose of God's knowledge in respect of us and our knowledge in respect of God, that is, of wisdom.

If, however, a particular discussion of the knowledge and wisdom of God's is justified, this justification comes, in our view, from the necessity to consider together: a) the various partial acts in which God's knowledge is manifested along with the bestowing of his knowledge on man; and b) the connection that exists between these acts and all the other acts of a comprehensive plan regarding the world. This connection and this comprehensive plan might be named the wisdom of God in a special way.

Of course, the wisdom of God is included in every act. For each knowing act on the part of God is connected with the whole ensemble of his plan regarding the world. This connection is only made to us, however, over the course of time. Moreover, the full knowledge of God is manifested in the connection of all of knowledge, that is, wisdom. Whoever has a partial knowledge, unconnected to the whole, not only lacks wisdom, but even the knowledge he does have about the partial matter in question is not full knowledge. Our knowledge and our incomplete wisdom are only a path towards the greatest possible knowledge and wisdom that come from our full union with God. For only in God will we know all things fully in their infinite causality and their connections with all things.

In the following exposition dedicated to the wisdom of God, we will focus our attention on the entirety of the plan God pursues in respect of the world. This plan of God regarding the world itself represents a kenosis for him. It is a descent of God to the dimensions, possibilities, and necessities of the world. Through wisdom God creates and sustains a harmony among the components of the world and through this harmony he preserves all of them without confusion or separation. This too reflects the intrinsic unity and distinctiveness of God. But in seeking the greatest and definite good of all the components of the world and of the world as a whole, God can only see this good — their closest and yet unconfused union — when, to the greatest possible extent, they come to abide in himself. That is why God's wisdom is not only his coming down to the world, to everyone and everything within it; it is also a totality of actions adequate to raise the world up continuously to a common and harmonious participation in the divine life and happiness. The culminating wisdom of God vis-à-vis the world becomes concrete in "the eternal counsel or plan" he has regarding the salvation of the world, the perfection of the world in himself, and the accomplishment of this plan.

The wisdom of God disclosed in revelation and, in a climactic way, in Christ who rose from the dead and opened the prospect of resurrection to us as well, does not contradict the essence of the order of the world, therefore, but restores and completes it, and raises it to a different plane. Yet inasmuch as it corrects the state into which we have fallen, it will often seem opposed to the state of the world.

To a judgement that sees only the rigid order of nature, the wisdom manifested in nature will seem superior to the wisdom revealed in that revelation which culminates in Christ; it may even seem to it to be the only true wisdom. But, according to our conception, a wisdom that reveals the order of the world as a basis for the development of the human being towards an eternal existence is, in reality, more profound. For this is the one that responds to the worth and longing of the human being; more profound yet is a wisdom that reveals the order of the world as a basis for a higher and eternal dialogue of the human being with God and his neighbors; still more profound therefore is a wisdom that reestablishes the human being with the higher and complex order of normal interpersonal relations sustained by the dialogue with God, a dialogue of endless exactingness, subtlety, and complexity, a dialogue that can shape even the order of nature in a higher direction.

What an abyss of wisdom is hidden in the incarnation of the Son of God as man, the one who opens up the prospect of an eternally deified life, an eternal and unutterable glory for the human being! Saint Paul the Apostle prays that the spirit of this wisdom may be given to the Christians of Ephesus so they might understand "what is the hope to which he has called you, what are the riches of his glorious inheritance in the saints" (Eph 1.18). What an abyss of wisdom is hidden in the fact that through the incarnation, one and the same person is both God and man at the same time, bearing in himself, as in all of us as well, the spiritual life of the human being and deepening it to the very measure of the divine infinity! What an abyss of wisdom is hidden in the cross and in the suffering that the very Son of God takes on himself for us, to make of it in our case too — through the renunciation of himself and the patience implied in it — the condition of our higher life, that is, of the relations between ourselves and God! What an abyss of wisdom is found in the prospect of eternal life, the prospect of resurrection thrown open and bestowed on us in Christ's resurrection! What endless depths of blessed meaning does the wisdom shown in the economy of Christ give to the order of the world, a world that by itself would remain fragmented in meaning and lead us nowhere! Within what limitless growth of meaning is God revealed to us as Person or Trinity of persons and as one who enters through the warmth of the endless communion of which he is capable into a relationship of love with us as persons, especially when compared with the simplistic, monotonous and lifeless "god" conceived according to the type of nature!

In the kenosis of love which only God as person can assume there is revealed to us, if we let ourselves be conquered by this love, what Saint Paul says: "that you, being rooted and grounded in love, may have power to comprehend with all the saints what is the breadth and length and height and depth, and to know the love of Christ which surpasses knowledge, that you may be filled with the fulness of God" (Eph 3.17-19).

Wisdom in this sense can have no other basis than the perfection of the Trinitarian communion. Through wisdom God wants to lead all things towards the perfection that radiates from that communion. Among us wisdom itself radiates from the intertrinitarian communion. The "One," in the abstract sense proper to some philosophies, cannot be wise. Where there is no interpersonal relationship, there is no balance and measure but exaggerating tendencies on one side and exclusivism. It is only life together that implies or demands the efforts made to achieve wisdom.

What we come to know in the course of our earthly life on the basis of the order of nature, and what we come to understand from the order of human spiritual life and even from the divine saving acts in our regard are only obscure rays from the knowledge and wisdom we can have here, a knowledge and a wisdom that guide us towards their full appropriation in our future union with God. "Therefore let us supremely praise this foolish 'wisdom,' which has neither reason nor intelligence (ἄλογον καὶ ἄνουν) and let us describe it as the Cause of all intelligence and reason, of all wisdom and understanding. All counsel belongs to it, from it come all knowledge and understanding, and 'in it are hid all the treasures of wisdom and knowledge.' From all that has been said above, it follows that the transcendently wise Cause is indeed the subsistence of absolute wisdom and of the sum total and individual manifestations of wisdom."[23]

Justice and Mercy

These two attributes cannot be separated in God's relations with us. Justice towards creatures has its foundation in the equality of the Trinitarian persons. But it is only by deigning to come down that God creates creatures and makes them share in his happiness according to a justice which reflects the equality of the divine persons.

God is not just without being merciful and is not merciful without being just. For it is through his free and merciful descent to us that he is just towards us. "Vindicate me, O Lord, my God, according to thy righteousness" says the Psalmist (Ps 35.24), or "my tongue shall tell of thy righteousness" (Ps 35.28). But he also says: "For thy steadfast mercy is before my eyes" (Ps 26.3), or "O continue thy steadfast mercy to those who know thee and thy justice to the upright of heart!" (Ps 36.10).

If he were only just, God would not be fully free; if he were only merciful, God would have no regard for human efforts nor would he encourage them. Human beings would be reduced to the state of being passive receptacles of his mercy. The created world would have no true and consistent reality and human beings could not grow through their own effort.

In his justice God wishes, on the one hand, that all men might be equal among themselves, while on the other hand he wishes to give them all as much of his own blessedness as they are able to receive according to their own efforts. For he made them all capable of these efforts when he himself had given them the capacity of being able to receive in the very highest degree what it is that creatures can receive. Through justice God has reference to us all, but he gives thought to each one in a distinctive way within the framework of all. Our yearning for justice begins from a model or an idea of justice and seeks its realization among all. God does not begin from an idea of justice but from the reality of justice in himself. If sin had not in part covered over our authentic human reality, we should not ourselves have to start from an idea of justice but we could begin from the reality of justice that is given within our own equality.

The feeling of justice in one who has the power to extend it to others consists in the propensity to do justice for others. In God this propensity is found in its culmination. But in one who is deprived of justice, this propensity towards justice consists particularly in the felt need of demanding that justice be done. Everyone desires that what is done to himself be taken into consideration, that is, into a consideration which is essentially equal to what is accorded everyone else. Before God, human beings do not manifest what is, strictly speaking, a sentiment of demanding justice, because it is only from God's benevolent will that they were brought into existence in order to share in his happiness. But God calls them to a justice even in their relation to him, inasmuch as he offers them all that he has, with the exception of the fact that he cannot make them to be as he himself is, that is, uncreated and sources of existence.

But a deep conviction exists among men that God does not violate justice in his relations with them, and on the basis of this conviction they have in themselves a feeling of legitimate expectation for justice and a propensity to seek it.

Taking our stand on this conviction we can make our prayer to God: "You, O Lord, who are just and have made me to be a sharer in your happiness, in justice fulfill this your intention in me also! You have made me for this justice but you can see the injustice that I suffer. Fulfill in me your justice for which you have made me!" But along with this we must also say: "I thank you because you have made me in order to fulfill your justice in me!" In other words, we must ask justice from God in our prayers of petition and thank him for it in our prayers of thanksgiving. From this it follows that when we pray to God to make us sharers in his happiness, we must ask him, in justice, to make others share his happiness too. Man's yearning after justice for himself, based on the conviction that God is just, must be joined to an equal desire that justice be done for others; it must not be forgotten that God — who is merciful and just — has made them too so that, in justice, they might enjoy his happiness.

Man can demand justice, especially from his neighbors, for himself and for others and in doing this he can take his stand on the fact that God created all men with the right to enjoy equally the goods that he gave them through creation, goods which can be increased through their own efforts. In demanding justice from his neighbors, moreover, man no longer needs to combine this with a plea for their mercy, for they are not the ones who made him; rather they are creatures equal with himself, and as such they commit an abuse if, for themselves, they hold on to a state that is higher either from a material point of view or in honor. Furthermore man can have the conviction that God supports him in demanding justice from others. Naturally, in demanding justice from others he is not to lose his love for them. Similarly, those who make special efforts on behalf of the good of all should enjoy a particular honor. In addition to all this, a Christian also knows that the most precious goods are spiritual goods and it is on these that his salvation depends, not on the material ones. Spiritual goods are developed through the efforts of the one who possesses them; they do not depend on what others give him. Nevertheless, others must not hinder him from the possibility of developing his spiritual goods through his own efforts.

With regard to the happiness that comes from God, the Christian knows that by creating all men with the right to share in it, God has linked this happiness with certain efforts that everyone has to make: "the kingdom of heaven has suffered violence" (Mt 11.12). But it is just that the distribution of material goods should be carried out according to a certain equality on the one hand, while, on the other hand, account has to be taken of the efforts men make. We must force ourselves to be just before God, to be open and loyal in our relationship with him, free from all deception. We must give to him too what is due to him on our part, that is, the praise and thanksgiving that are his due together with our own effort to obtain happiness in proportion to the spiritual level that we have attained.

Since he is just, God asks us also to be just. Only "the just one" in this sense can enjoy the justice of God. God must be acknowledged as just in all respects. It is not only that he bestows gifts according to justice but also that he seeks justice for himself and for our neighbors. Whoever, on his part, does not fulfill the condition for justice required by God, whoever does not acknowledge God as the source of justice and the one who demands it, whoever is not just in relationship to God and to his own neighbors as God wills — such a one cannot expect to share in the happiness that comes from God. Thus the complete meaning of justice is: everyone receives from the just God according to his own justice or injustice. In this area too God wants us to grow towards participation in his deepest justice and mercy through our own advancement in being just and merciful towards others. But the fact that we never attain a justice that corresponds to the one we ask for from God is another reason why we are not seeking only the justice of God (and hence only his judgement according to our own justice) but his mercy as well (Dan 9.18); "... all our righteous deeds are like a polluted garment" (Is 64.6).

Christ alone as man has attained complete justice. From his justice we absorb power to make progress in assimilating — in the life to come — the justice that belongs to him and is the human form of the divine justice (1 Cor 1.30; 2 Cor 5.21; Eph 6.14). From the fact that the justice we possess is from the mercy of God and that, due to the inadequacy of our efforts to receive it, we never possess justice fully, there results the further necessity of humility on our part.

Although our humility also enters into what is true "justice," a "righteousness" in the sight of God, that is, the acknowledgement that it is from God, from his mercy, that we have all things, nevertheless, to ask for the mercy of God does not contradict our asking to share, according to justice, in his happiness. In fact, the acknowledgement that God shares his happiness with us according to justice, on the basis of his benevolence and mercy, must be included in our asking for justice from God; on the other hand, when he is being merciful to us, God does not act high-handedly or arbitrarily in the bestowal of his happiness, as Calvinist teaching affirms. God is merciful, but he is also "the just judge" who puts great value on both the creature and his efforts. Whoever asks for God's mercy is, by that very fact, just, because he makes an effort of humility and acknowledges what he has received from God on the basis of his mercy, and thus shares, according to justice, in his happiness.

We are not speaking here of justice on the plane of worldly situations. That depends on other conditions. Whoever is wrongly treated on this plane is justified in demanding justice from others rather than requesting their mercy. He is even justified in rebuking those who are unjust, those who trample on justice for their own benefit, and protesting against their deeds. But he must not himself be the loser on the spiritual plane because of the manner in which he does this. Hence it is good to seek this justice not so much for oneself as for others. This belongs to love of neighbor.

The Christian must never forget that there exists another justice, one that comes from God and is shared out according to a "justice" of the human being. It differs from one person to the other according to the "justice" of each. Whoever is treated unjustly in the order of the world, therefore, enjoys a justice from God provided he himself is just in God's sight, and vice versa. Those who are more or less equal on the plan of worldly order might be quite distinct in respect of the happiness from God in which they become sharers. This comes about not because God would not wish that all men receive the same justice from him, but because through their own efforts or their lack of effort they become capable of a distinction in their happiness.

Inequality in the social order is caused by others; inequality in the spiritual order depends on each one individually. That is why the former can be overcome by means of struggle against others whereas the latter can be overcome only through the struggle with oneself. If all were to carry on this struggle with themselves, not only would justice and equality be realized in the spiritual order, but true justice would also be achieved in the external order. In the section above on the foreknowledge of God we gave a quotation from Saint John Chrysostom which shows how much God desires justice among men in both these respects and how much the obtaining of justice depends on their own efforts. He says the same thing when he gives it the further name of the mercy of God. "He is a God of loving kindness and of mercy. Just as the woman in labor is eager to give birth to her child, so God desires to pour forth his mercy, but our sins stop him."[24]

Those who are just will enjoy the full justice that comes from God, particularly in the life to come, as the parable of the unmerciful rich man and Lazarus, the poor man, shows (Lk 16.25).

God sustains this yearning for true justice but he does not grant it right away because we ourselves must draw close to it through our own continuous efforts and thus also draw close to him. God also sustains this advance towards true justice, among other things, by the fact that he punishes those who deprive others, especially the "just," of justice. Jesus, who was most just and suffered the greatest injustice from the world — the greatest precisely because he was himself the most just — and yet was also raised up to heavenly glory because of his justice, is the one who supports the struggle for true justice in history in the most effective way.

Furthermore, by punishing those who are unjust, God maintains — to a certain extent — a balance in the world and thereby the possibility for all to enjoy the goods bestowed by him for the sake of all. Since the justice of God, therefore, is a dynamic attribute or an energy, God has created the world according to justice and wants to bring it back to justice in all respects.

Those who participate in the energies of God (among which is numbered the energy of justice) first through their being and then through grace — by which their being is reestablished and strengthened — are themselves also animated by the impulse to bring about justice. And they also urge others to do justice. Saint Isaak the Syrian says: "Do not separate the rich from the poor, nor try to discriminate the worthy from the unworthy, but let all men be equal in your eyes for a good deed. In this way you can draw even the unworthy toward the good.... The Lord ate at table with publicans and harlots and did not alienate the unworthy, that he might in this way bring all to the fear of God, and that through bodily things they would approach the spiritual."[25]

The desire of the spiritual man is not only that an interior justice be realized among men, but an exterior one as well. For he knows that the exterior injustice can hinder the realization of love among men, and hence of interior justice too. But exterior justice is not the ultimate purpose; justice in the spiritual order is higher than this. And the spiritual man sets an example by fighting for more than exterior justice alone. Saint Isaak the Syrian says: "The man who becomes destitute of the things of this world will be rich in God."[26]

Genuine, complete justice will also mean the reestablishment of the perfect balance between all created things, the full reflection of the justice of God who loves them all.[27]

But because justice, as proper relation among us and between us and God, is a reality and a full reciprocal honoring, it is the condition for open, unhindered communicability. The just man has no reason to hide, in the way that the unjust man and the one who has suffered injustice have reason to hide their thoughts from each other.

Our perfect justice in the sight of God has been fulfilled in Christ. But the perfect reward from God for this justice has also taken place in Christ. For all that Christ suffered from the world because he kept himself just in the eyes of God, there has been given to him eternal glory above everyone and everything (Phil 2.9). And all of us who are united with him and follow his example will partake of his glory. In the Gospel of Christ "the righteousness of God is revealed" (Rom 1.17). God has made Jesus Christ "our wisdom, our righteousness and sanctification and redemption" (1 Cor 1.30). In him justice has been revealed in gift, and in him we have this justice/righteousness in the abundance of grace and free gift (Rom 5.17). In him the highest justice has been shown to us, a justice which is at the same time the greatest, most overwhelming mercy (Eph 2.4; Rom 9.23; Tit 3.5).

But it would be wrong to think, as Protestants do, that from his mercy God has displayed his justice in Christ upon a passive humanity. In that case, not justice too, but only the mercy of God would have been shown in Christ. In Christ, however, the most complete justice of God has crowned the most complete justice of man, and a full correspondence between the two has been realized. It is here that the importance of the human will of Christ appears. If God were to manifest his mercy apart from justice, he would no longer be accomplishing a pedagogical task with us and our own growth would no longer interest him. Instead this would show that he did not create us as beings capable of spiritual growth. His own creative power would appear as enormously diminished. As man, Christ fulfills justice because he is our representative, the representative of all, while, as God, he rewards this justice with justice. He accomplishes both of these because he is one and the same hypostasis for the divinity and for the humanity, and because he wants us to share not only in his justice as God, or in God's justice granted in him out of mercy — more precisely, therefore, out of God's mercy apart from justice, a mercy received by us passively — but he also wants us to share in his justice as man through our own effort, helped, of course, by the grace of Christ, that is, by his Spirit. All our members must be offered to God (or by God) "as instruments of righteousness" (Rom 6.13). Thus God brings about perfect justice in Christ not only because he fills Christ as man with all the glory and brightness of the divine persons, but also because he fills us too with this happiness in Christ, inasmuch as we have conquered in him. "He who conquers, I will grant him to sit with me on my throne, as I myself conquered and sat down with my Father on his throne" (Rev 3.21).

The justice of God will be able to fill the earth because it will be shown both from the side of God and from our side. Only thus can God's intention truly be achieved, that the world be filled with justice: a justice radiating both from within us and from above us. Only thus can the world truly become the kingdom of God which is "righteousness and peace and joy in the Holy Spirit" (Rom 14.17).

Holiness

The holiness of God both expresses a quality of God in Trinity and is also manifested in the world and becomes a quality in which human beings participate. Under the first aspect it is entirely apophatic and undefinable, while under the second, it is perceived, though in a manner that is difficult to define rationally, which is to say, in an apophatic-cataphatic manner. Under the first aspect we ought rather to call it supra-holiness, while under the second, as the relationship of God with his creatures, we should call it simply holiness. In this section we are speaking rather of the holiness that has been revealed and manifested in the world through God's condescension to it, through his uncreated energies.

In the holiness manifested in the world the same combination of the transcendent and the revealed, of elevation and condescension in God is revealed. If God has not revealed himself while preserving some of his transcendence in this descent, we would not know this quality in him; if he had not descended without ceasing to be transcendent, the world would not be able to bear the holiness of God nor come to be a sharer in it.

Nevertheless, by revealing himself and coming down to us, God shows something that surpasses all that is of this world, something that is of another order. If holiness were not transcendent, it could not give us the power to transcend ourselves unceasingly; if it had not come down to us, we would not strive to acquire it; it would be for us entirely inaccessible. As often as the light of the divine transcendence glints in our conscience, it impresses itself upon us with that quality of a holiness come down to us, difficult to define in concepts or words, yet somehow experienced nevertheless. Holiness itself is something that transcends the would and draws us upwards. The very holiness present in the world is the proof of the existence of a transcendent order. Perhaps that "wholly other" (*das ganz Andere*), that "awe-inspiring mystery" (*mysterium tremendum*) of the divine reality is to be experienced nowhere more directly than in the holiness which envelops God's revealing of himself. This revealed divinity we almost identify with holiness. Holiness can be said to reveal to us all the divine qualities in a concentrated way. It is the luminous and active mystery of the divine presence. In it there is concentrated all that distinguishes God from the world.

Nevertheless, holiness is not the attribute of an impersonal mystery. It is the attribute of transcendence as person. For before the holy mystery, as a supreme conscience or tribunal that calls us to account, we experience a certain fear or shame. The holy Transcendent is transcendent-person and strengthens our personal conscience, making us take thought of our sinfulness. The holiness of God appears as a grandeur that produces in man an infinite humility. The same is true with genuine self-consciousness. "When the soul is imprinted and immersed through the Spirit in the depths of Christ's humility, forgetting about the world and everything in it and looking only at itself and at its own, and persisting in this meditation and getting used to it, it sees only itself in its nothingness and humility and is convinced that nobody else in the world is so unworthy."[28]

Holiness fills us with a kind of awe different from any human awe, a thrill that is not experienced in relation to the realities of the world, mixed with fear, horror, and shame before all that is defiled within us. Faced with this personal holiness we feel as if we had been uncovered in all our uncleanness and nakedness. Yet at the same time this holiness attracts us. Dionysios the Areopagite identifies the holiness of God with his absolute purity, and our action of sanctification with the action of purification (*The Ecclesiastical Hierarchy*). But this absolute divine purity simultaneously has within it something transcendent, something divine.

Both the awe and the fear, however, are the awe and the fear before a person. Moreover, the state of discovery in which they place us is also a discovery of what is good in ourselves and this too demands of us the purification of our own conscience in the face of another conscience. Man is captivated by the charm of his true being, for, when God's holiness appears before man's being, he discovers within it a desire for purity and a relationship with God. We have a feeling of well-being, for the holy One has known us in our true being and yet he does not reject us even though we are in a sinful state, but calls us to purity. We are happy, for we feel unburdened and that nothing hinders us from manifesting ourselves in all sincerity before him; we are no longer acting out a role that leads us to a point where we end up no longer knowing ourselves and living always in the fear of being unmasked. We are no longer acting out a role which leads us to want to imagine that we are not sinners, though of course we are not successful in this, but only in keeping our defilement covered up. We liberate our reality as subject for genuine communion. Those who feel themselves cleansed in the sight of the holy God are given a "boldness" (παρρησία), an opening of conscience, a sincerity of communicability which has nothing rash or cynical in it but resembles the boldness of the child innocent of sin, while in addition it possesses maturity of conscience and the joy of it. When we ourselves feel defiled, therefore, we pray to the saints who have this "boldness" with God so that they will speak and mediate for us. Thus, by communicating holiness to us, God brings us back to the true state of being a subject, and reestablishes our reality as subject in its open functioning. He can do this, moreover, only because he makes himself known to us as loving subject. He awakens the responsibility of our reality as subject by entering, as transcendent subject, into a familiar relationship with us. Thus holiness is not the quality of an object, but the quality *par excellence* of the subject who is supreme and loving and, as such, all-pure and demanding.

Only through sustained perseverance and the consciousness of the presence of God as loving person is this "boldness" acquired, for this is the way purity is acquired. That is the only reason why boldness becomes habitual in saints. Once the consciousness of God's presence is lost, and with it, therefore, consciousness of self and of one's sinfulness, then this "boldness" is also lost because the defiling passions have entered it. For this reason, when man wishes to approach God anew, he does it with difficulty or with fear. Saint Isaak the Syrian says: "Seat yourself before the Lord continually, keeping the memory of him in your heart, lest having lingered outside his memory, you are unable to speak boldly when you enter in before him, because boldness with God comes from constant conversing with him and from much prayer."[29]

Boldness is a familiarity with God, but one that implies no weakening of sensibility to the extraordinariness of communicating with him, for this familiarity is accompanied by a continual consciousness of God's greatness and by a fear of interrupting communication with him through any kind of concealment from or disloyalty towards him.

Any human being over whom there projects a ray from the transcendence of the divine subject becomes holy as a result of his effort at responsible purification and at keeping his conscience steadfast before the presence of God. "For Thou our God art holy, and dost find rest in the saints," as the liturgy of the Orthodox Church says. God's "rest" in the saints is for them a permanent fact of consciousness. All Christians are called by Saint Paul "saints" if they preserve their consciousness of the fact that, at baptism, Christ took up his dwelling within them and if, with the help of the grace of baptism and of the other sacraments, they struggle for purification. The preservation of the consciousness of this fact and the effort of purification, however, are accomplished through the Holy Spirit.

It is sometimes asserted today that we cannot share in the holiness of God, and in more recent times this opinion has developed into the theory of secularism according to which Christianity has done away with the "sacred" as a quality of persons, places, special objects, and has made everything "profane," and also that, by becoming incarnate as man among men, the Son of God has himself been "secularized".

It is true that in some sense, inasmuch as Christianity has given to all the possibility of becoming saints, it has abolished the boundary between the sacred and the profane. To a certain extent even the Old Testament had done this. Hence the disappearance of this boundary does not mean a universal secularization but that the possibility of holiness is opened to all. In the Old Testament the whole people of Israel was consecrated to God and called to holiness. "Say to all the congregation of the people of Israel, You shall be holy; for I the Lord your God am holy" (Lev 19.2). We have seen that Saint Paul calls all Christians "saints," and Saint Peter calls them "a holy nation" (1 Pet 2.9). All of us have access to holiness, for since Christ is the Son of God who became man, we can all be united with Christ through the Holy Spirit. To deny the possibility of access to holiness for all is to deny that the Son of God, by becoming man, has kept his divinity active in the humanity he assumed and to deny that he is united with us in this quality, that is, as God incarnate. More significantly, we all have access to holiness because God, as the subject of an absolute purity, has become the human subject of a culminating purity, sensibility, and communicability, and thus helps us also to discover, in his communication with us, our own subjective sensibility.

In Christianity our nature was given back the experience of the mystery of its own existence as subject and, along with it, an awe in the face of our own person and that of others along with the obligation to care for its purity and to work for its eternity. The experience of this mystery became possible, moreover, through man's intimacy with the supreme subject in human form, for man has entered into a relationship with the absolute subject in human form who is holy *par excellence*. God has become accessible to us as an absolute subject of this kind, that is to say, absolutely holy, and has thereby also made our own reality as subject evident to our experience. In principle, Christianity has abolished the boundary between the sacred and the profane and has opened for all the access to holiness on a twofold basis: firstly, because although it does affirm that holiness comes from God — that where there is holiness there is God — Christianity has nevertheless acknowledged in our being both a yearning for holiness, for communication in purity between our own subject and the divine subject, and also a capacity for holiness, an inner urging towards communion with the absolute subject in purity and delicacy; secondly, because this access has been opened up to us through the incarnation of the Son of God as man and through his abiding in everyone who wishes to receive him.

The Fathers saw in holiness a great likeness of man with God through purification from the passions and through the virtues which culminate in love. But inasmuch as both the cleansing from passions and the virtues can only be acquired through the energy of the grace which strengthens human powers, likeness also means a radiation of the presence of God from within man. In those who love one another and are found within a reciprocal interiority, the face of the one is stamped with the features of the other and these features shine forth actively from within him. Now inasmuch as these divine features are growing and foreshadow the full degree in which they will overwhelm the human features, the faces of the saints even on earth have something of the eschatological plane of eternity in their appearance, that plane through which God's features will be fully reflected and his energies will radiate. Through these energies can be seen the eternal life of the future age, life reflected from within God. The good things from beyond nature have "various modes of the virtues as images and foreshadowing feature. . . . Therefore, blessed is he who has transformed, through wisdom, the God-man into himself. For after he has accomplished the fulfillment of this mystery, he suffers his

The Spiritual Attributes of God

deification by grace, and this will never have an end."[30] "There can be no doubt that the essence of virtue found in each one is the one subsisting Word of God; for the essence of all virtues is our Lord Jesus Christ himself."[31]

This stamping of the active divine features on us is equivalent to our deification, but simultaneously also to the humanization of God in us. Because in us God is being humanized, our deification comes to mean our own simultaneous humanization in the highest possible degree. According to Christian doctrine, if we act in the likeness of the God who is totally loving towards all, we act like men come to the highest point of their own realization, for our hearts are full of the most fervent love of all, God's love. In this the sensitivity to the pain of anyone else is heart-rending, greater even than for our own pain. And this is to comprehend the others more intensely in one's own self. Saint Isaak the Syrian asks: " 'And what is a merciful heart?' It is the heart's burning for the sake of the entire creation, for men, for birds, for animals ... and for every created thing; and by the recollection and sight of them the eyes of a merciful man pour forth abundant tears. From the strong and vehement mercy which grips his heart and from his great compassion, his heart is humbled and he cannot bear to hear or to see any injury or slight sorrow in creation. For this reason he offers up tearful prayer continually even for irrational beasts, for the enemies of the truth, and for those who harm him. . . . "[32]

From within the personal God there radiates our goodness, the purity of his disinterest towards himself — or, more positively, of his interest in man — transparence, and communicability. He thereby attracts into communion with himself any person who desires this, transmitting to him the same goodness, transparence, and communicability. From one perspective we give the name "purity from passions" to this goodness, transparence, and communicability, from another, "virtue." For there can be no virtue where there is passion. Passion is the blindness of exclusive concern with self. Hence, freedom from passions or dispassion — without which there is no virtue — is not the absence of sensibility but rather a supreme sensibility for others. To be able to acquire sensibility, you must suffer in the struggle against your own passions. Only through the cross do we attain the sensibility of sinlessness, that is, of virtue, for virtue means living for others. According to their rank the virtues receive different names. The virtue of love represents the culmination of goodness, transparence, and communicability. In itself all the virtues are concentrated, namely, that dispassionate sensibility which is sinless *par excellence*. It is the virtue identical with deification which is simultaneously identical with the highest degree of humanization. Only in God can man become fully man, as the definition of Chalcedon demonstrates.

But it is in prayer that the soul attains to the supreme likeness with God. For in true prayer it is united with God and cleansed from any other thought. The presence of God in the soul that prays unceasingly, hence in the soul of the saint, is itself unceasing. This soul "is enlightened" by the divine presence.[33] The transparence of the saint is the very transparence of God within him.

The light that radiates from within the saints is precisely this transparence of communication with God and with their neighbors, that is, of their participation in God. The most transparent is God for he is the one who communicates himself the most. But whoever does not open himself to the communication of God cannot experience this transparence of God. Whoever opens himself to it becomes a saint because he too becomes transparent. In general, when people become transparent to one another through that goodness that comes from their communication with God, they become saints. And from the Christian point of view this is the truly human condition. People who avoid one another do this because they are evil. Evil makes them opaque, darkened, closed up, insincere, hypocritical. The saint is the new or renewed, and therefore luminous, creation.[34] Saint Symeon the New Theologian says that the light of holiness in the soul makes the body transparent too. But on earth this comes about only in part. It is only in the life to come that bodies also will be fully transparent. "The bodies of the saints under the action of the soul united with grace, that is, partaking of the divine fire, are sanctified and become transparent by incandescence, being more different from and much more honored than the other bodies. But when the soul departs and is separated from the body, then the latter too is given to corruption and is slowly decomposed. . .[though some are preserved] in view of the final resurrection. . . ."[35]

But transparence, which is an effect of the overwhelming of matter by spirit and in its climactic stage is equivalent to the resurrection, is not a physical phenomenon of a spectacular character, but rather a communication and existential irradiation of love and interest for the rest of mankind and a participation in the sorrows and troubles of their lives. It is vibrant sympathy in the highest degree; it is peace and the discovery of our own great love for them — a love that causes others to bear their sufferings more easily. In this sensibility of participation the saint lives his humanity in the highest degree. And one who is glad of the saint's participation in his sufferings and problems also experiences this humanity of the saint. The personal character of holiness is revealed in this way.

Saint Cyril of Alexandria has linked holiness closely to sacrifice. Whoever passes over into the state of sacrifice, passes over into the state of holiness. The Greek word *hieron* means both "sacrifice" and "sacred." By the very fact that Christians give themselves to God or sacrifice themselves to him — meaning their complete self-offering as subjects to the divine subject — they become saints, are enveloped in the holiness or self-giving purity of God and open themselves to it. But they are able to sacrifice themselves in a manner that is pure or entire only if they partake of the pure or entire sacrifice of Christ who, by sacrificing or offering himself as man to the Father in total purity, has consecrated himself so that we too may be consecrated through our union with him in a state of sacrifice. Thus, in purity, the saints have access to God, to communion with the supreme subject: "And for their sake I consecrate myself, that they also may be consecrated in truth" (Jn 17.19).

Holiness comes, therefore, from the total surrender of the human subject to absolute Person. You can yield yourself only to a person. Only in the direction of a person can you truly transcend yourself. In the impulse towards inner purity and delicacy there is implied a tendency to be pure and delicate in relation to others, to surrender and open yourself to them sincerely and completely. But you can only achieve absolute surrender for the sake of an absolute person. And the power of absolute surrender you can only receive by being united with an absolute person who also surrenders himself. It is only by yielding ourselves to God and it is only because we succeed in doing this in union with the Son of God who became man and as such surrendered himself to God that we can become saints through our own absolute surrender, aided by the absolute Person through whom we thus surrender ourselves to absolute Person.[36] Total communicability before God is identical with complete surrender to him. At the same time, it is purity and transparency towards God and men. No thought contrary to God or to men forces the saint to hide, to try to make himself impenetrable, to put on a disguise or play a role.

Holiness comes from God, from the absolute as person, from the completely pure Personal reality who harbors no evil thought against us. But it also comes from him through the fact that we as persons yearn to surrender ourselves totally to this absolute Person who is of an absolute goodness towards us, and we achieve this surrender through the Son of God who, as man, surrenders himself along with us by an absolute decision. If by means of such an absolute decision you were to surrender yourself merely to a person, to one who lacked that character of absolute benevolence and communicability, you would be making an idol of that person and attributing to him the power of a communication of life that he does not in fact have. In itself, surrender to an idol cannot be definitive, for you soon discover its relativity, moreover you do not possess within yourself the power of absolute surrender, nor can you get it from another person like yourself who, as such, lacks the power of absolute benevolence and communication. The power of total surrender comes to you from the acceptance of this surrender with absolute love, from the encounter with the absolute love of the person to whom you surrender yourself.

Moreover, holiness comes only from an absolute person because only before that person can you be ashamed in a manner that is absolute and feel the impulse towards an absolute purity, sincerity, and absolute transparency dependent on the absolute power and, therefore, the absolute purity which you are encountering. Before an impersonal "absolute" you cannot be ashamed; before a person who is not absolute you cannot feel shame in a way that is terrible, absolute, as you tremble before that One who is holy and all-loving or before a person transparent of the holy One, and this is so because a person who is not absolute has in himself so many imperfections and restraints in his ability to communicate that these keep him at your own level. Only forgiveness from absolute Person can give you total and definitive peace of conscience through real cleansing of sins and through that person alone who speaks in the name of God and by his humility confirms that it is God alone who is speaking through him. Only an absolute as a person can be pure in being and can encounter you in the delicacy of total purity. If, in paganism, the sacred was a quality of things, in the Old Testament it became a quality of absolute Person and, in a certain measure, of the people as a whole made up as it was of persons, while still more in Christianity it became the quality of the human person to the extent to which the latter is filled with the Holy Spirit. This depends on the fact that in Christ absolute Person has become the person of what is human also, communicating his Holy Spirit to those who believe in him or, through that communication, absolute Person himself comes to dwell in them.

Purity cannot properly be attributed to an impersonal absolute, for purity itself is also a matter of intention, of thoughts, of subjective interiority, and of delicacy in relation with other persons in conscious acts. Only an absolute as person can be definitively and wholly pure in himself for he is pure by nature, not by effort or in a limited sense. Only a person is able to attract us, to awaken a real interest within us, for he is able to surrender himself to us and we are able to surrender ourselves to him in a total delicacy. Moreover, only absolute person is able to attract our absolute interest and exercise over us an attraction that is absolute and deliberate and thus make us surrender ourselves to him with an absolute sincerity and "consecrate" ourselves to him.

This surrender to absolute Person is a sanctifying self-sacrifice, for it is a transcending of self which goes beyond all that is relative. Any human being who is lifted up beyond himself towards supreme Person and offers himself to him, thereby renounces himself and tramples under foot all that is selfish or mean, all that is merely narrow interest or appetite directed passionately towards finite things, and thus he is consecrated and enters through that Person into a fully unlimited condition and complete freedom. He is consecrated because he forgets himself and is raised beyond himself in his own genuinely free communication with absolute Person and on the basis of the power of this absolute Person which comes from his side to meet him in the encounter. But since in this way the person realizes his own self in the most authentic manner, holiness — from our point of view — can be said to be the most fitting realization of the human, the discovery and valuing of its most intimate sanctuary.[37]

If the human being becomes holy because he gives or consecrates himself to supreme Person and to the service of the pure good, of the truth and justice willed by that Personal reality, the act of "consecration" or of "sacrifice" is a priestly act. All who sacrifice themselves or give themselves to supreme Person are priests and are sanctified through their act of offering to God.[38] Moreover, in offering their very selves, they give as gift the entire world with which they are joined; hence they consecrate it.[39] He who is sanctified helps all with whom he comes into contact to be sanctified by drawing them into a delicate and transparent relationship which is pure in its feelings and thoughts.

The elements and objects consecrated in church also receive a holiness of their own through the relation which holy persons have to them in God, but this holiness is not given in an exclusive way for the sake of the objects and elements themselves, a way which would separate them from the other elements of the world, as though from a sphere that was profane. They are consecrated on behalf of all the objects and things in the world, in a way that makes them represent all. Those who bestow them as a gift to God show delicacy in their dealing with them because these elements and objects are the gifts given by God and returned by those persons to him with thanksgiving. But the delicacy of our dealings with them gives us the power to achieve the same kind of behavior towards all things; it opens our eyes to see all things as gifts of God, gifts we must use with reverence, purity, and gratitude. Through the bread, water, wine, oil or wheat blessed in church, all bread, water, or wine used in the lives of men is blessed. An Orthodox Christian reverently makes the sign of the Cross over the loaf of bread as he begins to use it, conscious that it is the gift of God. All the faithful pray when they sit down at table. All things are presented in their relation to God. The Orthodox Church has special services for the blessing of wells, fields, yards, houses, animals. The eucharistic bread casts an aura of holiness over all bread. Moreover, the priests receive a consecration as ministers of the sanctification of all, as active points through whom all have occasion to enter into sanctifying communion with Christ, the divine-human person, as the focal point of pure relations among all men.

Through his self-offering to Christ, through his communion with Christ and through Christ, with all men, the saint restores his humanity completely, in a way that is freed from any hidden thought or interest.

But how is this made visible concretely? In the saint there exists nothing that is trivial, nothing coarse, nothing base, nothing affected, nothing insincere. In him the culmination of delicacy, sensibility, transparency, purity, reverence, attention before the mystery of his fellow men (a characteristic proper to what is human) comes into actual being, for he brings this forth from his communication with supreme Person. The saint grasps the various conditions of the soul in others and avoids all that would upset them, although he does not avoid helping them overcome their weaknesses. He reads the least articulated need of others and fulfills it promptly, just as he reads their impurities too, however skillfully hidden, and, through the delicate power itself of his own purity, exercising upon them a purifying action. From the saint there continually radiates a spirit of self-giving and of sacrifice for the sake of all, with no concern for himself, a spirit that gives warmth to others and assures them that they are not alone. He is the innocent lamb prepared for the conscious sacrifice of himself, the immovable wall that offers a support that does not deceive.

And yet there is no one more humble, more simple, no one less artificial, less theatrical or hypocritical, no one more "natural" in his behavior, accepting of all that is truly human and creating an atmosphere that is pure and familiar. The saint has overcome any duality in himself, as Saint Maximos the Confessor puts it.[40] He has overcome the struggle between soul and body, the divergence between good intentions and deeds that do not correspond to them, between deceptive appearance and hidden thoughts, between what claims to be the case and what is the case. He has become simple, therefore, because he has surrendered himself entirely to God. That is why he can surrender himself entirely in communication with others.

The saint always lends courage; at times, through a humor marked by this same delicacy, he shrinks the delusions created by fears or pride or the passions. He smiles, but does not laugh sarcastically; he is serious but not frightened. He finds value in the most humble persons, considering them all great mysteries created by God and destined to eternal communion with him. Through humility the saint makes himself almost unobserved, but he appears when there is need for consolation, for encouragement, or help. For him no difficulty is insurmountable, because he believes firmly in the help of God sought through prayer. He is the most human and most humble of beings, yet at the same time of an appearance that is unusual and amazing and gives rise in others to the sense of discovering in him, and in themselves too, what is most naturally human. He is a presence simultaneously most dear and, unintentionally, most impressing, the one who draws the most attention. For you he becomes the most intimate one of all and the most understanding; you never feel more at ease than near him, yet at the same time he forces you into a corner and makes you see your moral inadequacies and failings. He overwhelms you with the simple greatness of his purity and with the warmth of his goodness and makes you ashamed of how far you have fallen away from what is truly human, of how low you have sunk in your impurity, artificiality, superficiality, and duplicity, for these appear in sharp relief in the comparison you make unwillingly between yourself and him. He exercises no worldly power; he gives no harsh commands, but you feel in him an unyielding firmness in his convictions, in his life, in the advice he gives, and so his opinion about what you should do, expressed with delicacy or by a discreet look, becomes for you a command and to fulfill that command you find yourself capable of any effort or sacrifice.

In the delicacy of a saint the authority of God is transparent. At the same time his recommendation gives you a power that frees you from the powerlessness in which you have found yourself, from the lack of confidence you have had in yourself, because you perceive it as a divine power. You feel that he gives you light and power from the ultimate fount of light and power, with a goodness that comes from the ultimate source of goodness and wishes to save you. You fear his gazing into your soul, just as you fear the discovery of the truth by a doctor whose skill and friendship cannot be doubted, yet you wait for that gaze just as you wait for the doctor's gaze, for you know that along with the diagnosis he will give you the medicine for your recovery from serious illness. In his utmost delicacy, mildness, and humility you feel a power to help which no earthly power can deflect, a power that comes to him from God, from his total surrender to God and from his will, at God's command and by God's mission, to serve his fellow men so they may be saved. Whoever approaches a saint discovers in him the peak of goodness, purity, and spiritual power covered over by the veil of humility. You have to go to great pains to discover the mighty deeds of his *askesis* and of his love for men, yet his eminence imposes itself through the air of goodness and purity that surrounds him. He is the illustration of the greatness and power in kenosis.

From the saint there radiates an imperturbable quiet or peace and simultaneously a participation in the pain of others that reaches to the point of tears. He is rooted in the loving and suffering stability of God incarnate and rests in the eternity of the power and goodness of God, as Saint Maximos the Confessor says, and, like Melchizedek, is totally imbued with the presence of God.⁴¹ This eternity of his unshakenness in love for God and for men does not exclude his participation in the sufferings of men, just as Christ does not cease to offer his sacrifice for them, nor do the angels cease to offer their assistance continually to men. For persistence in that love which suffers and helps is itself an eternity. This is the "rest," the stability, or the "sabbath" into which the saints have entered (Heb 3.18; 14.11) as those who have come out of the Egypt of the passions; it is not the sabbath of a nirvana of insensibility. For the saint's rest in the eternity of God's unshaken love for men has the force to draw others also towards it and therefore to help them overcome pain courageously and not to succumb in despair.

Thus the saint is one who goes before and helps others on the path that leads towards the future of eschatological perfection.

He has triumphed in some way over time, while being powerfully present within time. In this way he has won a supreme degree of likeness to God, and has God within himself along with God's stability in the good and in his love for mankind. In God the saint has reached the fullness of the human essence. He has reached the point where the human essence is one with existence, as Evdokimov declares.⁴²

The saint represents the human in its purified state through whose subtlety of spirit and body shines his model of infinite goodness and power, that is, God. The saint is the restored image of the living and personal absolute, a peak at once staggeringly close and staggeringly exalted and sublime, capable of a completely open and uninterrupted dialogue with the Trinitarian communion.

The saint anticipates the dawning lights of the eternal and perfected humanity. The face of Christ, the model-face for all human faces, shines through the faces of all the saints. In themselves — as particular hypostatizations of it — the saints reveal and make effective the climactic humanity of Christ. More than this even: inasmuch as true humanity is the image of God, they reveal God, God made man, in human form.

If holiness is the pure and communicative transparency of one person for another person, it has its ultimate source in the tripersonality of God. The subject of holiness can only be a person in his pure relation with another person. Holiness comes about in the purity and delicacy of the perfect relation of one person towards another person. For, in other terms, purity and delicacy are the total fidelity, transparency, and attention of one person towards other persons, total self-transcendence towards them. From eternity this fidelity and self-transcendence find their supreme degree among the divine persons. The Spirit, as Spirit of the Father and of the Son, as the same Spirit in both, expressing as person this perfect fidelity between both, is called Holy in a special way.

From the perfection of reciprocal Trinitarian fidelity and attention, the power of fidelity and attention is imparted to us too through the Holy Spirit, towards God in the first place and, through him, among us also. Whoever dedicates himself with fidelity to God, therefore, is "consecrated" and "sanctified," and this comes about through the reception of the Holy Spirit and always for the sake of God and for the sake of the mission of bringing other people to God. This causes us to be in one Spirit with the Father and the Son. Things too can be consecrated so that they may be used faithfully for God. But the one who uses them faithfully for God is the one who believes. In such a one man's total faithfulness towards God and his character as one delegated by God with the administration of material things for the glory of God and the salvation of his fellow men is manifested. For the one who is totally faithful to God becomes totally faithful to his fellows, and includes his fidelity to them within the framework of his fidelity to God, as Christ did: "For their sake I consecrate myself" (Jn 17.19). Man can become totally faithful to God because of Christ's fidelity to man: "You shall be holy; for I the Lord your God am holy" (Lev 19.2). For this reason man's relation with God is likened to the bond between bride and bridegroom. Now the Church is holy because she is the faithful bride of Christ. The people of Israel were defiled when they forgot their fidelity towards God, when they made God's presence through Israel into something which was not transparent.

But the one who is totally faithful to God and, through this, to his fellows is humanized or receives a higher measure of human sensibility. Thus to be sanctified means to be humanized and any genuine humanization is at the same time sanctification.

The full holiness, the full priesthood of man has been realized in Christ. It is through this, moreover, that humanization in the highest degree has been realized in Christ as well, for he gave himself entirely to God through his life of obedience without compromise and through his sacrifice. But precisely in this way he gave himself to us too in just as total a fashion. As man he has placed himself within that same transparency and fidelity towards God and towards us in which he exists as God, but within a transparency fully accessible to us. In Christ the intertrinitarian fidelity has come down among us in a divine person so that it might also become something proper to the humanity he assumed, as fidelity towards God and towards us, and so that it might communicate its power to us too in order for us to make it our own in both directions. That is why the divine hypostasis of the eternal perfect fidelity has become also the hypostasis of humanity, that is to say, the human hypostasis of this same fidelity.

Christ transmits to us this power of fidelity through the Holy Spirit who, of the Trinity, has passed into him also as man. In his sacrifice is the power of our sacrifice, in his priesthood the power of our priesthood. In his very incarnation there is achieved an ultimate surrender of the human. "And since man only exists to the extent to which he abandons himself [we would say sanctifies himself], the Incarnation of God [in whom the human accepts to go beyond itself, receiving as its hypostasis the divine hypostasis in order to become fully transparent and the abode of the general human transparence], thus appears as the supreme and unique case of the essential fulfillment of the human reality."[43]

Because he is supreme holiness in human form, Christ is also the man for others in the highest and most exemplary degree. If the saint is a man *for* others, inasmuch as he is in the first place a man *for* God, Christ is the man for others in the highest degree, not so as to dispense us from the duty of sanctification, but so that we too might achieve holiness, that is, active fidelity towards God and towards our fellow men.

In his work *Adoration and Worship in Spirit and Truth*, Saint Cyril of Alexandria stressed the fact that we cannot become saints except in Christ, because he takes us into himself in his state as the sacrifice offered to God, and breathes into us that same act and state of sacrifice — or self-transcendence, or total fidelity towards God — in which he himself exists.

Through Christ, holiness, as the supreme reciprocal transparency of the persons of the Holy Trinity, is communicated to us as the perfect sensibility of the relation between the human person and God, and thus among human persons also.

God wants the whole world to be filled with saints; he wants the whole world to be sanctified so that his holiness may be seen and glorified everywhere in the world and the world become a new heaven and a new earth where justice — that is, fidelity, openness, holiness — abides because it has been extended into the world from the Holy Trinity.

Orthodoxy believes that through spirituality, through the penetration into the world of the uncreated energies, the world is transfigured, a transfiguration which also depends on efforts towards holiness made by believers who are strengthened by these energies. For in these energies, which have come to belong to men also, God in Trinity is made transparent.

It is only in the experience of holiness that our nature, filled with the effective presence of God, has not only a theoretical knowledge of God but one that comes through the experience of his presence, power, and love. "Strive for peace with all men, and for the holiness without which no one will see the Lord" (Heb 12.14). In this way whoever exists in holiness, exists also in the truth, in the knowledge of God through the experience of God, in God himself, the *Truth* that sanctifies: "Sanctify them in Thy truth" (Jn 17.17). "I consecrate myself, that they also may be consecrated in truth" (Jn 17.19). The saints know God in his presence at work in them and in the world. They know him in the sweetness of goodness and peace, in his transforming, transfiguring, and perfecting power in them and in all things. Holiness is not something static and individual but a process of unending Christian humanization through deification which is brought about in the relations between men and God, among men themselves, and between them and the cosmos as a whole.

Goodness and Love

Dionysios the Areopagite holds that the most proper name that is worthy of the divine subsistence and also makes it distinct from all others, is that of goodness, or goodness beyond the good. Thus through its very existence or supra-existence it extends the good as essential good (τὸ εἶναι ἀγαθόν, τὸ οὐσιῶδες ἀγαθόν) to all existences, just as the sun illuminates all things not because of any decision it has made, but by its very existence. Through the rays of the goodness of the supra-existent Sun all things exist: essences, powers, activities, from the highest and most spiritual to the lowest and most material. Through the rays of this goodness all things are maintained in unity and progress in the good.[44] The good who is beyond goodness gives

The Spiritual Attributes of God 239

existence and form to all things. In him there is that which is above essence, life, wisdom, or mind. Even what does not yet exist in the good, or does not exist completely, tends towards the good and strives to reach and to exist in the good, above being.[45]

From Dionysios' whole conception of the distinction between the divine supraexistence and the existences that have their origin in it, it is plain that he does not think that the existence of all degrees is extended as a good from the supraexistent deity by means of an emanation in the Neoplatonic, pantheist sense, but in the sense that the deity proceeds to the act of creation due to his supra-existent goodness, and in the sense that this creation can only be good given that the deity too is good through its very existence or supra-existence. Dionysios puts this in a more direct way when he declares that God is "also carried outside of himself in the loving care he has for everything."[46] But providential care is a willed act.

Dionysios speaks of the movement through which God goes out of himself, after all things have been brought into existence. Then he is in some fashion attracted by what is his own, or rather the God who has not gone out of himself is attracted by his presence which has gone out of himself and which is found in creatures.

Dionysios the Areopagite makes no distinction between goodness, love (*agapê*), and *erôs*. "The sacred writers lift up a hymn of praise to this Good. They call it beautiful, beauty, love, and beloved."[47] "For, in my opinion, the sacred writers regard 'yearning' and 'love' as having one and the same meaning."[48] "To those listening properly to the divine things the name 'love' is used by the sacred writers in divine revelation with the exact same meaning as the term 'yearning!' What is signified is a capacity to effect a unity, an alliance, and a particular commingling in the Beautiful and the Good. It is a capacity which preexists through the Beautiful and the Good. It is dealt out from the Beautiful and the Good."[49]

The unifying force of good, or of love, or of *erôs* lies in the fact that the divine yearning *(erôs)* "brings ecstasy so that the lover belongs not to self but to the beloved."[50] This tendency, whether it is called *good* or *agapê* or *erôs*, does not merely urge the creature towards God, but also God towards the creature. Properly speaking, this tendency pertains first and foremost to God being urged towards creatures. The texts of Dionysios in this sense are so clear that they provide no foundation for the Protestant interpretation that it is only the creature who is attracted to God through *erôs* and hence salvation would be a natural work of the creature. The creature too tends towards God only because it has its origin in God who has implanted this tendency within it. But inasmuch as sin has weakened this tendency, it was necessary for it to be recreated by the grace of the *erôs* or love of God. Through *erôs*, therefore, there is expressed that same descent of God towards creatures which is also expressed through love (*agapê*).

The divine love is, therefore, God's movement towards creatures, towards union with them. But for there to be movement towards someone, an eternal movement of this kind must exist in God. If, in general, *erôs* means the movement full of longing on two sides, it cannot exist where only one of the sides is person while the other is passive object of longing and love.

This means that in God there is a community of persons among whom love is manifested. Love in God would itself also imply a movement from one person towards the other. But since in God no movement exists which has as its purpose the surpassing of one degree of love for the sake of a more intense degree — and hence also the overcoming of a distance that might exist between the divine persons — or which aims at a fuller union between the persons, the movement of love in God is united in a paradoxical way with immobility. Dionysios himself says this, declaring that God is above not only movement but also immobility,[51] just as Saint Maximos, his commentator, will say the same thing, stating that God must not be thought of in the immobility that we know or can imagine. He specifies: "Then, properly speaking, God neither moves at all nor stands, for this is proper to those who are limited by nature and have a beginning of their existence ... for by nature he is above any movement and stability."[52]

But already Saint Gregory of Nyssa had said: "This is the most marvelous thing of all: how the same thing is both a standing still and a moving."[53] Each divine person goes out of himself totally towards the others. But it is precisely through this that he makes no movement which has as its purpose the realization of a greater going out from himself. For he is totally with the others or has the others totally in himself. Because they are all within the same integral movement, they can be said to be unmoved. Yet since they are not confused with each other, love is still a going out, hence a movement from one to the other. It is persistence in the same going out to the other persons, a going out which is permanently at the limit of its desire.

In this reciprocal, total, and hence stable going out of the divine persons the possibility is given of their common movement towards personal creatures, while love is realized as the going out of each towards the other. God desires to reach the created person, or his union with him, not only through his ecstasy towards the person, but also through the person's ecstasy towards him. Although the creature by its nature exists in God, because of its inadequate love it remains at a distance from him, and for this reason he empties himself by coming down to the creature and by accepting that the creature has its place at a certain distance from himself, and that to the overcoming of this distance the person should also make a willing contribution. For in order to bring about a love with created being too, God brought into existence not only a world of objects, but also a world of subjects who exist before his face at a distance which they can make either smaller or larger.

God's wish is that the interval (*diastasis*) between himself and these persons be overcome not only through his movement, but also through their own free movement towards him. For as long as the creature manifests a will which is not in accord with God's will, the distance between himself and the creature remains.[54] By moving towards God the creature puts its will in accord with its nature where God has implanted the desire of love for himself and the power to move towards himself. But this is a nature to which God has given back its original "powers" untainted or "the power of love through which it can renew the union with God and with its neighbors, since it opposes the love of self."[55]

Thus on the one hand God sets his power in motion in relationship with his creatures; on the other hand, through this movement of his love for them, he breathes into them their own love for him, once, through creation, he has given them this capacity and reestablished it moreover through the grace of Christ. By bringing them into existence and endowing them with so many gifts, including that of knowledge, God appears before their eyes as worthy of love — itself another form through which he sets them within the movement of love for himself. However, because this movement grew weak through sin, new instances of God's going out towards them were made necessary if their movement towards him was to be reestablished. Properly speaking, it is hard to separate the creation of love in creatures, through the fact that God seems worthy of love because of the gifts given them in the act of creation, and the activity of providence and of the recreation of their powers from God's new, permanent, and loving going out towards his creatures in Christ. All these three kinds of going out are manifestations of his love for creatures, but at the same time they are actions through which he makes himself worthy of their love and thus actions that produce the love of creatures for him.

From God's love for his creatures springs their love for him and thus their love for him cannot be separated from his love for them. That is why the Fathers make no distinction between them. The love of creatures for God is the gift of God, produced by the love God has for them, which returns bearing the fruit of their love for God. The love by which they themselves move towards him is the love by which God moves them towards himself.

Two persons who love one another no longer know what in this love belongs to each person from his own side or from the other person. If the other person did not love him, he would have no power to love the other; and if he did not love the other, the other would have no power to love him either. Each one makes the other capable of loving him through his own love and at the same time through an attraction exercised over the other. But even this attraction exercised over the other comes from his love for the other.

"Why is it, however, that theologians sometimes refer to God as Yearning (ἔρως) and Love and sometimes as the yearned-for and the Beloved? On the one hand he causes, produces, and generates what is being referred to, and, on the other hand, he is the thing itself. He is stirred by it and he stirs it. He is moved to it and he moves it. So they call him. . . yearning and love because he is the power moving and lifting all things up to himself. . . . "[56]

But even in this going out, God goes out by means of a power that still remains in himself. "And, in truth, it must be said too that the very cause of the universe in the beautiful, good superabundance of his benign yearning (δι' ὑπερβολὴν τῆς ἀγαθότητος) for all is also carried outside of himself in the loving care he has for everything. He is, as it were, beguiled by goodness, by love, and by yearning and is enticed away from his transcendent dwelling place and comes to abide within all things, and he does so by virtue of his supernatural and ecstatic capacity to remain, nevertheless, within himself."[57]

The fullest loving going out towards creatures was carried out by God through the incarnation of his Son who assumed human nature. But simultaneously the Son filled human nature with his divine love for the Father. Through love the Holy Spirit unites us with God and among ourselves and becomes the bearer of love from God to us and from us to God and one another, just as God's incarnate Son is too. The Spirit moves us from within through his love which he has from the Father and brings to us the love of the Father and the love between himself and the Father, while at the same time implanting in us too his own love for the Father and for all men.

In our life on earth we are on the path towards perfect love of God and of our neighbors. We will reach this perfect love and union with God and our neighbors in the life to come if we strive for it in this life. Creation is on the path of love; it receives its power from the trinitarian love and advances towards its own perfection in the union with the holy Trinity and with all men.

NOTES

1. *The Divine Names* 7.2, PG 3.869A-B; ET Luibheid/Rorem, pp. 107-108.
2. Ibid. 1.1, PG 3.588B; ET Luibheid/Rorem, p.50.
3. Ibid. 7.1, PG 3.865B; ET Luibheid/Rorem, p. 105.
4. Ibid. 7.2, PG 3.869A; ET Luibheid/Rorem, p. 107.
5. Ibid. 7.2, PG 3.869A-B; ET Luibheid/Rorem, pp. 107, 108.
6. *Church Dogmatics*, vol. 2. 1 pp. 551-553.
7. Ludwig Ott, *Fundamentals of Catholic Dogma*, ed. J. Bastible (Cork, 1955), p. 39.
8. *The Divine Names* 7.2, PG 3.869C; ET Luibheid/Rorem, p. 108.
9. Maximus the Confessor, *The Ambigua*, PG 91.1216B-C.
10. *The Ambigua*, PG 91.1240A-41C.
11. *The Divine Names* 7.4, PG 3.872D.
12. Cf. *Kosmische Liturgie,*/Einsiedeln 1961 2 rev, pp. 76-78, 84-90.
13. *The Divine Names* 7.1, PG 3.865C-868A; ET Luibheid/Rorem, p. 106.
14. *Homily* 15; ET p. 85.
15. *Oration* 31.14, PG 36.149A; ET Hardy/Richardson, p. 202.
16. Ibid. 31.12, PG 36.148A; ET Hardy/Richardson, p. 201.
17. Cf. *The Divine Names* 4.4, 6, PG 3.697B-700A, 700B-701B; ET Luibheid/Rorem, pp. 74-76.
18. Ibid. 4.6, PG 3.701A-B; ET Luibheid/Rorem, p. 76.
19. Ibid. 7.3, PG 3.872A; ET Luibheid/Rorem, pp. 108-09.
20. Ibid. 7.3, PG 3.872A; ET Luibheid/Rorem, p. 109.

21. *The Orthodox Faith* 2.30, PG 94.969B-972A; ET Chase, p. 263.
22. *The Incomprehensible Nature of God* 8.5, PG 48.775; ET Harkins [= 8.38], p. 228.
23. *The Divine Names* 7.1, PG 3.868A; ET Luibheid/Rorem, p. 106.
24. *The Incomprehensible Nature of God* 6.4, PG 48.754; ET Harkins [= 6.33], p. 180.
25. *Homily* 4; ET p. 37.
26. Ibid. 15; ET p. 86.
27. *The Divine Names* 8.7, PG 3.893D-896B; ET Luibheid/Rorem, p. 113.
28. Symeon the New Theologian, *Ethical Discourse* 9.485-492, ed. Darrouzès, *SC* 129, p. 254.
29. *Homily* 5; ET p. 48.
30. Maximus the Confessor, *Questions to Thalassius* 22, PG 90.321B.
31. *The Ambigua* PG 91.1081C-D.
32. *Homily* 71; ET pp. 344-345.
33. Ibid. 4; ET p. 36.
34. Symeon the New Theologian, *Ethical Discourse* 1.3.99-119, ed. Darrouzès, *SC* 122, pp. 202/204.
35. *Ethical Discourse* 1.3.108-115, 117-118, ed. Darrouzès, *SC* 122, p. 204.
36. See the texts of Cyril of Alexandria, *Adoration and Worship in Spirit and Truth*, cited in n. 29, p. 196 above.
37. Cf. Mühlen, *Entsakralisierung*, pp. 10-12.
38. Alexander Schmemann, *For the Life of the World* (NY 1963) p. 69.
39. Schmemann, *For the Life of the World*, pp. 3-7.
40. *The Ambigua*, PG 91.1193C-1196C.
41. Ibid. PG 91.1144A-C.
42. *La femme et le salut du monde*, p. 221.
43. Karl Rahner, "Considérations générales sur la christologie," in *Problèmes actuels de christologie*, ed. H. Bouëssé, (Bruges 1965) p. 21.
44. *The Divine Names* 4.1, PG 3.693B-696A; ET Luibheid/Rorem, pp. 71-72.
45. Ibid. 4.3, PG 3.697A; ET Luibheid/Rorem, p. 73.
46. Ibid. 4.13, PG 3.712A-B; ET Luibheid/Rorem, p. 82.
47. Ibid. 4.7, PG 3.701C.; ET Luibheid/Rorem, p. 76.
48. Ibid. 4.12, PG 3.709B; ET Luibheid/Rorem, p. 81.
49. Ibid. 4.12, PG 3.709C-D; ET Luibheid/Rorem, p. 81. Dionysios does not know the distinction between *erôs* and *agapê* made by Protestant theologians (for example, Nygren) who consider the former as the natural attraction felt by creatures towards God, and the latter as the benevolent inclination of God towards creatures. They attribute to the Fathers a Platonism opposed to Christianity, inasmuch as it loses sight of the love of God who bends down towards creatures (*agapê*). We leave to one side the fact that this distinction hides the Protestant criticism of patristic thought in the name of an exaggerated conception of man's sinfulness.
50. Ibid. 4.13, PG 3.712A; ET Luibheid/Rorem, p. 82.
51. Ibid. 4.10, PG 3.705C; ET Luibheid/Rorem, p. 79.
52. *The Ambigua*, PG 91.1221A-B.
53. *The Life of Moses*, PG 44.405C; ET Malherbe/Ferguson [= 243], p. 117.
54. Maximos the Confessor, *Letter* 2, PG 91.396B-D.
55. *Letter* 2, PG 91.397C.
56. *The Divine Names* 4.14, PG 3.712C; ET Luibheid/Rorem, p. 82.
57. Ibid. 4.13, PG 3.712A-B; ET Luibheid/Rorem, p. 82.

Chapter Ten

The Holy Trinity: Structure of Supreme Love

The Mystery of the Holy Trinity

Love always presupposes two "I's" who love one another or one "I" loving another who receives that love, or of whom the lover knows that he is aware of his love. And this in reciprocity. At the same time, however, love unites these two "I's" in proportion to the love between them, though without confusing them with one another, for that would put an end to love. Thus, perfect love is a paradoxical union of these two things: on the one hand, many "I's" who love one another while remaining unconfused, and, on the other hand, the highest degree of unity among them. Apart from the existence of a perfect eternal love there can be no explanation for love in the world, nor is the purpose of the world at all evident. Love in the world presupposes as its origin and purpose the eternal perfect love between a number of divine persons. This love does not produce the divine persons, as Catholic theology affirms, but presupposes them. Otherwise it would be possible to conceive of an impersonal love that produced and dissolved human persons. From eternity the divine persons remain perfect, for their love is that perfection of love which is not able to increase the communion among them. Were this not the case, the origin of all things would have begun from utmost separation, from absence of love. Love, however, presupposes a common being in three persons, as Christian teaching tells us.

In its turn, reciprocal love among men implies that there are many persons capable of loving on the basis of an essence which, in a certain meaure, is common to them all. This unperfected love between us presupposes, however, the perfect love between divine persons with a common being. Our love finds its explanation in the fact that we are created in the image of the Holy Trinity, the origin of our love.

From supernatural revelation we know that God is essence subsisting in three persons. But nothing like this exists in the created order, and even if it did exist, it would differ wholly from the tripersonal subsistence of the infinite and uncreated essence. Hence, even expressed in this way, it remains a mystery. That is why we must not imagine that we have completely understood the reality of the Trinity. This is to remain at the level of our earthly understanding and the Trinity then becomes an idol for us, halting the movement of our spirit towards that mystery of the plenitude of life which transcends understanding. On the other hand, however, there is no need for us to give up this expression altogether, as if it said nothing real in reference to God. We would then either sink down into the world of the undefined which gives us certainty about nothing at all — and thus no certitude about eternal existence through communion with the divine Personal reality — or else we would be left with the formula for an impersonal or unipersonal god who does not possess the spirit of communion within himself, and hence is neither apt for, nor disposed towards, communion with created persons.

In the view of Dionysios the Areopagite, developing here a statement of Saint Paul (Eph 3.15), only a God who is Father and Son explains the whole reality of earthly paternity and sonship. The warmth of differentiated human relationships derives from the existence of a God who is no stranger to the affection of such relationships. Moreover, these relations receive a spiritual quality from God through the Holy Spirit. Conversely, therefore, relations among the divine persons transcend paternal and human relations among human beings to an incomparable degree just as the Spirit who perfects these relations is incomparably transcendent. Dionysios says: "The procession of our intellectual activity can at least go this far, that all fatherhood and all sonship are gifts bestowed by that supreme source of Fatherhood and Sonship on us and on the celestial powers. . . . Fatherhood and Sonship of this kind are brought to perfection in a spiritual fashion, that is incorporeally, immaterially, and in the domain of mind, and this is the work of the divine Spirit, which is located beyond all conceptual immateriality and all divinization, and it is the work too of the Father and of the Son who supremely transcend all divine Fatherhood and Sonship."[1]

The dogmatic formula concerning the deity as one in being and threefold in persons is, like any dogmatic formula, the confession of faith in a reality which saves us and consequently — given the infinite abyss of the Godhead - provides our understanding with at least a minimum of content. It defines the Christian teaching about God

Holy Trinity: Structure of Supreme Love 247

over against other teachings only in the sense that such a deity, as the basis for loving communion with us in eternity, can alone be a saving God. But in what this dogmatic formula provides for our understanding, it comprises the framework of genuine infinity and opens for us the prospect of our personal participation in the Godhead for all eternity. For it is within the perfect and eternal communion of the three persons, in whom the unique supra-essence of the Godhead subsists, that the infinity and perfection which mark the loving life of the Trinity and of each divine person are given. Moreover, only through the Trinity is our eternal communion with the infinite love of God assured as such, together with communion among ourselves as those who partake of this infinity and yet remain distinct. The Trinity thereby assures our continuance and perfection as persons to all eternity. As something simultaneously revealed to us and yet transcending all understanding, the doctrine of the Trinity constitutes the foundation, infinite reservoir, power, and model of our growing eternal communion; yet it also spurs us on to grow and think continuously in spirit, and helps us both pass continually beyond any level we may already have reached in our personal communion with God and among ourselves, and also strive for an ever more profound grasp of the mystery of supreme communion.

Thus Dionysios the Areopagite affirms the certainty of irreducible distinction among the three divine persons within the unity of being just as powerfully as he asserts the character of the divine being as a mystery inaccessible to our understanding.

"The unified names apply to the entire Godhead.... Hence, titles such as the following — the transcendently good, the transcendently divine, the transcendently existing, the transcendently living, the transcendently wise. These and similar terms concern a denial in the sense of a superabundance.... Then there are the names expressing distinctions, the transcendent name and proper activity of the Father, of the Son, of the Spirit. Here the titles cannot be interchanged, nor are they held in common."[2]

Holding in what follows to the framework provided by these two essential patristic directions, we will refrain from explaining the generation of the Son and the procession of the Holy Spirit, that is, the mode of being of the three persons. Instead we will confine ourselves only to casting their unity of being and of love into relief. Thus we seek to avoid the psychologizing explanations of Catholic theology which has recourse to these only from its desire to find human arguments in favor of the *Filioque*, the doctrine that the Holy Spirit proceeds also from the Son.

As a work of raising up believers to intimate communion with God, salvation and deification are nothing other than the extension to conscious creatures of the relations that obtain between the divine persons. That is why the Trinity reveals itself essentially in the work of salvation and that is why the Trinity is the basis on which salvation stands. Only because a triune god exists does one of the divine persons — namely the one who stands in relationship as Son vis-à-vis the other and, as man too, can remain within this affectionate relationship as Son — become incarnate, placing all his human brothers within this relationship as sons to the heavenly Father, or indeed placing his Father within a paternal relationship to all men. Saint John of Damascus suggests that the incarnation is the mode of union between two subsistences, proper only to the only begotten Son and the Word so that his personal attribute might remain unchanged,[3] or so that as man too he might remain in filial relationship to the Father.

Saint Gregory the Theologian says: "Be reconciled to God (2 Cor 5.20) and do not quench the Spirit (1 Thess 5.19); or rather may Christ be reconciled to you, and may the Spirit enlighten you. But if you are too fond of your quarrel, we at any rate will hold fast to the Trinity, and by the Trinity may we be saved."[4]

Through the incarnate Son we enter into filial communion with the Father, while through the Spirit we pray to the Father or speak with him as sons. For the Spirit unites himself with us in prayer. "It is the Spirit in whom we worship, and in whom we pray. . . . Therefore, to adore or to pray in the Spirit seems to me to be simply himself offering prayer or adoration to himself."[5] But this prayer which the Spirit offers, within us, he offers to himself in our name, and into this prayer we too are drawn. Through grace the Spirit identifies himself with us so that, through grace, we may identify ourselves with him. Through grace the Spirit eliminates the distance between our "I" and his "I," creating between us and the Father, through grace, the same relation he has by nature with the Father and the Son. If in the incarnate Son we have become sons by grace, in the Spirit we gain the consciousness and boldness that come from being sons.

By becoming incarnate the Son is also avowing as man his filial love of the Father, but is an obedient love; likewise he reveals the Father to men so that they may love him precisely as Father. At the same time, to the Son in his character as incarnate Son, and through the Son to us as well, the Father is avowing his own love as Father. Moreover, the Holy Spirit makes spiritual the humanity assumed by the Son and deifies it, which is to say, makes it fit to participate in the love which the divine hypostasis of the Son has toward his Father. The revelation of the Trinity, occasioned by the incarnation and earthly activity of the Son, has no other purpose than to draw us after grace, to draw us through the Holy Spirit into the filial relationship the Son has with the Father. The trinitarian acts of revelation are acts that save and deify, acts that raise us up into communion with the persons of the Holy Trinity. For this reason the Fathers take all their proofs for the Holy Trinity from the work of salvation accomplished in Christ.

A unipersonal god would not have within himself that eternal love or communion into which he would wish to introduce us too. Nor would such a god become incarnate; instead he would instruct us from afar about how we were to live rightly. Indeed, were he to become incarnate, he would not, as man, be established in relationship with God as with a different person, but, even as man, would impart to himself the consciousness of being the supreme reality. Furthermore, such a god would either impart this same consciousness to all men or, even in his character as man, would appear devoid of that humility a human being has in relation to God whom he approaches not as his own hypostasis, but as one distinct from himself. In Christ, however, we are saved because in him we have a relationship to God which is at once correct and intimate. We are saved in Christ because in him and from him we possess the fullness of exaltation and the fullness of humility; we experience the total warmth of communion and yet are maintained eternally each in his own personal reality. Christ is the Son who is equal in being with the Father while standing in filial relation to the Father, and at the same time he is the man who prays and sacrifices himself to the Father for the sake of his human brothers, teaching them how they are to pray and sacrifice themselves in their turn.

An incarnate god who was not the Son of a Father would not remain as person through relationship with another person equal to himself. The humanity such a god had assumed would sink down within him as into some impersonal abyss and have no share in the love of the Son for the Father.

There was a time when the coincidence of opposites was considered incompatible with reason. Wherever a synthesis of such a kind was encountered — and the whole of reality is like this — reason would break it up into irreconcilable and contradictory notions, setting up some elements over against others or trying to melt them all down by force into one new element. In the understanding of reality, however, reason has now become accustomed to unifying the principles of distinction and unity to such an extent that it is no longer hard to see the antinomic model of being that characterizes the whole of reality. It is an accepted fact for reason that plurality does not break apart unity, nor does unity do away with plurality. In fact, plurality necessarily exists within unity, or, to express it another way, unity is manifested in plurality. It is a fact that plurality maintains unity and unity maintains plurality, and that the decline of either of them means the weakness or disappearance of the life or existence of any individual entity. This conception of the mode of being of reality is recognized today as superior to former ideas of what was rational, while under the pressure of reality the idea of what is rational has itself become complex and antinomic. Assertions formerly considered irrational because of their apparently contradictory character are now recognized as indications of a natural stage towards which reason must strive, for the understanding of this stage constitutes the natural destiny of reason, and the stage is itself an image of the supernatural character of that perfect unity of what is distinct within the Holy Trinity.

Today many see the plurality of the entire creation as something made specific in all manner of trinities. Bernhard Philberth, for example, declares that the whole of creation is a threefold reflection of the Trinity.[6]

The effort to understand the constitution of reality as both unitary and distinct helps us rise towards the suprarational paradox of that perfect unity of three distinct persons which is represented by the unity of being of the three divine persons. As we rise towards this understanding, we move also to promote an ever greater unity among ourselves as distinct human persons. For the most suitable image for the Holy Trinity is found in human unity of being and personal distinction. Naturally this effort we make is not enough to raise us up towards a greater understanding of the Holy Trinity, known through revelation, and make unity among us a deeper thing. For that we must be helped by the very grace of the Holy Trinity, which is to say, by the power of the Trinity that strengthens unity within us without simultanously weakening us as persons, and so aids us in understanding more deeply a supreme unity of this kind between persons who remain unconfounded.

If we are to grasp this supreme unity of a number of distinct persons, we have need of power from that very unity itself, and must make use of the imperfect unity among human persons as an obscure image of the Holy Trinity.

Replying to those who objected that human beings also form a single humanity while men are many, and, consequently, that in the Godhead too we must admit that there are three gods, Saint Gregory of Nazianzos says: "In this case the common nature has a unity which is only conceivable in thought; and the individuals are parted from one another very far indeed, both by time and by dispositions, and by power."[7] When he affirms the unity of God in Trinity by contrast with the many gods of the Greeks, Saint Gregory declares: "To us there is one God, for the Godhead is one, and all that proceeds from him is referred to one, though we believe in three persons. For one is not more and another less God; nor is one before and another after; nor are they divided in will or parted in power; nor can you find here any of the qualities of divisible things; but the Godhead is, to speak concisely, undivided in separate persons; and there is one mingling of lights, as it were of three suns joined to each other. When, then, we look at the Godhead, or the first cause, or the *monarchia*, that which we conceive is one; but when we look at the persons in whom the Godhead dwells, and at those who timelessly and with equal glory have their being from the first cause, there are three whom we worship."[8]

Saint John of Damascus states the same: "In three suns joined together without any intervening interval there is one blending and the vision of the light." And a troparion from the Orthodox liturgy of burial has the following expression, "one Godhead in triple splendor."

Saint Basil the Great says that in the case of men being is dispersed and in hypostases we see this dispersed being.[10] In the persons of the Holy Trinity, however, "a continuous and infinite community is visible."[11] Now thought conveys no gradation that might exist as a space between Father, Son, and Holy Spirit, "for there is nothing inserted between them; nor beyond the divine nature is there anything so subsisting (πρᾶγμα ὑφεστώς) as to be able to divide that nature from itself by the interposition of any foreign matter. Neither is there any vacuum of interval, void of subsistence, which can make a break in the mutual harmony of the divine essence, and solve the continuity by the interjection of emptiness."[12] When we think of the Father as incomprehensible and uncreated, we think also of the Son and the Holy Spirit, for the infinity, glory, and wisdom of the Father are not separated from those of the Son and of the Spirit, but in them is contemplated what is uninterruptedly and undividedly common: "For it is in no wise possible to entertain the idea of severance or division, in such a way as that the Son should be thought of apart from the Father, or the Spirit be disjoined from the Son. But the communion and the distinction apprehended in them are, in a certain sense, ineffable and inconceivable, the continuity of nature being never rent asunder by the distinction of the hypostases, nor the notes of proper distinction confounded in the community of essence."[13]

Moreover, Saint Athanasios too declares: "Yet, in saying that the Son is in himself (καθ' ἑαυτόν) and both lives and exists like the Father, we do not on that account separate him from the Father, imagining place and interval between their union in the way of bodies. For we believe that they are united with each other without mediation or distance, and that they exist inseparable; all the Father embosoming the Son, and all the Son hanging from and adhering to the Father, and alone resting on the Father's breast continually."[14]

In fact continuity of nature exists even among us men. The Holy Fathers did not see this completely, for the degree of development that marked the consciousness of nature and spiritual reflection in their time gave them no possibility of observing it. In comparison with the unity of God's being, however, the unity of our nature is much reduced. "For we are not only compound beings, but also contrasted beings, both with one another and with ourselves; nor do we remain entirely the same for a single day, to say nothing of a whole lifetime, but both in body and in soul are in a perpetual state of flow and change."[15] "For in these (Father, Son and Holy Spirit) there is no distinction in time, nor are they torn away from their connection with each other. . . . "[16]

Each person of the Holy Trinity, revealing himself in the world and active in and among human beings, manifests perfect unity vis-à-vis the other two persons both through his own being and through his perfect love for them. Yet at the same time, from the love he has for the other persons, each person also conveys his love to men. The love we have among ourselves is not perfect, because the unity of being among us is not perfect either. We are called to grow in perfect love among ourselves and in perfect love for God through the uncreated divine energies, for these represent God's unity of being which is conveyed among us and extends the unity of our own human being.

The continuity of human nature subsisting concretely in many hypostases can be imagined graphically as a string on which the hypostases appear, one after the other, like different knots. The knots are not separated by total emptiness, but by a thinness or diminution of the nature that appears in the knots in thickened form, that is, in the actualization of all its potencies. Without that continuity between human persons, represented by the attenuated string of nature, the various concrete forms nature takes in persons could neither be grasped nor preserved. Nevertheless we cannot say that the string exists first and only then come the knots, or that the attenuated string between the knots does not belong to the latter in common. Nor can it be said that the knots produce the string between them. Both string and knots — or at least some of the knots — exist simultaneously. The knots communicate through the string and bring one another into existence. They are able to become more and more interior to one another. In a way, each human hypostasis bears the whole of nature as this is made real in the hypostatic knots and the string which unites them. Individual human beings, in the proper sense, cannot be spoken of as if they were concrete expressions of human nature existing in total isolation. Each hypostasis is linked ontologically with the other and this bond finds expression in the need they all have to be in relation. They are thereby characterized as persons and they develop genuinely when they develop as persons by strengthening continuously the communication between themselves.

When this relationship is a positive one the string between the knots can grow thicker, whereas distance and struggle between the knots makes the string grow thinner until human nature almost snaps or is torn asunder, not as an ontological unity, but as a unity which is called to show itself also in the unity of the will. Saint Maximos the Confessor says: "We were created at the beginning in the unity of nature, but the devil divided us and separated us from God and divided our nature into many opinions and fantasies by making use of the choice of our will."[17]

By means of the fine string of human nature linking human

persons a continuous movement from one person to the other occurs, a mutual penetration and reception that goes on without each person ceasing to maintain his own distinctiveness by preserving this bridge between them.

Yet among human persons there is more than just one such linear string. If there were only the one, then each person could relate directly only to one other person distinct from himself. In fact, however, threads lead out from each person towards all other persons, and these threads can be made actual through direct relations or they can remain at the level of potentiality only. Like a star, every person is the center of endless rays, and through their rays persons are joined together as in a huge net of mesh. Through their rays they both give and receive, and in this way their rays are something they have in common, while the persons themselves remain distinct centers of those rays which go out from them and come towards them. Within this mesh each person is the center of as many actual threads as there are persons in relationship with him, and the center of so many virtual or potential threads as there are persons who could be brought into relationship with him. Moreover, each person can function as center in relation to any other person at all, and so this netting of mesh grows continually from within itself, one part passing, another being added on, as the mesh comes to resemble a sphere of greater and greater density.

Human consubstantiality does not consist, therefore, only in the fact that one and the same nature is possessed by persons who are remote from one another. It consists also in a unique being which all the hypostases bear in solidarity with one another, even though some persons, engulfed by the Spirit of Christ, are being saved, whereas others are not.

The definition of Chalcedon tells us this same thing when it states that Christ is consubstantial with us according to manhood.

Thus, in the created human order — just as in the order of the other genera and species — there unfolds the paradox of unity in plurality.

But the hypostases of the Holy Trinity are not united in the same nature only through such fine threads as these which would bind them together but, to a certain extent, also keep them apart. No kind of attenuation of the divine nature is conceivable among the persons. All three are perfectly one in the other, together possessing in common the whole of the divine nature with no weakening of the continuity between them. In order to have even any understanding of this we must keep in mind that the divine nature is entirely spiritual, and that its spirituality is of a kind that transcends all spirituality known or imagined by us. As such the divine hypostases are free of any of that impermeability or persistent tendency to annex the other from which human hypostases — whom we have accordingly imagined as knots on a string — are never wholly exempt.

The divine hypostases are totally transparent one to another even within the interiority of perfect love. Their consubstantiality is neither preserved nor developed by those fine threads which, on the human analogy, might unite them as bearers of the same being. Rather, each one bears the entire nature in common with the others. They are thereby wholly interior to one another and have no need to leap over even the thinnest of bridges between them so as to achieve a greater unity among themselves by means of such communication. The infinity of each leaves no possibility for any such attenuation of the divine nature among them. They might be likened, after the fashion of the Fathers, to three surpassingly bright and transparent suns which are reciprocally comprised in and appear in one another, bearing undividedly the whole of a single and infinite light. "He who has seen me has seen the Father. . . . Believe me that I am in the Father and the Father in me," said our Savior (Jn 14.9, 11), and Saint Basil declares: "He who has, as it were, mental apprehension of the form of the Son, prints the express image of the Father's hypostasis . . . gazing at the unbegotten beauty in the Begotten."[18]

The Father — the sun in the sense of the paternal subsistence of infinite light — causes the Son to appear in him, that is, the sun in the sense of a reflection of the whole of that infinite light which subsists in the Father. The Father projects himself within himself as a filial sun and views himself henceforth through the latter while comprising the latter in himself, or better, while revealing himself still more luminously through the latter. Moreover, the Father also projects himself within himself as another sun, as Holy Spirit, revealing himself even more luminously as paternal sun and revealing the Son in the same fashion as filial sun. They are three real hypostases, three real modes in which the same infinite light subsists. Each appears shining through the other two as bearer of the same infinite light, being himself interior to them and having them interior to himself.

But in the spiritual order the subsistence of the light as sun implies a conscious subject. The subject cannot be divided from consciousness, nor consciousness from the subject, for consciousness is at one and the same time reality and power inasmuch as it is always the predicate of a subject.

The fact that we speak of the divine hypostases as subjects does not mean that we are reducing the divine nature to a nonsubjective reality. The person does not bring the character of subject (as though this character were something new) to divine nature. For the person is nothing other than the mode of real subsistence that belongs to a nature. But neither does this mean that there exists an impersonal being which gives itself the character of subject. Being does not exist really except in a hypostasis,[19] or — in the case of spiritual being — in the conscious subject.

We can say more: the spiritual essence that is subsistent only in a subject always implies a conscious relation between subjects, and consequently a hypostatization of that essence in numerous subjects, in perfect reciprocal interpenetration and transparence — what Saint John of Damascus termed *perichôrêsis*. For a subject can have no joy in existence apart from communion with other subjects. In the perfect unity of the Trinity the consciousness of the other two subjects, and thereby the very subjects themselves who bear that consciousness, must be perfectly comprised and transparent in the consciousness of each subject.

Hence that subsistent essence which is supreme and spiritual is not a singular conscious subject but a community of subjects who are fully transparent. The Trinity of the divine persons belongs to the divine essence and yet the three persons are not confused with the unity of the essence. Saint Athanasios declares: "But to say of the Son, 'He might not have been,' is an irreligious presumption reaching even to the essence of the Father, as if what is his own might not have been. For it is the same as saying, 'The Father might not have been good.' And as the Father is always good by nature, so is he always generative by nature; and to say 'The Father's good pleasure is the Son,' and 'The Word's good pleasure is the Father,' implies, not a precedent will, but genuineness of nature, and propriety and likeness of essence."[20] And Saint Basil says that what is good is always present with God who is over all, and that it is good to be the Father of such a Son, — that hence what is good was never absent from him, nor was it the Father's will to be without the Son; when he willed he did not lack the power, but having the power and the will to be in the mode in which it seemed good to him, he also always possessed the Son by reason of his always willing that which is good.[21]

In these two texts the existence of the divine persons is inferred from the goodness of God. But in Scholastic dogmatics goodness is held to be an attribute of the divine being. The thought of the Fathers, however, is more complex. They do not conceive of the divine being separately from person; for them the goodness of the being shows itself in the relationship between persons. Of course, they do not thereby confuse the persons, for generation is an incommunicable property of the Father. But in the act of generation there is sumultaneously manifested, in a certain personal way, the attribute of goodness belonging to the divine being. From his own position each person manifests those attributes common to the being.

A lone "I" cannot experience the fullness of existence proper to the divine being, a fullness on which depend that complete joy and happiness found only in the form of pure subjectivity. The joy of the lone "I" is not a complete joy and, therefore, not the fullness of existence. And the joy of existence communicated by one "I" to another "I" must be just as full in the one who receives as in the one who gives. Hence there is also fullness of existence. But this implies the complete self-giving of one "I" to another "I," not merely the giving of something from oneself or from what one possesses. There must be a correlation of total giving and receiving between two "I's" who nevertheless remain distinct within this very possession.

In perfect love persons do not merely engage in a reciprocal exchange of self; they also affirm themselves reciprocally and personally, and establish themselves in existence through giving and receiving. But the divine love is all efficacious. The Father therefore establishes the Son in existence from all eternity by his integral self-giving, while the Son continually affirms the Father as Father from all eternity by the fact that he both accepts his own coming into existence through the Father and also gives himself to the Father as Son. The acts through which the divine persons, in their distinction and through perfect love, affirm one another reciprocally in existence are eternal acts and have a totally personal character, although they are acts in which the divine persons are active together.

If love belongs essentially to God, then the reciprocal relationship in which the love of the persons manifests itself must also have an essential basis, even though the positions occupied by the persons in this relationship do not change among themselves. In God there must be Father, Son, and Holy Spirit. But the persons do not change these positions among themselves. On the other hand, since the being is one and is perfect love, the relationship is that of equal to equal, not that of superior to inferior or stranger to stranger. If God needed to relate to something outside himself, this would imply that he lacked something distinct from himself. Divine relations must take place in God himself, although between distinct "I's," so that the relation and hence the love may be real.[22]

In order to maintain the definition of love as the essential divine act and, simultaneously, the definition of this act as a relation while the divine being remains one, we must see the divine being at one and the same time as unity and as relation, as relation in the very heart of unity. Unity must not be destroyed for the sake of relation, nor relation abolished in favor of unity. Now the Holy Trinity transcends the distinction between unity and relation as we understand them. Reciprocal reference is act, and in God this act is essential and points simultaneously to a distinction of those who have reference one to the other. Reference is common in God, although each person has a different position in this common act of reference: "The true subject is a relation of the three but a relation which appears as essence, that is, a substantial relation."[23]

To each subject of the Trinity the others are interior and at the same time perfectly transparent as other "I's" of his own. Through the act of generation the Son appears in the consciousness of the Father as another self (ἄλλον ἑαυτόν).[24] According to patristic tradition, the self of the Father would not know itself if it did not have the Son in the mirror of its consciousness as another consciousness of its own. This does not mean that the Son brings the Father knowledge of himself from outside, but that the Father knows himself only inasmuch as he is the subsistence of the divine essence as Father, hence inasmuch as he is the begetter of the Son. In other words, the divine essence is light only inasmuch as it subsists really as three hypostases. The fact that it is light appears in that is subsists in three hypostases who together know one another. Saint Athanasios says: "Is God wise and not word-less, or on the contrary, is he wisdom-less and word-less? If the latter, there is an absurdity at once; if the former, we must ask, how is he wise and not word-less? Does he possess the Word and the

Wisdom from without, or from himself? If from without, there must be one who first gave to him, and before he received he was wisdom-less and word-less."[25] And Saint Gregory of Nyssa observes that if the Son, as the Scripture says, is the power, and the wisdom, and the truth, and the light, and the holiness, and the peace, and all the like, before the Son was, as the heretics think, these would not have been either. And without these, they of course will understand the Father's bosom as devoid of all these things."[26]

The self of the Father knows itself by the fact that it knows itself from its image, from the Son, just as the Son knows himself by observing himself in the Father as his model. The subject of the Father begets an image of his own, so that through it he may know himself. The condition of this real knowledge he has, however, is given him not by a simple image he himself conceives, but by a real image which shows the Father, through its existence, not only what he can conceive, but also what he can do and how he can love. That is to say, it is an image which itself also receives thereby the being of the Father. The Father knows himself in the Son and through the Son only inasmuch as the Son — as real image of the Father — projects towards the Father his existence as Son of the Father; but it is in this way that the Son also knows himself. The Father knows himself in the Son not as in a passive image of his own, but as in an active image which also turns back towards the Father its own knowledge of him, knowledge which has become possible inasmuch as it took birth as a real and perfect image of the Father.

Knowledge generally unites in itself two things: the common character of knowledge and the birth of one of the two partners in knowledge from the other. I know myself from what I have produced, because it resembles me. But I know myself best in the one who reproduces the perfect image of me through generation, and so confronts me with my image not only in a passive way but by communicating it to me in an active way.

The begetting of the Son by the Father is the premise for the knowledge which the Father has of himself, a knowledge brought about in common with the Son.

Each one of us knows himself not only from the one whom he has begotten, but also in conjunction with any of his fellow creatures who possesses the same hypostatized nature as his own. In God, however, the second hypostasis can come forth from the first alone because the unity in God is perfect and has its ultimate source in God himself; there is no reference to a higher source. The divine nature is hypostatized in the second hypostasis through his generation from the first, and in the third hypostasis through his procession from the first. No single hypostasis of the Holy Trinity comes forth from two hypostases. Inasmuch, however, as human nature subsists in many hypostases — and in each with certain insufficiencies — and inasmuch as human nature does not arise in its subsistent entities from a single hypostasis directly, and indeed manifests certain intervening distances, each human hypostasis knows himself in the measure in which he knows various other hypostases and overcomes the distance between himself and them. In God, however, the Father possesses the entire hypostatized nature only in the Son and in the Holy Spirit; and between these and himself there is no distance of any kind.

The Divine Intersubjectivity

The spiritual character of the transparency or interpenetration of the divine persons, which is also a compenetration of the consciousness of each, can be still more fully expressed by the term "intersubjectivity".

God is pure subject or Trinity of pure subjects. The entire divine essence, a spiritual essence subsistent in threefold fashion, possesses the quality of being subject or threefold subject. The subsistence of the divine being is nothing other than the concrete existence of divine subjectivity in three modes which compenetrate each other, hence in a threefold subjectivity. Not one of the three subjects sees anything as object in the persons of the others nor in himself; he experiences them as pure subjects and experiences himself too as pure subject. If there were anything in them which had the character of object, this would diminish their full openness to the other two subjects, and so they would not possess themselves as the consciousness of three subjects perfectly interior to one another. Moreover, this would cause them to treat one another as objects to a certain extent, and hence no complete communion would exist among them. This would in turn cause each subject not to be fully open or transparent or in perfect communion with the others.

Full communion comes about only between persons who are and make themselves transparent as pure subjects. The more they are subjects and appear as subjects, the more the relations between them are characterized by a greater and freer degree of communication and communion and by a more evident interiority and conscious reciprocal compenetration, thus bringing into being a still greater intersubjectivity.

The pure character of the divine subjects implies their complete intersubjectivity. That is why we can speak of a single God and three "I's." The three subjects do not detach themselves from one another, each from the consciousness of the others, so as to display the Godhead subsisting separately. Consequently the subjectivity of none of the divine "I's" is diminished. Rather it expands and, in a certain way, comes to take in the others. Each experiences the modes in which the others live the divine being, yet not as his own but as theirs.

By begetting the Son eternally the Father does not thereby somehow make him an object of his own. That is why Christian teaching also makes use of the expression: "the Son takes his birth from the Father" in addition to "the Father begets the Son." Now this begetting/taking birth is eternal and indicates that the Son too has the same character of being pure subject. The generation of the Son from the Father expresses only the unchanged position of the Father as giver and of the Son as receiver of existence, just as it also expresses the relation between them through the act of generation. Both live this act eternally as subjects, but they live it in common or within an intersubjectivity which does not confuse them, for each lives the act from the position that is his own.

For this reason the Catholic terminology of *generatio activa* and *generatio passiva* — the former attributed to the Father, the latter to the Son — is foreign to Orthodox theology. The Son is not passive in his generation from the Father, although he is not the subject who begets but the subject who takes his birth. Neither does the term "procession" in reference to the Holy Spirit mark any passivity on the part of the Holy Spirit such as would make him an object of the Father. The Savior said that the Spirit "proceeds from the Father" (Jn 15.26). The Spirit is eternally in the movement of proceeding from the Father, just as the Son exists eternally in the movement of taking birth from the Father. But neither does this mean that the Father is placed in a state of passivity. The Spirit proceeds, but the Father also causes him to proceed. The procession of the Spirit from the Father is itself an act of pure intersubjectivity of Father and Spirit, without there being any confusion between them. Moreover, as the Father in incomprehensible fashion is the source of both the Son and the Spirit, each of them together with the Father not only lives the act of his own coming forth from the Father, but also joyfully participates along with the other — though from his own position — in living that act whereby the other comes forth from the Father. All three in intersubjectivity experience the act of the Son's generation and of the Spirit's procession, but each from his own position. Once again this forms a community between the three hypostases.

The term "intersubjectivity" stresses the positive communion which takes place between the persons of the Holy Trinity and between the act of generation and that of procession, while the expression *oppositio relationis* used by Catholic theology since Thomas Aquinas to indicate the relations produced by these acts between the divine persons places less emphasis on this reciprocal communication and communion. Saint Basil also spoke of this *oppositio*, but he took care to affirm with equal vigor that in these acts of coming forth there persisted the unity of being of the persons who are "opposed."[27]

But the divine community manifests itself not only through the being of God but also through what is proper to the persons. The "opposition" between them is the specific characteristic each brings to communion; it is the mode whereby one person communicates with another in the act of his coming forth, both giving and receiving. In this way, moreover, the persons sustain themselves in what they are. But communion does not always have need of acts like this in which one person comes forth from the other. In order to achieve communication between himself and the Son and to share intersubjectivity with him, the Holy Spirit has no need of an act whereby he comes forth from the Son. Both are within this intersubjectivity by virtue of the fact that both are from the Father and in the Father, and each, along with the other, rejoices in the Father not only for that act through which he himself has his origin, but also for the act whereby the other one takes his origin, while each rejoices simultaneously with the other in the fact that both have their origin in one and the same source. Some of the Byzantine Fathers and writers have expressed this by speaking of the Spirit "shining forth" from the Son or "coming to rest" upon the Son.[28] Each of the two who come forth rejoices in company with the Father for the fact that he comes forth from him, but he rejoices also in company with the other fot the fact of this coming forth. The pure intersubjectivity of the

Holy Trinity: Structure of Supreme Love   263

three persons also finds manifestation in their reciprocal affirmation of one another as distinct persons.

But there is no longer any place for this reciprocal affirmation of the three subjects as distinct persons in that teaching according to which the Father and the Son, as a single principle, cause the Holy Spirit to proceed.

Intersubjectivity and reciprocal affirmation bring it about that the Father, as he experiences himself as Father, experiences simultaneously — as Father — all the filial subjectivity of the Son. The subjectivity of the Son is interior to him, but as to a Father. It is infinitely more interior to him than is the filial subjectivity of an earthly son to an earthly father, or to an earthly mother which makes her able to substitute herself for her son and live his own joys and sorrows with even more intensity than he himself does. But just as the divine Father experiences the subjectivity of the Son in his own subjectivity as parent, without mingling the two but rather intensifying them, so too does the Son experience the paternal subjectivity of the Father in his own filial subjectivity, that is, as Son. In the Holy Trinity all is common and perichoretic, and yet in this common movement of the subjectivity of the one in the other there is no confusion of the distinct modes in which this subjectivity is experienced together.

The aspiration and, in part, the realized capacity of the human "I" to be a simple unity while simultaneously containing all things and to be in ontological and dialogical relation with other "I's" and thus to have them, in this sense, within himself as subjects is a reality that is perfectly realized in God from all eternity. Otherwise the mode which we have discussed whereby human "I's" are ontologically irreducible and one would be inexplicable, as would also be their dialogical relationship.

In God each "I" is and contains all, but his perfect happiness consists in the fact that each "I' who is the all contains the other "I's" who are themselves also the all, each being the all in this reciprocal act of containing. These "I's" do not encounter one another from the outside, as is the case with human "I's," even though the latter are satisfying an inner necessity. From eternity they are completely interior to one another but not identical, just as human "I's" aspire to become. The divine all (or the infinite divine being) is not multiplied externally, as is true with men, since if this were the case the Godhead would no longer be absolute. It remains perfectly one and nevertheless subsists in three personal modes, each mode containing perfectly in itself the other modes as well. The divine all exists within an ontological dialogue among the three. No partner in the dialogue furnishes any content from outside the dialogue. Each possesses the infinite divine all in dialogical communion with the other two "I's."

For us the difficulty of understanding rests in the fact that in God an "I" has title to what belongs to another "I," while in our case each "I" has title to a content that differs in large measure from that of the other "I."

It is as if another "I" interior to my own "I" had title to all that I am, while I myself remained in possession of what I am and made use of it as the perfect and identical content of a dialogue, the dialogue of a giving and receiving or of an indefatigable love.

In God it is not possible for an "I" to assert himself over against another "I"; instead he continually considers the other as a substitute for himself. Each sees himself only in relation to the other, or regards only the other, or sees himself only in the other. The Father sees himself only as subject of the love for the Son. But the "I" of the Father is not lost because of this, for it is affirmed by the Son who in his turn knows himself only as he fulfills the will of the Father. Yet precisely through this the sense of paternity grows stronger in the Father, and the quality of sonship in the Son. This is the circular movement of each "I" around the other as center ($perich\hat{o}r\hat{e}sis$ = $circumincessio$). Each person discloses not his own "I," but two together reveal the other; nor does each pair of persons disclose their own "I's" in an exclusive way, but they place the other "I" in the forefront, making themselves transparent for that one or hiding themselves (as it were) beneath him. Thus in each hypostasis the other two are also visible. Saint Basil says: "See how sometimes the Father reveals the Son, other times the Son reveals the Father. . . . Thus the entire Godhead is revealed to you sometimes in the Father, other times in the Son and in the Holy Spirit."[29]

In this self-forgetting of each person for the other perfect love is manifested and only this makes possible that unity which is opposed to individualism. The sin of individualism hinders us from understanding that fullness of love and unity which is characteristic of the holy Trinity and is at the same time compatible with the preservation of personal identity.

Holy Trinity: Structure of Supreme Love 265

Only this desire of Christ dwelling within us to substitute the "I" of the Spirit for his own "I," and vice versa, carries us along too into the impulse of substituting the "I" of the Spirit and of Christ and of our neighbor for our own "I," thus reestablishing that unity of our nature which had been dissolved away by sin. As a work of our unification in God and among ourselves, therefore, the work of our salvation can only be the work of the holy Trinity. Saint Maximos the Confessor says: "[Because of love] everyone attracts willingly his neighbor to him and prefers him as much as he rejected him before and wanted to be ahead of him.... [Now] by stripping himself willingly of himself because of love through the separation from the thoughts and the attributes arbitrarily considered as his own, and by bringing himself to simplicity and identity, through which he is not at all separated from what is common but everyone belongs to everyone and all to all, and all belong rather to God than to each other, they have all become one, having through them the one reason of existence which is shown as unique in nature and in will.... This was perhaps achieved by the great Abraham who restored himself within the reason of nature, or the reason of nature in himself, and by this he gave himself to God and has received God.... By this he became worthy to see and to receive God as man coming from the love for men as guests, through the perfect reason according to nature. And he raised himself towards this, leaving behind the characteristic of those which divide and are divided, and no longer thinking of the other man as of another one than himself but of the one as all, and all as one."[30]

The affirmation of the filial "I" through the paternal "I" and vice versa can be seen as it relates to creation not only in the identity of the will but also in the fact that all the works of the Father are accomplished by the Son and vice versa.

Nothing exists in total separation from other things and no unity exists without containing some distinction within it. In consequence, all numbers are at the same time a unity and every unity is at the same time a number; any one thing, moreover, is also a multiple as well and any multiple is also one thing. Both the one and the other are relative. Indeed, reality transcends the one and the many.

This characteristic belongs supremely to God. He is in an eminent way one and three, or rather he transcends the mode in which one and three exist in our experience. The three subjects are so interior in their unity as Being that knows no dispersal that they can in no way be separated so as to be counted as three entities having a certain discontinuity between them. Saint Basil declares: "For we do not count by way of addition, gradually making increase from unity to multitude, and saying one, two, and three, nor yet first, second, and third. For 'I, God, am the first, and I am the last' (Is 44.6). And hitherto we have never, even at the present time, heard of a second God. Worshipping as we do God of God, we both confess the distinction of the Persons, and at the same time abide by the Monarchy. We do not fritter away the theology in a divided plurality."[31]

The number, however, which *par excellence* represents distinction in unity or unity made explicit is three. The number two does not tell us what is contained strictly speaking in unity, whereas in the strict sense unity can be seen in the sphere of subjects. Here is to be seen the true significance of distinction in unity or of unity in things which are distinct — along with the purpose of this paradoxical constitution of reality.

A subject who was unique in an absolute sense would lack the joy and hence the meaning of existence. He would be doubtful even of his own existence which would become something mingled with dreams. According to our Christian teaching, if a subject and an object are together, or if a subject is even confronted with a whole world of objects, that subject is kept within a loneliness devoid of all joy and meaning to existence. "What will it profit a man if he gains the whole world and forfeits his life?" (Mt 16.26). A subject and an object are not complementary halves, for the object does not deliver the subject from the uncertainty of existence.

Two subjects, however, do bring about through their communion a certain solidity together with a joy and a meaning to existence.

But even this real complementarity of two, which is at the same time a dialogical unity based on the unity of being, is insufficient. Communion in two is itself a limitation from a double point of view. Firstly, this kind of communion does not open up the entire horizon which is implied in existence, for not only do the two open themselves the one to the other, they also close themselves off. The other becomes both a window and a wall for me. Two cannot live only from their own resources. They must have an awareness of a horizon which extends beyond themselves though it is linked with both of them. Nor can this horizon be constituted by an object or a world of objects, for that would not deliver the two from the monotony of a limited vision or of a loneliness à *deux*. Only the third subject — and one who can be a partner in communion and does not stand over against them as object — takes the two out of their uninterrupted loneliness as couple.

If the "I" without any relation can be represented as a point, and the relation between two subjects as a line drawn from one point to another, their relation with a third subject can be represented as a surface, or rather as a triangle, containing within it the all. This intentionality finds its realization in the divine Trinitarian communion.

The limited horizon of an exclusive communion between two persons is bound up with a love which has a limited objective. This is why a communion of such a kind, if it does not satisfy men, is that much less satisfying to God. Although Father and Son give themselves integrally the one to the other in their love, any idea of an egoism à *deux* which contradicts the divine infinity must be far removed from this love.[32] Such an egoism locates all that is external to the two or different from them within an eternal nothingness or, at the most, reduces it to a level of eternal inferiority. This kind of exclusive love vis-à-vis the other always implies within itself fear, uncertainty, and jealousy.[33] The third is the trial by fire for the genuineness of love between the two.

It is only through the third that the love between the two proves itself generous and capable of extending itself to subjects outside themselves. Exclusiveness between the two makes the act of a generous overflow beyond the prison walls of the couple impossible.

This is the sense in which the name of the Holy Spirit is so closely associated with love, inasmuch as that name is the sign of perfect love in God. Only the third implies complete deliverance of love from selfishness. Through the Holy Spirit the love of the Trinity proves itself as genuinely holy. Only because a third exists can the two become simultaneously one, not merely through the reciprocity of their love alone, but also through their common self-forgetfulness in favor of the third. Only the existence of a third in God explains the creation of a world of many "I's" and the fact that these "I's" have been elevated to the level of deified partners of Father and Son in love through the Holy Spirit, their equal. Only through the Holy Spirit, therefore, does the divine love radiate to the outside. It is not to no purpose that created "I's" are brought forward and raised to the level of being partners in the dialogue with Father and Son through the Holy Spirit. The Holy Spirit represents the possibility of extending the love between Father and Son to other subjects, and at the same time he represents the right which a third has to a part in the loving dialogue of the two, a right with which the Spirit invests created subjects.

If previously we have made use of the term "pure subjectivity" to describe God's mode of being, so as to remove far from him any sign of the character of object, we did so while understanding by "subjectivity" not some illusory content which a subject can give it, but God's absolutely free mode of being through himself and of deciding through himself. In the case of God, however, this mode means the mode of reality which is most consistent of all: he is an objective subjectivity, or a subjective objectivity. He transcends the distinction between subjectivity and objectivity, for a person is more than just intellection; the person is the most intensive reality that is. God surpasses the subjectivity and objectivity familiar to us, for he is the one inasmuch as he is the other. Saint Maximos the Confessor says: "Any thought is a synthesis of those who think and of those that are conceived of, but God is neither among those who think, nor among those that are conceived of. He is above them. For otherwise he would be circumscribed as a subject who thinks and would need the relation with what is thought, and as a thought object he would naturally fall under the vision of him who thinks, because of the relation."[34]

But this subjective-objective consistency is fully assured in God by the fact that he exists in three persons. A single person might be taken to be merely a process of intellection; two persons immersed in their exclusive communion can have the impression that they have departed from reality. Only a third person assures them that they are within an objective reality and that in this reality they surpass their own dual subjectivity. For although a third person is also experienced as subject, nevertheless the fact that he is experienced by the two gives them the sense of their own objectivity. Were some common object necessary to them, it would circumscribe them, but a person who is their equal leaves them uncircumscribed and even extends their condition of being uncircumscribed, making it for them a fully "objective" thing.

The third fulfills the role of "object" or horizon, assuring the sense of objectivity for the two by the fact that he keeps the two from becoming confused within an indistinct unity because of the exclusiveness of their love, an exclusiveness which can flow from the conviction of each that nothing worthy of love exists outside the other. When a third of the same worth exists, neither of the two who love each other loses sight of the merit of loving that belongs to the third, and both are thereby kept from becoming confused, the one in the other. In the case of human beings, the third can have the role of keeping the other two not only from immersing themselves in each other, but also from falling into a lethal boredom because their finite character makes it impossible for them to keep up their reciprocal interest in one another permanently. With men, therefore, the third person has the role of offering to one or the other of the two — and to both together — the newness of another communion from which they can return, with interest refreshed and enriched, to the communion that exists between themselves.

In the case of God there can be no question of the third person playing a role in rekindling the love between the other two, but only in preserving them in their personal distinction, accompanied by the enduring love that persists in them by reason of their infinite character. The reference they have to the third person coincides with the confirmation of their subjective objectivity and with the simultaneous assurance of their distinction as persons. In the three persons there is fully confirmed the "truth" of God's existence, a truth which, in the case of two, would be confirmed only in part, and in the case of one alone would remain uncertain. Hence in a special way the Holy Spirit is named "the Spirit of truth" (Jn 15.26; 16.13), and has as his task to strengthen in truth. The troparion of the Epiphany proclaims in regard to the incarnate Son: "The Spirit in the form of a dove has testified to the strengthening of the Word" of the Father.

Inasmuch as the existence of God is attested through the Holy Spirit, as third person, he receives the further name of the "Spirit of love," and for creatures this signifies "the giver of life" and "the comforter," or "the Holy Spirit" and "the sanctifier" (Jn 17.17, 19).

In the case of God, the Spirit cannot have the role — such as is found among human beings — of attracting one of the two into alternative communion with himself in order to rekindle the love between them; instead his role is only to preserve them as distinct, for all three divine persons stand face to face. With men this happens only rarely and incompletely, for in their case, when three persons are present, the gaze must always be shifted in order to look from one to another. Occasionally, however, when the love between three persons is full and equal, something similar to the divine relationship occurs even among human beings. Parents look together upon their child, while the child looks simultaneously upon the faces of its parents, or one parent may gaze simultaneously at the face of the child and at that of the spouse. When all three are present, none of them becomes "he" for the others. None of them is, strictly speaking, "third" when it comes to matters of order, love, or honor. In such cases the two are "we" for the third, while the third is "thou," or the two are "you" for the third. In God the Three are somehow simultaneously "I," "thou," "thou."

In God this relation is perfect and permanent, since no one is third in the strict sense, that is, in the sense that he would be outside the direct "I — thou" relation. This is all the more true as each person sees the other through each person, or sees the others as himself. In God the "we — thou" or "I — you" relations all obtain simultaneously with the "I — thou" relation. Each divine subject is capable of this simultaneous attentiveness to the others, whether seen as distinct or in pairs. To make the fullness of existence something actual and to confirm the two in existence, a "fourth" is not a further necessity. The third represents all that can exist over and above the two, the entire reality in which the two can be confirmed. A fourth in God would disperse and limit the third and diminish his importance. The existence of a fourth would mean that the whole of the objective horizon in which the two are found is no longer concentrated within one person.

With men this fourth dimension is possible and indeeds promotes their spiritual enrichment and the overcoming of that monotony which is experienced in regard to any human person at all by reason of human limitation. An "I" must always be drawing more and more persons included under the category of "he" into the role of the "thou." Moreover, the "he" must represent more than one other, for both "I" and "thou" are limited. Even in the case of human beings, however, there can never be more than the three categories "I," "thou," and "he" — or their multiple into which more persons would be assimilated (whether as "I," "thou," or "he") in the forms "we," "you," and "they." From the perspective of the "I — thou" relation there can be no progress beyond the "he," for there is nowhere else to go. Florensky says: "I will be asked, 'Why are there exactly three hypostases?' I speak of the number 'three' as immanent to Truth, as internally inseparable from it... ["I" cannot exist apart from the relation with "Thee," and apart from a horizon which confirms "Us."] It is only in the unity of the Three that each hypostasis receives an absolute foundation which establishes it as such. Outside the Three there is none existing alone; there is no Subject of Truth. But more than three? Yes, there can be more than three hypostases, if they receive new ones within the bosom of the Trinitarian life. But these new hypostases are no more members on whom the Subject of Truth rests, and that is why they are no longer interiorly necessary for its absoluteness. They are conditioned hypostases which may or may not exist within the Subject of Truth [and even for the sake of confirming me in the truth of earthly existence to the limit, a limit surpassed in my eternal existence through the divine Trinity]. Hence they cannot be called hypostases properly speaking; it would be better to designate them with some such term as deified persons."[35]

Catholic teaching on the procession of the Holy Spirit from the Father and from the Son as from a single principle — which was formulated with the intention of strengthening the communion between the Father and the Son — offends against the two points treated above: the generous extension of the love between Father and Son, and the preservation of their distinction as persons, particularly in the case of the person of the Holy Spirit.

By emphasizing the love between the Father and the Son to the point of confusing them into a single principle of the Holy Spirit's procession, Catholic theology no longer sees them as being distinct persons. But the effect of this is to make impossible even the love between them, for, as in the act of the procession of the Holy Spirit, they no longer exist as two persons, Father and Son can no longer love one another properly speaking. Moreover, the existence of the Spirit as the third, or his role as the one who shows forth the greatness of the love between Father and Son and who preserves their distinction as persons, ceases to have any object. In this misunderstanding of the Trinity the Holy Spirit is no longer, strictly speaking, the third, but the second. He appears rather as the one who drowns the two within an indistinct unity. And if, in order to be the common cause of the procession of the Holy Spirit, the two are indeed drowned within some indistinct whole, then the Spirit — as one who results from this indistinct whole — cannot be person either.

In fact the expressions some Catholic theologians use regarding the Holy Spirit are so ambiguous that it is hard to say any longer whether they consider him a person or not. Others do declare him a person, but their speculations rather suggest the conclusion that he is not. What leads them all to this conclusion is that speculative tradition whereby they identify the generation of the Son and the procession of the Holy Spirit with the soul's act of intellection and will — in particular, the necessity to establish through these acts the procession of the Holy Spirit from Father and Son as from a single principle. This necessity has compelled Catholic theology to identify the Son with that image which the Father has of himself through knowledge, and the procession of the Spirit with the love between Father and Son. As this love no longer preserves two different persons in existence, it is itself the common person of the Father and Son. Thus in this act Father and Son are merged into a dual person, a "we," and thus cease to be any longer two persons properly speaking; this merged, and hence impersonal, reality is itself simultaneously held to be the Holy Spirit.

Among contemporary Catholic theologians who identify the Spirit with that "we" constituted by the Father and the Son we mention Herbert Mühlen. He declares: "One can say that the Holy Spirit is the common act (*Wir-Akt*) between the Father and the Son, namely, 'we' as person (*'Wir' in Person*), respectively 'the intertrinitarian relation we.' "[36] "The Holy Spirit is the intertrinitarian relation 'we,' since the common act (*Wir-Akt*) of the Father and the Son subsists in himself."[37]

As is evident from these passages Mühlen nevertheless persists in calling the Holy Spirit a person. But it is an odd thing, this person who is nothing other than the dual person of the Father and Son. "In the Holy Spirit the personal unity of the Father and of the Son becomes a person." "The Holy Spirit is the unity in person between the Father and the Son; it is, so to speak, the interdivine perichoresis (compenetration) in person."[38] "The distinction of the Holy Spirit from the Father and the Son consists in the fact that He is the absolute approach of two realities in one person."[39]

Mühlen wishes, however, to preserve the Father and Son as distinct persons. He believes that the distinction between them is assured by the fact that concomitantly with the "we relation" that obtains between them — which is one and the same thing with the Holy Spirit — there exists also an "I — thou" relation between Father and Son; or, put another way, before the "we — relation" that obtains between them there is affirmed the "I — thou" relation. "The Father and the Son do not form a 'we' in the full sense, before (in a moment logically later than that of their respective constitution as persons) they spirate the Holy Spirit. The reciprocity of the 'I — thou' is not yet *as such* the mutuality of the 'we' . . . . Rather is this formulation only an expression of the fact that Father and Son stand in a closer relationship in respect of the Holy Spirit than the Spirit and the Son in respect of the Father."[40]

On the other hand, Mühlen holds that the "we-relation" between Father and Son, which is one and the same thing with the Holy Spirit, is an act of the divine being. "In *spiratio activa* is shown the divine nature which is one, as an act of 'we' . . . The Father and the Son are in the Holy Spirit (and in his procession) not on the basis of everyone's constitution as person, but on the basis of the unity of the divine nature."[41]

In other words, the Father and the Son are two persons in the "I — thou" relation between them, while the one divine nature exists concomitantly in "their relation as 'we' " — this latter being identical with the Holy Spirit. This conception reveals plainly that the divine being is equated with person, first of all with the two persons of Father and Son, and then with the person of the Holy Spirit: Father + Son = the divine being = the Holy Spirit. This scheme leads particularly to the melting away of the person of the Holy Spirit who, as we have shown previously, is maintained as person precisely because of the fact that he proceeds from one person — the Father (Jn 15.26).

We have here, in another form, the Catholic theory that began with Tertullian: in the procession of the first to the second, God diversifies himself, so that in the procession which is continued in the direction of the Holy Spirit God becomes again one. Taking up this conception Thomas Aquinas too had said: "Through love [the divinity] returns to the substance from which it began through knowledge."[42] Le Guillou, moreover, though he declares insistently that the identification of the divine processions with the soul's functions of intellection and willing makes the personal character of God appear more clearly than does the patristic ontologist doctrine of the hypostasis, goes on to state: "The essence is that from which and through which everything is in God, including the Persons who are God."[43]

The full love between Father and Son as identical with the Holy Spirit, an identity of which Catholic theology makes so much, is nothing other than the submersion of the two persons within impersonal being, in a sense that recalls Plotinos or the doctrine of nirvana.

Orthodox theology has avoided the danger of falling into this kind of impersonalism and has simply received the Son and the Holy Spirit as real persons actually given through generation and procession. It is under no obligation to explain — through the processions of the soul — an unrevealed doctrine like that of the procession of the Holy Spirit from Father and Son as from a single principle, and it has not let itself be tempted into trying to explain the mode of origin of the divine persons after this analogy of the soul, but has expressed it through the apophatic terms generation and procession.

Carried away by the analogy it draws between generation/procession and the functions of the soul, Catholic theology has no longer treated these two acts as transcending those other acts of God which Orthodox theology observes on the plane of God's relations with the world. Thus, Catholic theology declares that as these other acts of God are common to all the divine persons because they come forth from their common being, so too the acts of generation and procession are common. In this way, therefore, Catholic theology no longer holds these acts as specific acts of persons and as constitutive for the divine persons. For this reason, from the order in which the divine persons are manifested in the world Catholic theology infers an order of their relations within the Godhead, and admits no freedom for that divine order by which the persons are active in the world, for — according to this view — divine acts in the world must strictly reproduce the order in which the persons are found within the divine life. This theology denies that the Son can be sent by the Holy Spirit, as the Lord says he is (Lk 4.18), because in the eternal sphere it is the Spirit who proceeds from the Son. We see here no understanding of the mystery of divine freedom, and an interpretation of God's work in the world that follows an order devoid of freedom. The identificaton of the sphere of person with the sphere of being and the derivation of the sphere of creation from the divine sphere of being bring the Catholic conception close to pantheism. Hence too the rationalism of Catholic theology.

Holy Trinity: Structure of Supreme Love 275

Mühlen rejects the doctrine according to which generation and procession would pertain to different persons: "This would mean that three centers of acts would refer between themselves. In Godhead there is only a unique center of acts, strictly common."[44] The result of this would be that in God there exists, properly speaking, neither Father nor Son, for there exists no generation as an act proper to the Father alone. The patristic writers too emphasized that in God there exists one principle only, one single center of acts, one single center of the acts of procession. In their teaching, however, this center is the Father, therefore a person who secures the personal character of all the persons, not that being which is common and so makes the distinction between persons relative and ambiguous.

If we simply accept the three divine persons and do not try to explain their origin according to the analogy of the functions of the soul, we come to understand the third principal significance of the Trinity of persons, without weakening the distinction between them as persons. This significance consists in the fact that Trinity of persons assures the fullness of their communion and makes this communion full of the joy one person finds in another. The joy that exists between two is not full unless it is communicated by each to the third. The Father rejoices in the Son, but he wishes to communicate this joy to a third so that it may be full. This does not mean that the Son must also give existence to another person distinct from the Father to whom he might communicate his own joy. Were that the case, then the Son would also be shutting himself off from the Father in any communion with another distinct person. With this end in view the Father causes the third subject to proceed who is directed together with the Father totally towards the Son. The shared joy which the Father has in the Son fills the Son with an increased joy in the Father. Besides this, the Son too imparts the joy he has in the Father to this third subject, yet without having to cause him to proceed once he exists through procession from the Father. The Spirit shares in the joy which the Father takes in the Son, inasmuch as he proceeds from the Father and has part in the joy which the Son takes in the Father, thereby shining forth from the Son.[45] The Son himself appears more radiant to the Father because he rejoices in the Father not only in his own right as the Father's steadfast image, but together with the Spirit as well. Saint Gregory Palamas says: "[The Spirit] belongs also to the Son who possesses him from the Father as Spirit of truth, wisdom, and word ... a Word which rejoices together with the Father who rejoices in him ... for this pre-eternal joy of the Father and the Son is the Holy Spirit in that he is common to them by mutual intimacy. Therefore, he is sent to the worthy from both, but in his coming to be he belongs to the Father alone and thus he also proceeds from him alone in his manner of coming to be."[46]

It is in this sense that the Holy Spirit joins Father and Son together, yet without ceasing to be a distinct person and without proceeding also from the Son. This is the sense in which the Spirit is also "the Spirit of the Son," but in this shining forth of the Spirit from himself the Son remains Son and does not become Father of the Spirit. The Spirit is not himself the joy. He is the one who, by participating in the joy which the Father has in the Son and the Son has in the Father, shows forth in its fullness the joy which the one has in the other, or the joy which all the three have in all three. Accordingly Saint Athanasios observes: "The Lord said that the Spirit is the Spirit of Truth and the Comforter; by this he showed that in him is the perfect Trinity."[47]

The Orthodox teaching concerning the procession of the Holy Spirit from the Father towards the Son and his shining forth from the Son towards the Father — a shining forth through which he keeps the Son illuminated before the eyes of the Father — itself implies that Son and Father are neither confused with nor separated from each other. The third person has this same role everywhere in relationship to the other two persons: because of the third person the two are neither blended together within a love which has no horizon in a pantheistic sense (as in Catholicism or in various impersonalist philosophies), nor are they separated from one another in an individualist sense (as in Protestantism); instead they remain in communion. Properly speaking, both pantheism and individualism represent a falling away into nature from the plane of a personal existence which is genuinely spiritual. That is why the passage from individualism to pantheism is an easy one, for the individual tends to melt the other down into himself. By themselves, however, persons cannot escape from this falling away into nature; they must have help from the personal — that is to say, Trinitarian — mode of existence which belongs to the transcendent reality, to God. The holy Trinity alone assures our existence as persons.

Since the Spirit is more than just he who participates in the joy the Father has in the Son and the Son in the Father, but is also the one in whom Father and Son find joy, he is not the third in any rigid sense of the word. Yet inasmuch as the Son has a distinct position as image of the Father, while the Spirit has been caused to proceed for the purpose of participating in the joy which the Father takes in the Son as image, the Spirit does have the special role — within the relationship of the other two persons — of one who was caused to proceed so that he might make of the joy each person has in the other a joy that is shared by the other. Only in this sense is he counted as the third. For he could otherwise just as well be called the second as the Son is (another second), or, since both Son and Spirit exist simultaneously with the Father and together with him, all are the first. In the Trinity there is neither "before" nor "after," for "the Three in God transcend all mathematical number."[48]

Because the Spirit is caused to proceed in order to give joy to each person, an ancient liturgical ekphonesis of the Church sets the particle "with" before his name. Saint Basil the Great remarks that this particle expresses the "dignity" of the Spirit.[49] That is to say, "with" implies equality in glory with the Father and the Son, but also signifies the special role which the Spirit has of bringing each person into relationship with the other so that he is not alone, but together "with" the other. Both these meanings are comprehended, it would seem, in the particle "together with" (συν-) by which the Holy Spirit is related to Father and Son in the Nicene-Constantinopolitan creed.

In this sense the Holy Spirit gives rise to "communion" in a special manner (2 Cor 13.14; Phil 2.1). The Spirit saves us from a loneliness that is deathly. For this reason he is the Comforter. Always he offers communion to each of us as a "thou," and in him anyone at all finds consolation. He it is who is always helping us and quickening our joy in God. He is the "giver of life." It is in the Spirit that we know and magnify God and find our joy in him.[50] The Spirit bears witness to our conscience before God (1 Cor 2.10-12) and through the Spirit as his gift God dwells in us (1 Cor 12.3-11). Saint Athanasios declares: "But we apart from the Spirit are strange and distant from God, and by participation of the Spirit we are knit into the Godhead; so that our being in the Father is not ours, but is the Spirit's which is in us and abides in us, while by the true confession we preserve it in us."[51]

By the fidelity with which he assists others and which he fosters in others as they stand before God and one another the Spirit is the Holy One and the Sanctifier. To participate as person and to make himself participated in as person, these belong to the Spirit. He is the expression of the generosity of God, of God's forgetfulness of himself as he "goes out" towards creatures. The Spirit is the joy God finds in them and they in God.

NOTES

1. *The Divine Names* 2.8, PG 3.645B-C; ET Luibheid/Rorem, p. 64.
2. Ibid. 2.3, PG 3.640B-C; ET Luibheid/Rorem, p. 60. The Greek Metropolitan Emilianos Timiades writes: "One might say that just as the Incarnation of the Logos in the life and actions of the historical Christ is a condescension of the Divinity towards human obscurity, through which are revealed 'things hidden from the foundation of the world,' so the same Logos, the Truth itself, condescends also to become 'incarnate' in religious forms and dogmas which serve man as a guide through the maze of confusion and ignorance in which he finds himself. In other words, doctrinal formulations have a double aspect. On the one hand, they 'reveal' the Truth in terms accessible to the human intelligence, and to this extent have an affirmative or cataphatic aspect, serving both as supports for man in his spiritual realization, and as defenses against misconceptions of things which the human intelligence may be tempted to have. On the other hand, they are not the Truth itself, but merely its expression in human terms, and in this respect they have a negative, or apophatic, aspect" ("Disregarded Causes of Disunity," *The Orthodox Observer* 36 [1970] Nr. 599, p. 10).
3. Cf. *Against the Jacobites* 78-80, PG 94.1473B-77B.
4. *Oration* 29.21, PG 36.104A-B; ET Hardy/ Richardson, p. 176.
5. *Ibid.* 31.12, PG 36.145C; ET Hardy/ Richardson, p. 201.
6. Cf. *Der Dreieine*, pp. 20-25.
7. *Oration* 31.15, PG 36.149B; ET Hardy/ Richardson, pp. 202-03.
8. *Ibid.* 31.14, PG 36.148D-49A; ET Hardy/ Richardson, p. 202.
9. *The Orthodox Faith* 1.8, PG 94.829B; ET Chase, p. 187.
10. Cf. *Letter* 38.3, PG 32.328A. [This letter is now usually ascribed to Gregory of Nyssa; cf. *Basil of Caesarea. Christian, Humanist, Ascetic.* ed. Paul Jonathan Fedwick (Toronto, 1981) Part One, p. xxx. Ed. note.]
11. *Letter* 38.4, PG 32.332A.
12. Ibid. 38.4, PG 32.332B; ET B. Jackson, *NPNF* 2nd Series, vol. 7, p. 139.
13. Ibid. 38.4, PG 32.332D-33A; ET Jackson, p. 139.
14. *The Councils of Ariminum and Seleucia* 26, PG 26.733B; ET J. H. Newman/A. Robertson, *NPNF* 2nd Series, vol. 4, p. 464.
15. Gregory of Nazianzos, *Oration,* 31.15, PG 36.149B; ET Hardy/ Richardson, p. 203.

16. *Ibid.* 31.31, PG 36.169A; ET Hardy/ Richardson, p. 213.
17. Cf. Maximos the Confessor, *Letter* 2, PG 91.396D.
18. *Letter* 38.8, PG 32.340B; ET Jackson, p. 141.
19. Cf. Maximos the Confessor, *Chapters on Essence and Nature, on Hypostasis and Person* 8, PG 91.264A: "There is no unhypostatized nature (φύσις ἀνυπόστατος)."
20. *Against the Arians* 3.66, PG 26.464B; ET Newman/Robertson, p. 430.
21. Cf. Gregory of Nyssa, *Against Eunomios* 8, PG 45.789C referring to Basil, *Against Eunomios* 2.12, PG 29.593A-B: ET W. Moore/H. Wilson, *NPNF* 2nd Series, vol. 5, p. 207.
22. Gregory of Nyssa, *Against Eunomios* 2, PG 45.493B; ET Moore/Wilson, p. 110: "then the Father begot another self, not passing out of himself, and at the same time appearing in his fulness in him."
23. Pavel Florensky, *Stolp i utverzhdenie istiny. Opyt pravoslavnoi feoditsei v dvenadtsati pis'makh* [*The Pillar and Ground of Truth. An Attempt at an Orthodox Theodicy in Twelve Letters*], rp. Farnborough 1970, p. 49. He is following Dionysios the Areopagite who defines the divine being as goodness, hence as relationship.
24. Gregory of Nyssa, *Against Eunomios* 2, PG 45.493B citing Basil, *Against Eunomios* 2.12, PG 29.593A-B.
25. *Against the Arians* 4.4, PG 26.472C: ET Newman/Robertson, p. 434.
26. Gregory of Nyssa, cf. *Against Eunomios* 8, PG 45.788B-789B.
27. "For the (personal) properties, like characters and forms considered in the substance, make a distinction within what is common, thanks to their individual characteristics, but they do not break the co-naturality of the substance.... Thus, when we hear of an unbegotten light, we think of the Father, and when we hear of the begotten light, we conceive the notion of the Son. Insofar as they are one light, there is no opposition between them, but insofar as they are begotten and unbegotten, we consider them under the aspect of an antithesis. Such, therefore, is the nature of the (personal) properties that they show forth otherness within the identity of the substance, and the properties themselves are distinguished one from the other sometimes by mutually opposing each other, and even by the forming of antithetical pairs, but they do not destroy the unity of the substance," Basil, *Against Eunomios* 2.28, PG 29.637B-C.
28. Staniloae, *Theology and the Church*, pp. 16-29 and p. 233, n. 25.
29. Basil, *Against Eunomios* 5.3, PG 29.756A; cf. Eugraphe Kovalevsky, "Saint Trinité," in *Cahiers de Saint Irénée*, Nr. 44, Jan/Feb 1964, p. 3: "The character of the hypostasis of the Holy Spirit is to love by eclipsing himself, as the Father by forgetting himself loves the Son in whom he has placed all his joy, and as the Son is beloved because he puts off his own 'I' in order that the Father may be made manifest and the Spirit shine forth."
30. *Letter* 2, PG 91.400A-C.
31. *The Holy Spirit* 18.45, PG 32.149B; ET Jackson, p. 28.
32. E. Kovalevsky, "Les nombres dans la Genèse," in *Cahiers de Saint Irénée*, Nr. 29, Jun/July 1961, p. 10: "The philosophy of the Middle Ages ... often analyzed the problem of the Three and One. Hugh of St. Victor proposes for us a marvelous definition of the One: 'The One,' he says, 'is, from the moral point of view, a satisfaction, an egotism, a thing closed in on itself, while Two somehow opens itself to love, to the compenetration of the one by the other, to the struggling of the one for the other. Two is already the love of the couple. It still contains imperfection because in loving the other, one is in the end loving oneself. The other reflects you. The One does not love itself; Two love each other. The charity which

is disinterested, ecstatic, sacrificial, radiant, open, without restriction, fruitful with love, genuinely appears only with the Three."

33. In *Little Eyolf*, Ibsen has portrayed this egotistical, ill-fated and uncertain love for her husband of a wife who was jealous even of her husband's love for their own son.

34. *Gnostic Chapters* 2.2, PG 90.1125C.

35. Florensky, *Stolp i utverzhdenie istiny*, p. 50.

36. *Der Heilige Geist als Person* 5.88 (Münster, 1963), p. 157.

37. Mühlen, *Der Heilige Geist* 5.92, p. 199.

38. Ibid. 5.100.12-17, p. 166.

39. Ibid. 5.100, p. 166.

40. Ibid. 5.94, p. 161.

41. Ibid. 5.98, 5.99, pp. 164, 165.

42. A.-M. de Monléon, "Le Saint Esprit comme Amour selon saint Thomas D'Aquin," *Istina* 17 (1972) p. 439.

43. Le Guillou, "Réflexions sur la théologie trinitaire," p. 462.

44. Mühlen, *Der Heilige Geist* 5.98, p. 165.

45. Gregory of Cyprus insisted in a special way upon the distinction between the "procession" of the Spirit from the Father and his "shining forth" from the Son; cf. Staniloae, *Theology and the Church*, pp. 16-29.

46. *The One Hundred and Fifty Chapters* 36.21-23, 24, 26-31, ed. R. Sinkewicz, *Saint Gregory Palamas. The One Hundred and Fifty Chapters* (Toronto, 1988), p. 122; ET Sinkewicz, p. 123.

47. *Letter to Serapion* 1.25, PG 26.589B.

48. Evdokimov, *L'Esprit Saint*, p. 44.

49. Basil, *The Holy Spirit* 27.68, PG 32.193B.

50. *The Holy Spirit* 28.69-70, PG 32.196B-200A.

51. *Against the Arians* 3.24, PG 26.373B-C; ET Newman/Robertson, p. 407.

www.ingramcontent.com/pod-product-compliance
Lightning Source LLC
Chambersburg PA
CBHW031429160426
43195CB00010BB/669